WITHDRAWN

Macromarketing

Macromarketing:
A CANADIAN PERSPECTIVE

Donald N. Thompson
York University
Patricia Simmie
York University
Louise Heslop
University of Guelph
Stanley J. Shapiro
McGill University

AMERICAN
MARKETING
ASSOCIATION

Proceedings Series

222 South Riverside Plaza   Chicago, Illinois 60606   (312) 648-0536

Cover Design by Mary Jo Krysinski

Library of Congress Cataloging in Publication Data

Main entry under title:
Macromarketing, a Canadian perspective

  Bibliography
  1. Marketing--Canada--Congresses. 2. Consumer protection
--Canada--Congresses. 3. Consumer protection--Law and
legislation--Canada--Congresses. I. Thompson, Donald N.

HF5415.12 C35M27   381   79-16031
ISBN 0-87757-124-4

215/1000/1279

TABLE OF CONTENTS

PART II - THE BUSINESS-CONSUMER EXCHANGE SYSTEM

PART III - THE NATURE-TECHNOLOGY ENVIRONMENT

PREFACE

In June of 1979, the Third Triennial Canadian Marketing Workshop was held on the campus of York University in Toronto. The workshop focussed on macromarketing, in a Canadian context, including the general areas of consumerism, consumer protection, public policy and its impact, social indicators, social issues, and the non-legislative regulatory process. The materials in this volume were presented in earlier form at the workshop. The revised papers reflect the input of discussion at the CMW meetings, contributed by 75 business executives and marketing scholars representing 40 universities and colleges, the federal government, and a number of corporations.

The papers presented were commissioned following a country-wide competition for proposals. Many of the authors received additional financial support from the federal government or other sources. Acknowledgement of such support is found in the individual papers.

The intention of the triennial workshops is to encourage the development of material in those areas of Canadian marketing where literature is not readily accessible. It was clear that macromarketing was such an area: a great deal of work was being done, but little material was publicly available in spite of the demand for it in marketing courses. The papers here cover a wide range of topics within the macromarketing area, from a discussion of government activities in developing a program for Canadian unity, to a discussion of markets and channels for contemporary art in Canada, to a ten year retrospective of marketing in the Canada Post Office.

The success of the workshop and the publication of this volume are the result of contributions, assistance, and support from a large number of people. Deserving of first mention is the financial sponsorship of the workshop, research papers, publication, and travel subsidies by John Labatt Ltd., Union Carbide Canada Limited, the Margaret Brown Byron Marketing Fund, and the Faculty of Administrative Studies Development Fund at York University. Personal thanks go to W.O. Johnson, R.H. Rastorp, and Chairman J.S. Dewar of Union Carbine, and Dean Wallace Crowston of the Faculty of Administrative Studies at York.

Colleagues in the planning and execution of the workshop were Patricia Simmie of York University, Louise Heslop of the

University of Guelph, and Stanley Shapiro of McGill University.

Sincere thanks go to Lynn Beard, who served as secretary and problem solver to the coordinating group; Shelagh Paul, who performed the editorial function; Terry-Lee Rach and Sharon Morrison, who both typed late on many evenings; and Thérèse Rochette, who provided the translation.

Each paper begins with a short summary of contents and major conclusions, in both english and french languages. The various papers have also undergone moderate editing in the interest of format, length and clarity. Apologies are extended in advance for any errors in translation or reproduction.

Earlier volumes in the workshop series are Canadian Marketing: Problems and Prospects (Wiley of Canada 1973) and Problems in Canadian Marketing (AMA 1977).

Donald N. Thompson
Toronto, September 1979

MACROMARKETING: DEVELOPING A FRAMEWORK FOR A CANADIAN PERSPECTIVE

Louise A. Heslop, University of Guelph
Patricia Simmie, York University

Marketing practitioners and theoreticians have found them-selves more and more involved with such issues as government regulation of marketing, demarketing, the social responsibility of marketers, marketing's impact on society, ecological market-ing, and consumerism. These concerns seem somehow far removed from involvement with market share, pricing, distribution, ad-vertising, etc. These two areas appear to be two separate sub-jects altogether, and so two new words have been devised to differentiate them. The term "macromarketing" has come to be applied to the former set of issues and "micromarketing" to the latter. This latter area has a fairly clearly established set of principles and modes of study attached to it, but the newly emerging field of macromarketing is still in its infancy; strug-gling to establish itself and its definition, scope and funda-mental concepts.

The overall field of marketing has been expanding in scope and application within the last ten years. Formerly, marketing was viewed as being concerned only with "business activities that plan, price, promote, and distribute want-satisfying pro-ducts and services to customers" (Mulvihill 1978). However, within the last few years the application of marketing tech-niques and concepts to the whole area of exchange relationships taking place in society has been more commonly accepted (Bag-ozzi 1974, 1975). Once the view of marketing as the study of exchange has been recognized, significant steps can be taken to broaden its appropriate range of interests. First, the applica-tion of marketing principles to the dissemination and accept-ance of ideas and concepts, such as those of conservation, birth control, political platforms, etc., becomes appropriate. Such activities have been termed "social marketing," and actu-ally involve the application of micromarketing principles to new fields.

Secondly, the interaction of marketplace activities and marketing techniques with the larger societal system becomes a set of concerns with a new base of operations and at the core of a newly established field. Indeed, such issues cannot be ignored. The pressures for public accountability and social

responsibility of marketers of goods, services, and ideas are
growing stronger and demand recognition. In fact, the increasing activity of regulators and public interest groups has left
many marketers dumbfounded as to why they are presently in such
a sea of controversy. They feel they are more regulated than
ever before, and yet the public is more cynical and demanding
of reforms than ever before (Anderson 1979).

Some effort needs to be made to develop a framework or
perspective for this increased macromarketing interest, i.e.,
of the interaction of marketplace activities and the application of marketing techniques with society. Such an overview
could aid marketers in understanding and appropriately respon-
ding to opportunities and restrictions in their environment.
It should also aid policymakers in properly assessing the impact of their efforts in regulating business activities.

Macromarketing Environment

Traditionally business marketers have been concerned with
aspects and institutions in society as they impact upon consumers and their own exchanges with consumers. In fact, the effects flow two ways. The reciprocal relationship is the effect
of interaction of business/marketer-consumer exchanges on other
exchanges going on in society.

Individuals and institutions enter into exchanges to satisfy needs. In our highly complex society most exchanges satisfy more than one need and have implications in more than one
field of human endeavor. When individuals, acting as consumers,
enter into exchanges with businesses, they do so to satisfy not
only economic/physical needs but also psychological needs for
self expression and social needs for love and esteem. Conversely, when individuals, as members of a social group, enter into exchanges with other group members, those exchanges will
most likely involve physical, social and psychological need
satisfaction. The patterns of need satisfaction through various exchanges in society can be very complex.

Because of these complex patterns, conflicts may arise as
to the acceptability of certain modes of interaction between institutions and individuals. One institution may feel that the
actions of another institution jeopardize its own relationship
with its client group. What ensues to resolve this situation
depends upon the positions of the groups vis-à-vis their members and the society.

Lately, business organizations have very often found themselves at the receiving end of much criticism. The methods
used by businesses to win customers have been attacked for

leading to materialistic, wasteful, environmentally dangerous, hedonistic, inane, unhealthy lifestyles. Essentially, businesses are being blamed for destroying sets of values established and held forward by other institutions in their exchanges with their clients.

The controversial area of advertising to children may serve as an illustration. It used to be that children had very little input to purchase decisions about what food the family would buy. The parent told the child what to eat and received compliance (within tolerable limits). There were few alternatives, and no one suggested that the child should have a say. The last thirty years has seen a substantial change in such attitudes. Cereal manufacturers and advertisers discovered children and children's television. A situation developed which eventually was viewed as objectionable by a substantial number of parents who felt that the products promoted and the methods used by the advertisers were inappropriate. These parents and their supporters are so vehement because they view the advertiser as intervening in their exchange with their child in the traditional pattern of parent-child relationships. The traditional interaction pattern was as illustrated in Figure 1, where business promoted only to the parent who chose what to communicate with the child.

Figure 1. Traditional Parent-Child-Business Interaction Mode

The new relationship looks more like Figure 2.

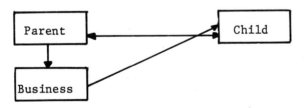

Figure 2. Revised Parent-Child-Business Interaction Mode

Now both the parent and the advertiser are providing information and direction to the child. The parent feels less in control of this latter situation and may reject the apparent loss of power.

3

There are several options, available for parents to regain this loss of control or to constrain the power of the advertiser. One means frequently used now is for the parents to seek support of another institution, often the government, either directly or by forming an intermediate group which can then approach government as illustrated in Figure 3. If the latter is sympathetic to the issue and sees support from still other institutions, it may take one or more of several courses to affect the advertiser-child relationship, for example, by imposing product restrictions or advertising bans.

Many other examples could serve to illustrate the overlap of function between institutions in the lives of individuals. Business marketers may be more sensitive to potential conflict areas if they recognize these areas of overlap as the source. They may also more fully appreciate the depth of commitment of the groups who may raise objections. These groups see the issues as ones of infringement of fundamental rights or jurisdiction in their exchanges.

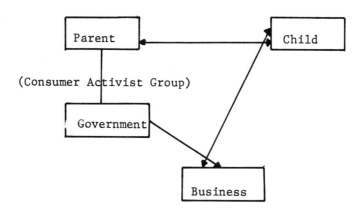

Figure 3. Interactions of some institutions with regards to advertising to children.

Figure 3 also helps to illustrate the placement of business as one of many institutions within society. This is more generically illustrated in Figure 4. This figure takes on the impossible task of trying to depict a very complex four-dimensional dynamic system in a two-dimensional static medium. The core of the system is the individual who changes roles in keeping with the particular institution with which the exchange is taking place. The individual is a customer to the business, a citizen to the government, a member of the congregation to the church, etc. The position and relative prominence of the enclosures depicting the many institutions in society vary across individuals over time, and across issues. The institutions

4

FIGURE 4: Macromarketing Model of Exchange System and their Environments.

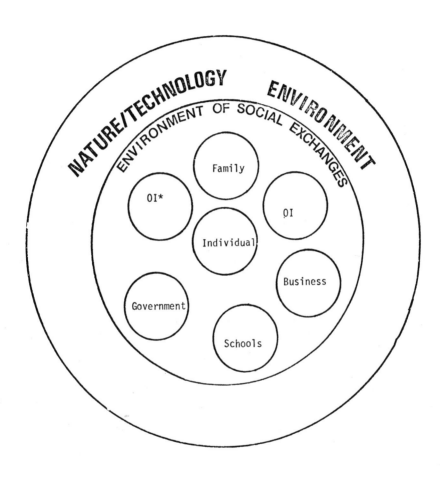

*OI -- Other Institutions

should be viewed as mobile and free to establish exchanges as appropriate with all other institutions, as well as individuals. At any given point of time, a dynamic equilibrium exists which is determined by the generally accepted set of roles attributed to the importance of each institution within the society. The patterns of exchanges that take place, the norms governing them and the ways in which they affect the relationship of business-es with their customers is one of the major domains of macro-marketing.

The second major domain recognizes the outer ring of Figure 4 – the nature/technology environment. All the institutions and their patterns of interaction are "nested" within this environment, affecting and being affected by it. If, for example, there are major changes in the availability of resources within this environment, pressures may be brought to bear to shift the nature of inter-institutional or individual-institutional relationships.

The field of macromarketing is concerned with these two major areas which are the "environment" of the micromarketing decision. First, it is concerned with the other institutions in society, their relationship to each other and to business and to the functions performed by business, the rules and norms which govern these relationships, and how all of these affect the business-consumer exchange system. Secondly, macro-marketing is concerned with how all of this "fits" into the nature/technology environment, affecting and being affected by it.

The remaining papers in this volume can be seen to be fitting into one of these two general areas. The bulk of the papers deal with topics in the first area. The overlap of the functions performed by marketing and other institutions is seen in articles by Cameron, "The Marketing of National Unity"; Courtney and Dixon, "Contemporary Art in Canada: Aspects of the Markets and Channels and Implications for Public Policy"; and Shapiro and Barnhill, "The Post Office in the Market Place: A Ten Year Retrospective." Governments and business are jointly involved in these endeavours because the products and services are an extremely complex mix of cultural, political and physical goods. For example, a contemporary artwork provides aesthetic value, as well as providing support for our national culture. The major reason for the joint involvement is the perceived importance of these commodities to the culture and workings of our society.

Aspects of the overall structure of the business-consumer exchange system are addressed in papers on competition policy development by Day and Tigert, "Marketing Aspects of Canadian

Merger Policy" and by Thompson, "Pricing and the Experience Curve Effect." The general structure of the interaction process is also the focus of two other papers addressing specific issues of "The Decline of the Independent Store in Canada: Some Public Policy Questions" by Moyer and Sernick and "Public Policy Aspects of Electronic Funds Transfer in Quebec" by Bennett and Calantone. The particular provincial locale of this latter research paper again exemplifies the impact of cultural and political institutions on marketplace exchanges.

The paper by Barnes and Kelloway, "Consumer Issues: Application of the Concept of Market Maturity" considers an interesting mix of impacts on the business-consumer exchange system as the result of a combination of nature environmental factors (geography) as well as what are likely to be cultural and political issues arising out of problems of regional disparities.

Specific conduct of the parties in business-consumer transactions is dealt with in papers by Loyns, "Marketing Boards: The Irrelevance and Irreverence of Economic Analysis", Forbes, "The Law and Canadian Consumers" and Kennedy, Pearce and Quelch, "Consumer Products Warranties: Perspectives and Issues." All of these concern themselves with the constraint systems governing the conduct of both parties in their exchanges.

The nature/technology environment is examined in two papers. Haines, Leonidas and Sommers in "Canadian Marketing Management in a Conserver Society" and Claxton, Anderson, McDougall and Ritchie in "Consumer Energy Consumption and Conservation Research" address the problems of responses of institutions to recent shortages that have become evident in that environment.

These papers present a Canadian perspective on some macro-marketing issues. This Canadian perspective does not mean that they are irrelevant to non-Canadians. It does mean that the particular national environment raises some issues that may not be raised elsewhere, and it also assumes or takes for its point of study certain exchange systems which may be of different forms elsewhere, either in their makeup or in the nature of the rules, norms and power relationships within which they operate.

REFERENCES

Anderson, Ronald (1979), "Government Arbitrates for Business and Society," The Globe and Mail, Toronto (August 30), B2.

Bagozzi, Richard P. (1974), "Marketing as an Organized Behavioural System of Exchange", Journal of Marketing 38 (Oct.)71-81.

_____ (1975), "Marketing as Exchange," Journal of Marketing 39 (Oct.) 32-39.

Mulvihill, Donald F. (1978), "The Quality of Life and a New Definition of Marketing" in Phillip O. White and Charles C. Slater, editors. Macromarketing: Distributive Processes from a Societal Perspective, An Elaboration of Issues. 2nd Macro-Marketing Seminar 1977. Boulder: University of Colorado, Business Research Division.

THE MARKETING OF NATIONAL UNITY

David   R. Cameron, Federal-Provincial Relations Office

ABSTRACT

Someone recently said that the unity issue constitutes the biggest macro-marketing challenge of them all. It may indeed be that, but it is more than that, for there are things that have gone wrong in our federal system that must be put right. This calls for more than a marketing approach.

In normal marketing situations the object of the exercise seems to be pretty clear: to get the consumer to consume what you are selling. This is not the case with national unity; it is not always clear what you are selling, and it is not always obvious when someone has bought it.

What _is_ clear is that unity in a democracy must be based on the consent of the country's citizens. It is not simply the preservation of the integrity of the state, but the maintenance of a voluntary union of peoples. Thus a marketing strategy needs to be aimed at informing Canadians about their country and its political system and at strengthening the sense of common identity and common purpose.

The Task Force on Canadian Unity, an independent commission established by the federal government, was not so much involved in promotional activities as it was in "animation" and the pro-vision of policy advice. It served as a conduit for the expres-sion of public opinion on the unity issue, and thus provided a data base on which to develop an understanding of Canada's prob-lems and possible responses to them.

The Canadian Unity Information Office, on the other hand, is a federal government organization with explicit information and communications functions. Through its publications, ex-hibitions and advertising and communications programs, the CUIO seeks to achieve the two goals indicated above: informing Canadians on unity questions and strengthening Canadian identity.

Il a été dit dernièrement que l'unité nationale constitue le plus grand de tous les défis rencontré dans le domaine du macro-marketing. En effet, cela est plus que vrai mais il faut aller plus loin encore et réaliser que certaines choses se sont gâtées dans notre système fédéral et qu'il faut y remédier. Et cela exige beaucoup plus qu'une méthode générale de marketing.

Dans les situations normales de marketing, l'objectif semble très clair: il s'agit de convaincre le client d'acheter ce que vous vendez. Tel n'est pas le cas quand il s'agit del'unité nationale; ce que vous vendez semble plutôt vague et il est difficile de savoir si l'idée a porte fruit et a été adoptée.

Ce qui est clair est que dans une démocratie, l'unité doit être basée sur le consentement des citoyens du pays. Il ne s'agit pas uniquement de préserver l'intégrité de l'état, mais aussi de maintenir l'union volontaire du peuple. Et c'est là que la stratégie de marketing doit viser à renseigner les canadiens sur leur pays et son système politique afin de renforcer l'idée d'une identité commune et de buts partagés.

La Commission Spéciale pour l'Unité Canadienne, une commission indépendante établie par le gouvernement fédéral, ne fut que très peu impliquée dans des activités visant à promouvoir l'unité; elle fut active surtout dans "l'animation" et la disposition de conseils sur les politiques à suivre. Elle servit aussi de conduit pour l'expression de l'opinion publique sur la question d'unité, et elle put ainsi fournir des données permettant de développer une compréhension d'ensemble et une réponse possible aux problèmes du Canada.

D'autre part, le Bureau d'Information sur l'Unité Canadienne est une organisation du gouvernement fédéral qui a fonction de fournir des informations et communications explicites. Grâce à ses publications, ses expositions et ses programmes de publicité, le BIUC tente d'atteindre les deux buts mentionnés ci-haut: renseigner les canadiens sur la question de l'unité nationale et renforcer l'identité canadienne.

NATIONAL UNITY AND MARKETING

Someone recently asserted that the unity crisis constituted the biggest macro-marketing challenge of them all. In this paper I plan to look at the crisis in Confederation from this angle. I propose to begin by making some general remarks and by entering a caveat - or should I say a caveat emptor - and then to proceed to describe the activities of two bodies, the Canadian Unity Information Office and the Task Force on Canadian Unity.

First the caveat. I am adopting what I understand to be a

marketing perspective for the purpose of discussion and to permit concentration on certain aspects of the 'unity debate,' as
it is often called. I remain agnostic (at the very least) as
to whether that is the most appropriate or comprehensive perspective for approaching the issues which are now troubling
Canada. I do not believe that, taken on its own, a marketing
perspective is at all an adequate framework within which to
confront Quebec nationalism and the strong regional pressures
of other parts of Canada.

A marketing perspective is not sufficient as the exclusive
or primary approach to national unity if it is the case, as I
think it is, that there are genuine inequities in the distribution of benefits and burdens among the people of Canada and
genuine deficiencies in our political system and public policy
processes. Our federal system, alas, is not the equivalent of
a Maytag washing machine which (so they say) never needs repair; we have got problems, and they need to be resolved. It
is therefore, I suspect, beyond the reach even of the arcane
and powerful arts of the advertising world to persuade people
that what is going wrong with their country is, in fact, going
right. I believe that our traditional political concepts and
vocabulary which refer to such things as the satisfying of
grievances, the righting of injustices and the achievement of
reform are more serviceable in this respect than the notions of
market research, product development and sales promotion.

It is nevertheless my impression that the marketing approach may help in understanding a good deal about the issue of
unity and may provide a line of action which bears directly on
certain significant aspects of the problem. What the approach
holds out for us is, first, a methodology for studying or analyzing the problem, and second, a strategy for solving the problem so analyzed.

As a methodology, marketing falls presumably within the
general realm of social psychology and directs our attention to
the springs of human behaviour, in this case, to the motivations of Canadians. What are the hopes and fears of the Québécois that animate and support the forces of nationalism in the
province? What are the attitudes of Canadians in other parts
of the country? How is the behaviour of one group interpreted
by the other and how does that contribute to disunity? If the
experience of the Task Force is any guide, such questions as
these are fascinating, important and extremely difficult to
handle systematically.

As a strategy, the marketing approach, as we will see in a
moment, presents a wide array of possible actions, all of them
designed to communicate information and to structure opinion in

ways that enhance the unity of the country. But what is Canadian unity? How does one establish what the factors are which contribute to disunity in a country? You would probably get more people in this country to agree that disunity is a problem than to agree on precisely what it entails or how important it is. Some would contend that it is at bottom a phony crisis, and is in reality the best trick yet devised by one part of the country to extract benefits from the rest. Some would identify the major threat to unity as being the intention of the Government of Quebec to hold a referendum. Others would argue that the referendum is merely symptomatic of deeper structural forces that are transforming Quebec society and the rest of the country and their relations with one another. Still others would insist that it is a problem of attitudes.

Who is right? And, more to the point, how does one decide who is right? One suspects intuitively that each opinion expresses a fragment of the whole, but that no such single point of view captures the truth of the matter comprehensively. While it is necessary to make use of all the resources of social science -- survey and interview data, historical scholarship, economic analysis and so forth -- one must go beyond this to arrive at even a rough appreciation of the thing itself. What we fall back on, faute de mieux, is our best judgment of people, circumstance and opportunity, our general experience of life, common sense -- in short, those non-quantifiable qualities which are an essential component of political wisdom.

There is another factor that bears on our discussion, and that is the difference between a practical definition of the problem and a theoretically satisfactory definition of the problem. While intellectually, one may appreciate the comprehensive nature of the issue and its manifold ramifications, in practice one will behave as if the issue was much narrower and more amenable to specific reform than it really is.

Most countries have had, at some point in their history, periods of acute difficulty in which the danger of fragmentation and even collapse has been great. Many have, in fact, collapsed. One has only to look at the forces of regional separation at work in such historic states as Britain, France and Spain to realize how prevalent they are. The United States fought a civil war in the last century on the subject of national unity; Nigeria and Pakistan fought civil wars in this century for the same reason. It is not just empires that rise and fall, but countries as well. The causes of such occurrences are as varied as human personality and circumstances themselves.

A crisis of national unity, in Canada or elsewhere, is typically a crisis of disintegration in which certain centrifugal forces threaten to break the country apart. To speak more

12

precisely of those centrifugal forces, I cannot do better than to quote the Task Force on Canadian Unity. In their final report, A Future Together, the Commissioners write:

"We believe that the heart of the present crisis is to be discovered in the intersecting conflicts created by two kinds of cleavages in Canadian society and by the political agencies which express and mediate them. The first and more pressing cleavage is that old Canadian division between 'the French' and 'the English'. We will consider the present configuration of this historic problem of Canadian duality in a moment. The second cleavage is that which divides the various regions of Canada and their populations from one another. Regionalism, like duality, also has an extended lineage in Canadian social, economic and political life, and we pursue this matter subsequently as well.

"Both duality and regionalism, then, are deeply rooted in our history and are major elements in the social and economic foundation of Canada. The shape of these two structural forces of Canadian life has altered quite rapidly in the last quarter of a century as power has shifted within and between various groups and as their aspirations have changed.

"In our judgment, the first and foremost challenge facing the country is to create an environment in which duality might flourish; the second is to provide a fresher and fuller expression of the forces of regionalism in Canada's constitutional system and power structure. We wish to emphasize that it is in the context of the present crisis that we assign priority to these two, and we do so for a very simple reason. Each, if ignored or left unsatisfied, has the power to break the country, and each must accept the other if a new period of harmony is to be achieved."

For the Task Force, the present crisis of unity is shaped primarily by the existance of significant linguistic, cultural and regional differentiation - in their vocabulary, by the forces of duality and regionalism. If one could pick and choose the kind of problems one would prefer to work on, these might not be the forces one would select, but they do seem to correspond fairly closely to the actual character and dynamic of the crisis as it has unfolded in Canada.

I have briefly explored the link between disunity and the threat of national disintegration. What of unity? It is enough to say that national unity exists and the problems

disappear when the forces of disintegration are stilled? Is
unity the absence of disunity? Obviously, one could be for-
given for thinking that something was going right if the voices
raised in regional and 'dualist' complaint fell silent.

But a certain kind of silence would make one uneasy. It
is important to understand the causal factors that lie behind
the expressions of grievance and the reason why they have
ceased, in order to be able to appreciate the character of the
problems the country faces and to assess whether they have been
genuinely resolved. There is, for example, the calm before the
storm, and the silence of fear or hopelessness. Neither of
these is soil in which the seed of national unity can be
readily sown.

Let us return for a moment to the words of the Task Force
Report. It speaks of unity as follows:

"It is the sum of conditions upon which the various communities and governments of Canada agree to support and
sustain the Canadian state. As such, it endows each of
the parts with something it would not have if it stood
alone. It is, then, a just union of constituent elements,
or, as one dictionary puts it, a harmonious combination
of parts."

The significant element in this definition is the notion of
consent of agreement, for it is that which supports and defines
the character of national unity. Canadians seek a union which
is grounded in the freely offered consent of the citizens of
the country.

The French writer, Ernest Renan, offered the following
definition of a nation: 'Une nation, c'est un plébiscite de
tous les jours.' The notion of a continuing, daily plebiscite
directs our attention not only to the quite serious limitations
attendant upon any single consultation with the people (such
as Quebec referendum), but also to the heart of what constitutes the unity of a country, namely, the sustaining consensus
expressed by individuals in everyday acts of loyalty and acceptance.

All this may seem to roam a long distance from the subject
of marketing, but it indicates the nature and outer limits of
activity in this field. It is my layman's belief that in normal marketing situations the object of the exercise is pretty
clear. No matter how lovingly the market survey is carried
out, or how sophisticated the sales pitch may be, the central
and sustaining goal is to get the consumer to consumer the product you are selling. And in most cases you know pretty

14

clearly what it is you are selling. That is not the case with
national unity; it is not always clear precisely what you are
selling, and it is not always obvious when someone has bought
it.

I would think this point of differentiation applies even
in comparison to such diffuse macromarketing projects as improving national fitness or educating the public to use energy
more efficiently. In those cases, a range of appropriate consequential behaviour, given the goal of the marketing operation,
would be fairly clear and fairly readily measurable. But what
would be appropriate 'unity behaviour' and how would one measure the degree to which it had emerged? It would appear that
in such a case as this, the challenge outreaches the methodology. It is here that a narrower definition of the problem renders the work at once more manageable and less comprehensive.
If one approaches unity from the perspective of the referendum
which is to be held in Quebec, it becomes quite easy to say
what 'unity behaviour' is, namely, opposing the referendum.
And yet we know perfectly well that that is only a part of the
truth.

In addition, with the marketing of national unity the consumer is a citizen in a democratic society and the issue is his
allegiance to the country of which he is a member. The goal
of the marketing operation, cannot be to instil unjustified
fear of to peddle phony propaganda about the country and its
prospects. It is one thing to advise that one fear what is
fearful, quite another to encourage fear where such an emo-
tion is without rational foundation. This will be something to
watch out for on all sides as the debate heats up in the months
prior to the referendum. Despite not infrequent charges of
'psychological terrorism' and 'fear campaigns,' it seems to me
that the national unity discussion so far has been remarkably
free from such tendencies. The next few months or years are
likely to provide a much stiffer test of the 'procedural fairness' in all of us.

It is obvious that the event which pushed the question of
national unity to the forefront was the election of the Parti
Québécois as the Government of Quebec on November 15, 1976. It
is the two and a half years since then that will be the period
on which this article will focus, and it is the activity of two
federally-based agencies that will receive direct attention.
One is the Canadian Unity Information Office, a unit within the
Government of Canada, and the other the Task Force on Canadian
Unity, an independent Commission of enquiry established by the
Government of Canada.

THE TASK FORCE ON CANADIAN UNITY

The Task Force on Canadian Unity was created during the summer of 1977 and received a mandate with three basic elements:
- to support, encourage and publicize the efforts of the general public, and particularly those of voluntary organizations, with regard to Canadian unity;

- to contribute the initiatives and views of the Commissioners concerning Canadian unity; and

- to advise the Government of Canada on unity issues.

It was created under the Inquiries Act and thus enjoyed the status and independence from Government of a royal commission. The eight commissioners held hearings and attended meetings of all kinds across Canada from September, 1977 to April, 1978. In the summer and fall of 1978, the Task Force consulted with experts, worked with its staff and tested its ideas with many people in informal meetings as it prepared its final reports.

These reports were published in the first three months of 1979. The first, which appeared in January, was A Future Together, and contained the observations and recommendations of the Task Force. The second, Coming to Terms, appeared in February and provided what was, in effect, a 'primer' for the unity debate -- that is, extended definitions of the meaning of critical terms and a good deal of information about the Canadian political system and the main constitutional options in contention. The third, A Time To Speak, was released in March and provided an account of the Task Force's national tour (in which many of the volume's readers would have themselves participated).

I would suggest that the 'promotional function' of the Task Force was much less important than its role as an 'animator' and as a policy body in the widest sense. If simply to raise the profile of an issue or thing is to market it, then clearly the Task Force was heavily involved in marketing, but I think the main contributions of the Task Force lay elsewhere.

During the winter of 1977/78 when it was engaged in its national tour, it functioned very much as a citizen 'animator' and as a conduit for the expression of public opinion on the unity issue. Its visit to each of fifteen cities across Canada served as a focal point for the activity of local unity groups and an opportunity for private citizens to speak their mind. The media provided extensive coverage, and thus helped to ensure that people in other parts of Canada heard what was on the minds of the people in a particular region.

Thus, the function of the tour and the active public discussion that it involved was to raise the consciousness of Canadians about the challenge to national unity and to permit Canadians to express their own views on their country and its prospects. It was not the function of the Task Force at that stage to promote a particular view of the country or of its constitutional system, but to permit the citizens of Canada to speak for themselves.

The second aspect of the Task Force's role was the provision of policy advice in the widest sense, that is to say, the sharing with the Government of Canada and with Canadians in general of its ideas on the country, its problems and possible reforms. That was the job which preoccupied the Task Force from the summer of 1978 until the conclusion of its work. One might say that the Task Force was more involved with the creation of the product than with its sale and promotion. Indeed, the irony is that, consistent with the customary practice of royal commissions, it wound up its operations just as the promotional phase was needed. It has been left to others, or to the Commissioners acting individually and privately, to 'sell' the final report and its recommendations.

With these points in mind, consider the other organization under discussion, the Canadian Unity Information Office. It was created at about the same time as the Task Force, but its responsibilities were significantly different and fell much more directly into a broadly defined marketing perspective.

THE CANADIAN UNITY INFORMATION OFFICE

The story of the Canadian Unity Information Office and its activities properly begins with the prior creation of another organization, the Coordination Group of the Federal-Provincial Relations Office. This unit, popularly known as the Tellier Group, was established three months after the election of the Parti Québécois. Headed by Paul Tellier, who is a Deputy Secretary to the Cabinet, and made up of a half-dozen senior officers, it was designed to provide a focus for the Government of Canada's thinking on national unity, to prepare information and advice to assist the Government in the decisions it was to make, and in general to develop and implement a Canadian unity strategy. After the PQ victory, the Canadian Government found, not surprisingly, that it was not organized to deal in a coherent fashion with the challenge from the Government of Quebec. The Coordination Group was the main organizational response to this lack within the federal public service.

To carry out its role, the Group has fulfilled the following functions:
-periodic general evaluation of the Canadian unity situation;

-anticipation of the strategy and tactics of the Parti
Québécois;

-ensuring the coordination from a Canadian unity point of
view of the activities of the main government departments
and agencies;

-assessing the criticism of federalism and the programs
and policies of the federal government expressed by the
Government of Quebec or the Parti Québécois and advising
the Government of Canada on possible reactions; and

-planning, developing and supervising the implementation of
an information program in the area of Canadian unity.

This last function really carries over into the domain of
the Canadian Unity Information Office. It soon became evident
to members of the Coordination Group and others that one thing
that was woefully lacking was a coherent, vigorous information
program on the part of the federal government. A great country-
wide surge of interest in Canadian unity followed in the wake
of the election of the PQ and revealed that Canadians concerned
about the future of their country had surprisingly little in
the way of documentation and analysis, displays, systems for
exchanges with people in other parts of the country, information kits for school children, and so forth, which would permit
productive discussion and citizen participation in the issue.
It also revealed that there was widespread ignorance of the
federal system of government and how it operated in Canada, an
ignorance to which government inactivity on this front was a
contributing factor. It was in this atmosphere that both the
CUIO and the Task Force on Canadian Unity were conceived and
born.

The CUIO was established in August, 1977 as the operational
information arm of the Coordination Group with a mandate to
carry out the following broad functions:
-to gather, develop and distribute information and documentation designed to acquaint Canadians with issues relating to Canadian unity;

-to respond to requests for information from individuals
and organizations on matters relating to Canadian unity;

-to guide and advise groups seeking assistance with

projects promoting Canadian unity; and

-to work in cooperation with federal departments to help
coordinate those components of their information programs
relating to Canadian unity.

At the outset, the CUIO was established with a staff of
fewer than two dozen people, limited financial resources and
an enormous, but very unfocussed assignment. In the period following its establishment, the small nucleus of staff at CUIO
sought to define its goals and organize its work and to determine who should be reached with what message.

It is at this point that the question of a comprehensive
as distinct from a narrow definition of the issue arose. If
the election of the PQ and the prospect of an impending referendum occasioned the creation of the CUIO, it was a genuine
question of whether and how these factors should define the
work of the Office. Partly because of these factors and partly
because of the limitation on resources, it was decided that the
primary target audience initially would be the population of
Quebec.

As for the 'message' which was to be conveyed to Quebeckers, it was decided that, during the indeterminate period which
was to precede the referendum campaign proper, the referendum
vote would not directly constitute the defining focus for the
Canadian Unity Information Office's activities. During the
first phase of operations a broader definition of the problem
was accepted, relating to the strength of attachment of Quebeckers to Canada and Confederation. The communications effort
was devoted to painting a portrait of Canada and of what
Quebeckers derive from being Canadians, showing that they benefit from the wide range of federal government services and
programs available to all citizens, and generally making them
more aware of the positive effects of federal government activity. It is obvious that this general communications strategy is more suitable to the period prior to the referendum
campaign, and that information and communications activities
more directly related to the actual vote would be more appropriate during the campaign itself for any body that chooses to
participate actively in that process.

There are three general activities in which the Canadian
Unity Information Office is engaged. First, there is its role
as a documentation centre, assembling kits on unity subjects
(of which some 23,000 have been distributed), summarizing and
analyzing speeches and papers on Canadian unity (of which some
600 have been done), and filing and cross-referencing under 200
subject heads data from publications, press, radio and T.V.

Second, there is the role of the CUIO as a research and analysis unit, preparing rebuttals to the major PQ criticisms of the federal system, drafting material for speakers' kits, and so on

The third role involves the unit in publishing, distribution and public relations, and this is an activity which is perhaps worthy of some expansion here. The five broad categories of work are as follows.

Publications and Distribution

CUIO has prepared a wide variety of publications dealing with Canada in general, its political system and federal programs and services. As of April 1979, 24 million copies of this material have been distributed via mailing lists, Members of Parliament, display stands in federal buildings, exhibitions and in response to advertising. This material is targeted at a wide audience, although there is as well a series of more technical studies designed to provide a data base for federalist spokesmen. Five papers in this latter series have been produced so far on trade realities and economic association, the concept of sovereignty-association, the textile industry, transportation and Quebec's access to capital markets.

Exhibitions

There are three main types of exhibits to be noted here. First, the CUIO has prepared and administers two travelling exhibitions, shown in shopping centres across Canada, entitled "Notre chez nous -- It's all ours," which feature Canada's beauty and natural characteristics as a country. Second, the Office has developed and administers five exhibitions entitled "Libre service - Self-service," which describe federal programmes and contributions to five regions of Quebec (Bas St. Laurent, Gaspesie, Mauricie Bois Francs, Sagenay-Lac-St. Jean, Montreal and Quebec). These exhibitions are tailored to each region and are shown in motorized trailers. Third, there are several information kiosks and special exhibits during the summer months which distribute information on Canadian unity.

Advertising

The CUIO has initiated several advertising campaigns designed to inform Quebeckers of the diversity of programmes and services offered by the federal government, and to inform Quebeckers of certain aspects of Canadian federalism. One specific example is 'the Beavers' campaign which publicizes the list of federal departments which are at the service of the people of Canada. Another example is the series of maps which appear in Quebec shopping centres and in the Monteal metro

informing citizens of the locations of federal offices. A
third example is the 'notes on federalism' series of advertisements which is being run in Quebec weekly newspapers.

The CUIO also plays a coordination role vis-a-vis the
advertising of the federal government, reviewing all major advertising programs of federal departments from a Canadian unity
point of view.

Audio-visual

The CUIO in connection with the National Film Board is
producing two 30-minute films, which will be ready for release
in September. One is aimed at Canadians in general and is designed to show with humour the foibles and prejudices of Canadians, while the other is directed at Quebeckers in particular,
and is designed to demonstrate that being a Quebecker and being
a Canadian are perfectly compatible. The Office has also been
developing a series of audio-visual presentations aimed at the
Quebec market dealing with aspects and advantages of the federal system and Canada. The Office, also, in conjunction with
the National Film Board, produced a film to accompany the music
of the national anthem and this film is used by many T.V. stations as their sign-off at the end of the day.

Liaison and Special Projects

Finally, the CUIO is working with 95 federal departments
and agencies and with crown corporations to ensure that their
information and publicity programmes inform Canadians about
Canada and the role of the Government of Canada as well as
about the specific services which the given department provides.

CONCLUDING REMARKS

One point that comes rapidly to mind in considering the
work and experience of these two organizations is that there is
a widespread and quite natural tendency among citizens and observers to regard government information and promotion programmes with a certain skepticism. Both the Task Force and the
Canadian Unity Information Office began their lives in the
midst of criticism that they were little more than propaganda
arms of the Liberal Government.

We have seen that the Task Force was structurally independent of the government and that its central role in any case
was not directly to promote Canadian unity, but to stimulate
public discussion of the subject, to study it and to offer
policy advice. The Task Force gradually extricated itself from

21

the atmosphere of suspicion in which it was born, and I should think that the publication of the final report washed away the last vestiges of such sentiment.

With the CUIO the structural situation was and remains today quite different, for it is properly and explicitly an agency of the Government of Canada. While one may choose to question the expenditure of public funds on such activities or the efficiency with which the funds have been spent, it must, at the same time, be recognized that it is inevitable that any institution involved in education, information or communications will have a point of view of some kind, and that the orientation of the CUIO is federal and Canadian. But surely one would not expect anything else from an agency of the Government of Canada. When looking at the actual activities of the Canadian Unity Information Office, it is evident that the vast majority of the things which it does fall into two broad categories: in the first category, the Office informs Canadians about Canada, about their federal system or government and about the role of the Government of Canada in their lives; in the second, it seeks ways of strengthening Canadian identity and the sense of patriotism of Canadians. The CUIO is thus in part trying to do what many Canadian educators have said for a long time needs desperately to be done. Canadians are notoriously ignorant of their country and lack a common attachment to national symbols; there seems little doubt that this renders the country more vulnerable to threats of disunity and fragmentation. The CUIO is attempting to repair some of the omissions of the past and to establish a more solid foundation of knowledge and sentiment for the future.

There is an irony in all of this. The Task Force and the CUIO would not have been created if the election of the PQ and the consequent threat to Canadian unity had not occurred. If the supporters of unity, as exemplified by such bodies as these, are successful in their efforts, we may end up with a country much stronger than before. If we do, who can deny that we will owe something to Mr. Levesque and his supporters for that advance?

This is simply yet another example of the application of Dr. Johnson's hoary dictum that, when a man knows he is to be hanged in a fortnight, it concentrates his mind wonderfully. Dr. Johnson ought to know. If I remember correctly, he wrote Rasselas in 48 hours to pay for his mother's funeral.

CONTEMPORARY ART IN CANADA:
ASPECTS OF THE MARKETS AND CHANNELS AND IMPLICATIONS
FOR PUBLIC POLICY[1]

Alice E. Courtney, York University
Brian Dixon, York University

ABSTRACT

The marketing of art currently being produced by Canadian artists represents a number of changes and issues current in marketing today. Although marketing art is clearly a commercial activity, with buyers and sellers and producers as in any other industry, much of the marketing activity is influenced by non-profit, non-market, social and political considerations.

The question of whether intervention in the visual arts is a public responsibility has long been a matter of controversy. The form of the intervention is also questioned, notably whether government patronage should ignore the market, or act as a substitute for it, or act to improve its effectiveness in producing income for artists and distributors.

This paper reports the results of a series of surveys undertaken to examine whether, through positive government intervention, artists' incomes could be improved through improving existing approaches to marketing Canadian contemporary art. The surveys were conducted among high potential buying groups, artists, and dealers to provide information useful for policy-making with respect to Canadian art.

Study results and analysis of their policy implications indicate that there can be a useful and positive role for government intervention in the visual arts, a role aimed at helping the existing market to function more effectively and to develop further. The data indicate clear opportunities for market growth, particularly if government can take a more active role in the educative and communication functions in the market.

---

1. The data in this paper are drawn in part from a study by Bailey, Robert, Alice E. Courtney and Brian Dixon (1976), Canadian Contemporary Art, A Market Study, Ottawa: Canada Council. The study is not available for general distribution.

La commercialisation de l'art qui est actuellement prod-
uite par les artistes canadiens, représente l'un des nombreux
changements et sujets de controverse qui existent présente-
ment dans le marketing. Bien que cette commercialisation soit
nettement une activité commerciale avec ses acheteurs, ses
vendeurs et ses producteurs comme dans toute autre industrie,
une grande partie de l'activité du marketing est influencée
par des considérations dont les motifs sont sans but lucratif
ou commercial et aussi par des considerations d'ordre social
et politique.

La question qu'une intervention dans les arts visuels est
une responsabilité publique fait depuis longtemps un sujet de
polémique. La forme d'intervention est aussi discutée, notam-
ment à savoir si le patronage gouvernemental devrait ignorer
la commercialisation actuelle ou s'y substituer, ou devrait
agir de facon à améliorer son efficacité à produire un revenu
adéquat pour les artistes et leurs distributeurs.

Cet article est le compte rendu des résultats d'une série
d'études faites pour déterminer si une intervention positive
du gouvernement permettrait d'augmenter les revenus des
artistes, en améliorant l'accès déjà existant au marketing de
l'art comtemporain canadien. Les études furent menées auprès
de groupes d'acheteurs hautement prometteurs, auprès d'artistes
et de vendeurs afin de recueillir l'information nécessaire à
l'établissement d'une politique concernant l'art canadien.

Les résultats des études et l'analyse de leurs implications indiquent qu'une intervention gouvernementale peut jouer
un rôle utile et positif dans les arts visuels, un rôle visant
à aider le marché actuel à fonctionner plus efficacement et à
se developper davantage. Les données démontrent qu'il existe
des opportunités évidentes pour le développement de ce marché,
surtout si le gouvernement décide de prendre un rôle plus
actif dans les fonctions d'éducation et de communication du
marché.

INTRODUCTION

The marketing of Canadian contemporary art (that is, art
currently being produced by Canadian artists) represents an
interesting series of interfaces which reflect a number of
changes and issues current in marketing today. Although
marketing art is clearly a commercial activity, with buyers
and sellers and producers as in any other industry, much of the
marketing activity is influenced by non-profit, non-market,

social and political considerations. Because of the significant value characteristics of art, it represents the integration of market and non-market factors to a particularly high
degree. This unusual blend is caused by the substantial
amount of non-monetary motivation on the part of the various
parties in the market for art: artists, buyers and dealers.
The product characteristics were, and are, in large measure
determined by direct aesthetic or other considerations, rather
than by the normal supply-demand interaction of the marketplace.

Public policy with regard to the market for art takes
place in a context somewhat different from most government
actions in the marketplace. Throughout most of history, the
visual artist has only partly operated in the direct marketplace. Traditionally, the artist was supported in large
measure by patronage. Up to the start of the Industrial Revolution, this patronage of artists was direct, from individuals
who, at one and the same time, combined economic and political
power. The status and income of the artist were determined
typically by his role in society. Rewards and output hinged
on the dictates of role.[2] With the Industrial Revolution and
the introduction of representative governments with attendant
bureaucracies, the role of patronage in general shifted to
governments acting through various bureaucratic agencies. As
a result, there has come a real separation of the artist's
support from the market and from patronage.

CANADIAN GOVERNMENT INTERVENTION IN THE VISUAL ART MARKET

The question of whether intervention in the visual arts is
a public responsibility has long been a matter for controversy
in Canada. Government intervention has been defended on the
basis that it is requred to develop and maintain the industry
and is critical for the preservation of our cultural heritage
and cultural sovereignty. However, critics have maintained
that government intervention creates a false and inflated market for Canadian art and results in a class of dependent
artists. The form of the intervention is also controversial
and raises a number of questions, notably whether the government patronage should ignore the market, or act as a substitute
for it, or act to improve its effectiveness in producing income
for artists and distributors.

---

2. For an expansion of the issue of status, see Dixon, Brian
   (1977), The Status of the Artist, A Personal View, Toronto:
   The Canadian Conference of the Arts.

Canadian governments have been involved in the visual arts almost since Confederation. With the establishment of the National Gallery in 1880, a pattern for indirectly subsidizing artists and distributors was established. Recent government initiatives in indirect benefits have included manufacturers' sales tax relief for artists and income tax benefits for donors of art to charitable institutions.

Direct government involvement in the visual arts is a modern phenomenon, beginning in 1957 with the founding of the Canada Council. The Canada Council's programme of direct grants to visual artists has been a form of intervention that ignores the marketplace through direct subsidy of art producers. In 1977, the Canada Council made over 300 grants to individual artists. In total, grants to artists, museums and public galleries amounted to $31.8 million in 1976-77 (Canada Council 1977). It is interesting to note that the governments of most western countries made their significant expansions in this area at about the same time, during the late 50's and early 60's.

Increasingly, there has been a movement for the government to act as a market substitute, for example through purchase of art for public buildings by the Department of Public Works and other government agencies, and by the Canada Council Art Bank. The Art Bank purchases works of art and then rents the purchased works to government departments. It also has made occasional public displays of some of these purchases. Art Bank acquisitions to March 1977 totalled $4 million, with 1976-77 purchases at $755,000 (Canada Council 1977).

When the government moves into the marketplace, and when the intervention takes the form of a market substitute, there is a pressure to continue the intervention. The government substitution tends to weaken rather than strengthen normal market channels. If, under these conditions, the government is forced to pull back, the effect is likely to be doubly negative - government purchases drop or cease and the normal market is left in a weakened state.

The problem of government withdrawal occurred recently with the Federal Government's elimination of funds for Art Bank and Public Works purchases from their estimates for 1979. The Canada Council refused to accept this and diverted some of its scarce resources to keep the Art Bank alive, an action which, in the face of continued funding restraints, can only provide a short-run solution. In the wake of this substantial withdrawal of government support, it appears that damage to the normal market has occurred. Many dealers are currently in

26

difficulty and artists report a reduction in sales. It is too early to assess if permanent damage has occurred and too early to assess the extent of the damage, but the reality of the cutbacks themselves suggests the active consideration of other forms of government intervention.

An alternate form of government intervention can be positive, that is, it can be intended to improve the operating efficiency of the existing marketplace. This approach has been encouraged not only by fiscal considerations, but also by indications that artists would prefer income from sales to income from grants. The study on which the data in this paper are based was executed to gather information useful to aid the government and its agencies in providing positive assistance for the contemporary Canadian art market.

STUDY OBJECTIVES AND METHODS

The specific objectives for the study, stated in marketing terms, were to ascertain whether, through positive government intervention, artists' incomes could be increased through improving the existing approaches to marketing Canadian contemporary art. The study was conducted in the following areas: a survey of producers - Canadian artists; a survey of distributors, with primary emphasis on commercial galleries; and a survey of consumers.

The study was designed to provide information useful for policy making, and for artists and dealers interested in improving the marketing process. Given this, the various samples were picked to be typical, or to give maximum useful information rather than to be representative in a predictive sense. Thus, the sample of art buyers was drawn from Toronto and Montreal, to get the highest possible concentration of potential buyers in the two major markets. The sample of artists was drawn from Art Bank lists so as to obtain a wide selection of artists from around the country who had been clearly identified as working artists. The dealer sample was drawn from a combination of members of the Professional Art Dealers Association of Canada and dealers who had been in contact with the Art Bank, selected so as to give a range of city sizes and regions of the country. In the case of the interviews and survey, pilot studies were conducted to test and adjust the questionnaires and interview techniques. In both the artist and dealer interviews, particular attention was given to allow for receipt of as much input from these professionals as possible and interviews were allowed to expand accordingly.

SURVEY OF ART BUYERS

The major objective of this phase of the research was to establish the public's perceptions about art in general and Canadian contemporary art in particular, and to examine attitudes towards the methods of distributing art to the buying public. The sample design used selected those areas which has considerably above average income levels, in order to increase the incidence of art buyers.

Just as there are many ways of defining art, there are as many ways of defining an art buyer. It is first necessary to decide what "art" to include. For example, should people be included who buy or have bought reproductions? What about the person who just bought a painting from his friend down the street who paints as a hobby? An additional set of problems is involved in defining the buyer. Is it someone who has purchased once in his life and never since or people who buy a certain number of works each year? The problems are endless and each potential solution has many drawbacks. The problem was eventually resolved by asking the question shown below:

"Have you ever purchased an original work of art? This would include paintings, drawings, sculpture or original graphics."

Total Sample	"Yes"	"No"
529	271	258
100%	51%	49%

In the very selective sample used in this study, roughly half qualified as buyers, in the broad sense of the term. Working within this group, a number of questions were asked to help refine the definition. These included the frequency of purchase, the type of art purchased, the name of the artist and the amount spent. Two separate attempts were made to use these data to provide a useful definition of buyers. In the first, the names of the artists were compared with a directory of Canadian artists. This led to a small sub-group of buyers who had purchased Canadian contemporary art. The second approach combined the frequency and dollar expenditure data to arrive, in essence, at a continuum of buying.

Characteristics of Buyers - The "Culture" Dimension

A fairly obvious hypothesis in examining the characteristics of people who buy art is that they are "more cultural." A number of questions were included in the survey which were

culled from a somewhat longer list of questions tested in the
pilot phase of this research. Two dimensions were identified
which are useful in analysing the phenomena of art buying.
The first is a cultural activity index and it combined four
statements which measured frequency of visits to museums, art
galleries, theatres, and classical concerts. The second dimension is an attitudinal dimension which included positive and
negative items such as, "It is worthwhile to pay a lot for a
good work of art even if it strains your budget." These attitudinal dimensions measure the extent of agreement with the
relatively high utilization of resources for artistic purposes,
these resources being both personal and public. Table 1 shows
the relationship between both the cultural activity index and
the attitudinal index, taken together, with the buying of
original works of art. The results shown clearly support the
hypothesis that one difference between people who buy art and
people who don't is a cultural one.

Socio-Economic Characteristics

A second hypothesis is that higher income groups in the
population are more likely to be buyers of original works of
art. The data show that this is clearly the case. However,
buying is also related to cultural activity. Table 2 shows
the relationship between buying of art and both income and
cultural activity. The entries in the table represent the
proportion of people in that cell who have purchased original
works of art. Although the effects of both variables are
related to some extent, there is still a separate impact; that
is, even among the lowest income households (i.e. under
$10,000) there are some families with high culture activity
indices and these households show a fairly high probability of
purchasing original art. Similarly, among households with a
low culture activity index, if we look at those households with
incomes over $15,000, again the probability is fairly high.
In fact, the probability of purchasing art appears to be a
function of both these factors, i.e. culture and economics,
(both influenced by education) taken together.

A very useful by-product of this matrix is that it can be
used to define a sub-group of non-buyers who are potential
buyers. Those non-buyers who fall in the upper-right corner
of this matrix (i.e. who have both a high income and are high
on a cultural activity index), are very similar to buyers.
If the reasons why they have not, until this point, purchased
original works of art can be identified, this may provide a
method of expanding the market toward art.

Relative profiles of buyers and non-buyers with respect

TABLE 1
RELATION OF CULTURAL ORIENTATION TO ART BUYING

	total	low 1	2	3	4	high 5
		Cultural Orientation Index*				
Percentage Base	529	141	87	98	69	134
Buyers	51%	32%	45%	49%	55%	75%
Non-buyers	49%	68%	55%	51%	45%	25%

*Combination of activities and attitudes

TABLE 2
RELATION OF ART BUYING
TO HOUSEHOLD INCOME AND CULTURAL ORIENTATION

Cultural Orientation Index	Household Income (000's)			
	under $10	$10-$15	$15-$20	$20 +
High 5	45%	54%	93%	81%
4	*	50	67	89
3	36	45	36	72
2	17	37	45	65
Low 1	14	29	45	40

* sample too small

% are buyers

to the stage in life cycle, education level and age group
were examined. The differences between buyers and non-buyers
are quite pronounced particularly in the proportion who are
single, with 12% of buyers being single compared to 21% of
non-buyers. This would suggest that buying of art is linked to
the stage in the life cycle and is higher among the more established families whose children have grown up.

The education differences between buyers and non-buyers
are very pronounced with more than 60% of buyers having some
university education as opposed to slightly over 30% of non-
buyers with the same educational background. This percentage
goes to a little over 40% in a higher potential segment of non-
buyers, but nevertheless there remains a significant difference
between non-buyers and buyers. Although people with higher
education are more inclined toward cultural activities, this
alone does not explain their purchasing of original art.

Why People Buy Art

One of the questions one would like to ask in a study of
this sort is "Why do you buy original works of art?" Unfortunately, if this question were put directly to people who do
buy· art, there is a strong possibility that they might give
reasons which they felt were socially acceptable or that represented themselves in a way they would like to be shown. The
approach taken for this study was to ask people why they
thought other people bought art. The results of this question
are contained in Table 3. The first item, visual pleasure, is
a combination of two responses: "to gain pleasure in looking
at the work," and "to make their home attractive," which were
highly correlated one with the other. In total, almost 80% of
respondents ascribed this motivation to the purchase of original works of art. The investment motivation is shown as the
next most important reason. If, in fact, one-half of the
population perceives art buying to be at least partially an
investment process, this has implications for the marketing of
art products.

At approximately the same level of response as the investment motivation, is that of obtaining possessions of which purchasers can be proud. This appears to have connotations of a
social status objective. Three items were combined together to
form one dimension which could be clearly labelled social
status. "A desire to impress friends," "because it is the done
thing," "to be like their friends" were identified as possible
reasons for buying original art by slightly over one-quarter of
the respondents.

The reasons given for purchasing Canadian contemporary art,

TABLE 3
PERCEIVED REASONS FOR BUYING ART

In response to question:
In general, why do you feel
people buy original works of
art?

	relative frequency %
Percentage base = 529	
Visual Pleasure	79
- to gain pleasure in looking at the work	65
- to make their home attractive	47
As an investment	53
To give them possessions they can be proud of	50
Social status	26
- to impress their friends	22
- because it's the "done" thing	6
- to be like their friends	4
As intellectual stimulation	17
Because they enjoy the actual process of buying art	15
To cover a wall	7
To support artists	7
As something to spend their money on	5
Other/not stated	2

Multiple mentions: May add to more than 100%

32

in particular, were basically the same as those mentioned earlier with one exception. For art in general, only 7% of the population mentioned a desire to support artists as a motivation for purchasing art. In the case of Canadian contemporary art, some four out of every ten respondents cited this particular reason. This difference is important, and has implications both for encouraging buying, and for justification of public expenditures to encourage it. A surprisingly large proportion of art in Montreal and Toronto is purchased directly from the artist, indicating that a perceived motivation for purchasing art stems from a desire to aid the artist directly.

When people are asked why they do not buy art, the overwhelming opinion is because it is too expensive, either in absolute terms or in terms of it being too expensive to purchase the type of work in which people are interested. The second area of concern particularly among non-buyers, is that people feel they cannot judge what is good. Allied to this is the concern over making a bad purchase. In this context, it is interesting to note that non-buyers do feel they lack knowledge about art and Canadian art specifically. Contrary to some initial hypotheses, there seems to be little concern among respondents about the actual place in which art is purchased. Neither buyers nor non-buyers feel that there are off-putting characteristics of outlets which deter potential buyers. In other words, people feel that it is the problems, monetary and informational, associated with the purchase itself which inhibit non-buyers and not the aura surrounding the place of purchase.

The Buying Process

From the total sample in this survey, some 271 respondents, or 51% had purchased an original work of art at least once. These respondents were asked a number of detailed questions about the very last work they purchased. Slightly over six out of ten last purchases were of paintings, 20% were sculptures, 9% graphics and 6% a drawing of some kind. A surprising finding is that 60% of last purchases were made directly from the artist, either from his studio/workshop (42%) or at an exhibition of his work (18%). Only one in five of respondents made his last purchase from an art dealer and virtually no one had purchased from a department store or other source. This finding indicates that direct contact with the artist is an important aspect in the distribtuion of art. The majority of such purchases are obviously made in Canada and from Canadian artists.

The high frequency of direct purchase appears to be an attempt at personalization of the art object by the buyer. In this way the buyer gets both more needed context and an insight into the artistic process, which for the artists, is generally of greater import than the product. The direct purchase also seems to have elements of a throwback to a pre-market patronage relationship. Thus, **a direct** purchase taps a number of significant positive motives. The problems here are both of reach and volume, limiting its use as a sales device. Its obvious power, however, suggests much effort should be placed on capitalizing on the technique, while watching not to overburden the artist, or try to turn him into a salesman and deflect him from his primary purpose.

The data given some indication that the more expensive works tend to be purchased through the dealer distribution channel. One possible reason for this difference seems to lie in the higher proportion of non-Canadian work being distributed via dealers. As Table 4 shows, there is a tendency for people who bought non-Canadian works to pay more than people who purchased Canadian art.

The Buying Decision

Art buyers were asked to describe the actual process they used in deciding to buy the last work of art they purchased. They did this by choosing between alternate descriptions of the process. The first choice was between whether they were actually looking for a work of art or saw it by chance and decided to buy it. The responses indicated that for most people (50%), the situation is best described by the latter phrase, with only 35% of respondents indicating that they were actually looking for a work of art at the time they purchased. This pattern of response is very much dependent on the particular place where the purchase was made. For those respondents purchasing directly from the artist, the purchase tended to be **unpremeditated;** those who purchased from a private dealer, on the other hand, were more likely to be actively looking for a work of art (48%).

The next pair of alternatives is concerned with the high amount of thought given by purchasers to the purchase itself, the alternatives being between "saw it and bought it on the spot," and "thought about it for a few days." The responses indicate that the majority of purchasers made what amounted to an impulse purchase, they saw the work and bought it then and there. About one-quarter of respondents indicated that they had considered the purchase for a period of **time** before making it. Again, this pattern is somewhat different when we consider those who purchased from a dealer and those who purchased directly; direct purchasers tend to be more "impulse" than dealer purchasers. To a surprising degree the purchase of works of art

TABLE 4

PRICE OF LAST ART PURCHASE
CANADIAN VS. NON-CANADIAN ART

In response to question:
Roughly how much did you pay for
the last original work you purchased?

	total	Canadian art	Non-Canadian art
Percentage Base	271	186	65
under $100	49%	52%	42%
$100 to $499	43	44	45
$500 to $999	4	3	9
$1,000 or more	1	–	3
did not state	3	1	1

TABLE 5

ATTITUDES TO ART OUTLETS
ALL ART VS. CANADIAN ART

Would send a friend to:	for all original art	for Canadian Contemporary art
Percentage base	529	529
public art gallery	30%	22%
artist studio	26	34
private dealer	21	19
department store	6	4
other kinds of art exhibit	10	9

is an unpremediated on-the-spot purchase especially when the individual is purchasing directly from an artist.

The last set of alternatives available for describing the process of buying concerned the people who might influence the decision to buy. The data indicated that the decision in most cases is either a personal one or a joint husband/wife decision. This latter combination is more common with purchasing from a private dealer.

Respondents were asked how easy they feel it is to obtain information about Canadian art. The opinions indicated that the majority of respondents (60%) feel that such information is readily available. A majority of people use direct visits to galleries, studios and exhibitions at least occasionally as a source of information. This is true for both buyers (30%) and non-buyers (60%), although the non-buyers visit such places less frequently than buyers. In addition, articles in newspapers and magazines reach a majority of people at least occasionally, but among non-buyers not much more often than that. Magazines and books specifically about art have virtually no effect and reach a very limited audience even among art buyers. Although almost a third of the population have taken some educational course about art at some time, one would speculate that a good proportion of these were taken during high school days. If this is in fact the case, then the benefits to be reaped from using educational channels to communicate information about Canadian contemporary art are probably long-term in nature.

Attitudes Towards Outlets for Art

Respondents, both buyers and non-buyers, were asked to give their reaction to a number of outlets for works of art. The type of outlets considered encompassed the artist's studio, private dealers, department stores, and other kinds of art exhibition. In addition, public art galleries were included in this list. As an overall measure of preference, respondents were asked to say where they might send a friend with similar tastes who had decided to buy a work of art. Table 5 presents these data for all original art and for Canadian contemporary art. In the first instance, choices are distributed among three outlets: public art galleries (30%), artists' studios (26%), and the private dealers (21%). The relatively high standing of public art galleries is quite interesting, and suggests two possible hypotheses. First, there may be some confusion with regard to the terminology to the extent that people may have understood this term to be synonymous with private art galleries, that is, galleries where the public may view art and purchase it. The second possibility is that public art galleries represent a good first step when looking for art in order to help the prospective purchaser define the kind of thing he or she would like. If this is in fact the case, then public art galleries may offer an interesting opportunity to promote Canadian contemporary art to the general public. Public art galleries could take an active role in directing purchasers to the artists themselves. In a previous study done by the authors, it was found that public galleries, in concentrating on the critical art history assessment function, provided less current context than much of the public wanted, and certainly [3] less than the useful informative role suggested by this study.

Respondents were asked to compare the same list of outlets on three dimensions: comfortable atmosphere, high quality art, and reasonable prices. In summary, it would seem that artists' studios and department stores are felt to have the most reasonable prices, public art galleries to have the most comfortable atmosphere and the highest quality art. It is interesting to examine how these perceptions relate to overall preference for one outlet over another. Typically, comfortable atmosphere is the most important characteristic in determining outlet preference. Taking the results as a whole, one would reach the conclusion that in evaluating outlets for art, people are likely to take into account the atmosphere in which the art can be viewed and then to some extent, the perceived quality of the art being carried. Only after this are they concerned about the reasonableness of the prices.

SURVEY OF ARTISTS

As an essential part of the investigation of the marketing of contemporary Canadian art, forty-four Canadian artists were interviewed. The purpose was to investigate artists' behaviours and perceptions with respect to their work and the way in which it is marketed. A related purpose was to learn their perceptions of the government's role in marketing art. A list of contemporary Canadian artists was developed from the files of the Canada Council Art Bank. From this list, a random selection of artists living in Quebec, Ontario, the Maritimes and the Western provinces was chosen for personal interview. The picture that emerged was one of highly individualized people with highly individualized behaviours and attitudes. There were no consistent differences in behaviours and attitudes in

---

3. From Dixon, Brian, Alice E. Courtney and Robert Bailey (1974), The Museum and the Canadian Public, Toronto: Culturcan Publications. Available from the Canadian Museums Association, Ottawa, or agencies of the Federal Government Printing Office.

different regions of the country, between more or less experienced and successful artists, between French and English, nor between the young and old, male and female. The clear finding is that each artist differs from every other in the work he produces, the way he views that work, and in the way he markets it. No one marketing system, therefore, is likely to be "ideal" or even suitable for every artist.

The average artist in the sample had more than five years experience as a professional. Only eight of those sampled had worked as professional artists for less than five years and a quarter of the sample had been professionals for fifteen or more years. With the exception of three of the artists interviewed who reported being self-taught, all had engaged in formal art training and many held degrees in art or art history. Many had other kinds of art experience as well. Despite this experience, more than half of those interviewed earned less than $6,000 last year from the sale of works of art. Five artists earned between $6,000 and $10,000, and nine earned over $10,000 a year from sales of art. For almost two thirds of the artists interviewed, sale of works of art accounted for less than 50% of total income. They augmented their income by a wide variety of means, but by far the most commonly cited was teaching art or art history. Some artists cited exhibition, rental, and jurying fees as additional sources of income, and several mentioned government grants.

Means of Sale

Most of the artists interviewed attempted to sell their works through more than one means. However, the primary means of sale for most artists was either through a dealer or direct from the studio. Thirty of those interviewd sold through dealers and thirty-three sold directly from their studios. Twenty-two sold through exhibition in public galleries. A variety of other means of sale was also used including artists' co-operatives, competitions, and art fairs.

Among those artists who sold primarily through their studios, a variety of reasons were given. Four of those interviewed stated that they felt that they were not yet ready for dealer exhibition. Two stated that dealers were not interested in their work, and one that his work did not sell in galleries. Several others stated that they did not like the pressure and other demands of the dealer relationship. Two artists in a western city stated that there was no good dealer in that city. Five of those interviewed stated that they resented dealer commissions and believed they could make more money selling directly. Among those who sold primarily through dealers, the

major reason cited was that dealers gave them access to more
people and therefore to a greater volume of sales. The second
most important reason cited was that these artists were dis-
interested in the selling function and felt that their time was
better spent producing works of art. Among artists with more
than ten years experience, 11 out of 16 sold primarily through
dealers.

Sales Through Dealers

Thirty of the forty-four artists interviewed sold·through
commercial art dealers. For twenty of these artists, dealers
were the primary means of sale. Most of those artists who
sold through dealers were represented by more than one dealer.
When an artist was represented by more than one dealer, the
reason, in some cases, was that the artist sold original works
of art through one dealer and graphics through another. More
often, however, the reason for being represented by more than
one dealer was to obtain a greater geographic coverage for the
artist and thus greater exposure and possibility of sale.

In only one case did the artist interviewed have a written
contract with his dealer. The artist was paid a monthly stipend by the dealer and in return the dealer received a 90% commission on sales. In all other cases the artists had informal,
unwritten contracts with their dealers. In 65% of cases, dealers charged the artist a 40% commission on sales. In approximately 25% of cases, a lower commission was charged, usually
33-1/3%. Six of the artists who sold through dealers stated
that their arrangement included a commitment to pay the dealer
a commission on all sales made, including those made directly
from the artist's studio. The commission rate for such sales
varied from 10% to 40%.

On average, dealers provided their more established and
experienced artists with the opportunity to offer a one-man
show approximately once every year and a half. For less experienced artists, the number and timing was similar but it was
usually a group show. In addition, most dealers also undertook
to keep some of the artist's work on display on a regular basis.
Typically, the works of art to be shown are chosen mutually by
the dealer and artist, although with more established artists
the dealer may accept whatever the artist wishes to show. Both
one-man and group shows run from three weeks on average to a
month in some cases.

There is no clear pattern concerning arrangements for
financing and promoting shows. What appears to be the most
common arrangement is for the artist to pay one-way transportation of his work, for the dealer to insure it while on show,

39

and for the artist and dealer to split costs of promotion 50/50. However, there are many different variations of financing arrangements and an artist can expect different arrangements from different dealers and even from the same dealer in different situations.

The promotional arrangements made for a show also vary widely, and artists themselves differ widely in their interest in and awareness of these arrangements. The extent of promotional activity varies widely from one dealer to another and one show to another. Some artists reported significant advertising and publicity efforts for their last show; others reported that no efforts were made beyond invitations to the opening of the show.

On the whole, the artists interviewed were satisfied with the job dealers were doing for them. Seventy percent of those selling through dealers reported that they were satisfied with the sales level achieved, and a similar percentage were satisfied with the terms of their informal agreement with the dealer. The great majority felt that their work was being shown sufficiently by the dealer and were also satisfied with financial arrangements and with the speed of payment from the dealer.

Direct Studio Sales

Thirty-three of the artists interviewed sold directly from their studios and for nineteen of these artists, studio sales were their primary means of getting their work to the public. Among the artists who sold directly from their studios, only one reported having a formal studio showing of his work. The artists used a variety of means to promote sales through their studios. Most often they rely on word-of-mouth from their friends and previous buyers to interest others in their work. In addition, the artists report that visitors come to their studios as a result of seeing their work on exhibition in public galleries, art fairs, competitions and so forth. Consequently, the artists who are most active in selling through their studios typically make efforts to insure that their work is exhibited in community, university and other public galleries. The artists who see smaller, and more select groups of buyers, tend to concentrate their efforts on showing their work to representatives of the Art Bank and other government departments and agencies. These artists will approach those agencies directly and request studio visits.

Public Galleries

Twenty-two of the artists interviewed reported that they exhibited their work in various kinds of public galleries in

order to stimulate sales. The kinds of galleries used for this
purpose were varied and included community galleries, university
galleries, art fairs and exhibitions in relatively large-scale
public galleries such as Glenbow or the Art Gallery of Ontario.
The great majority of these artists reported that less than 25%
of their sales resulted from such exhibitions. However, it is
important to note that prospective sale is only one of many
reasons artists wish to be represented in such galleries.
Other reasons include the need to be exhibited to the public,
the desire to develop a reputation and the desire to see their
work alongside that of other artists. Several younger, less
experienced artists reported that the reason they exhibited in
public galleries was that this was the only way they could get
public exposure for their art.

        In general, those artists who were exhibiting through
public galleries expressed satisfaction with their dealings
with these galleries and with their terms of agreement. Despite this, however, many artists interviewed seemed to believe
that public galleries could do much more to aid the contemporary
artist. For this reason, attitudes of the artists interviewed
toward public galleries often contained negative elements.
Artists felt that the public gallery was a difficult environment in which to gain entry and that it was conservative,
narrow and outdated. In particular, they cited the fact that
most visitors to public galleries are not aware of the fact that
the work exhibited can be purchased from the artists. The artists interviewed believed that the public gallery must take a
more active role in informing the public about potential purchase of the work it exhibits.

Artists' Attitudes Toward the Government Role

        All but three of the artists interviewed had had their
work purchased by the Canada Council Art Bank. The vast majority felt that the Art Bank had been a "fantastic idea." Most
of those interviewed believed that the influence of the Art
Bank had been widely felt and had not only supported the
artist himself but had also helped to encourage a growing
market for Canadian art.

        Despite this, negatives were also stated. Several of
those interviewed believed that the Art Bank had resulted in
overpricing of contemporary Canadian art and that the Art Bank
had therefore created a "false market" which could not long be
continued. Among the younger, less experienced artists, some
said "the government has become the market - what happens when
they stop buying?" Other criticisms came from some of the
Western artists who felt that officials of the Art Bank did not
visit their cities often enough. In addition, several artists

were concerned that works purchased by the Art Bank tend to disappear from public view and are not shown or exhibited **publicly.**

Attitudes toward government grants, loans and subsidies were mixed. Many of the younger and less established artists interviewed believed that such government aid was essential in the Canadian environment; a few stated that subsidizing meant that the market and the environment for Canadian art were not really very healthy. Another artist who admitted that grants had been beneficial, nevertheless saw them as "charity." For this reason, many of those interviewed felt that purchase of their work benefitted artists more than did grants. This presents a real conflict. Artists, as is understandable since they live in a market economy, would generally prefer to earn money in ways comparable to the rest of society. Yet, as has been indicated, much artistic activity and support is outside the market mechanism or motivation. This indicates a very subtle and difficult role for government and quasi-government agencies.

SURVEY OF DEALERS

The purpose of this part of the study was to determine the role of commercial galleries in the marketing of contemporary Canadian art. Thirty-seven personal interviews were conducted with a sample representing major art centres in Canada.

Twenty-five of the dealers indicated that between 90% and 100% of their sales were of contemporary Canadian art. Of the 37 galleries, 24 specialized in contemporary Canadian art; however, even of those 13 galleries which did not specialize in contemporary Canadian art, 6 indicated that sales of contemporary Canadian art accounted for 70% or more of their total sales. Of all the galleries interviewed only five indicated that the sale of contemporary Canadian art accounted for less than 50% of their total sales. Most dealers indicated that Canadians buy Canadian art and that the art market is essentially local. As one dealer pointed out "Canadians buy Canadian and Canadians buy American but Americans don't buy Canadian." In effect, it was generally acknowledged that there is not a substantial international market for Canadian art.

The differences among galleries stood out more strongly than the similarities. The galleries ranged from those carrying well-known contemporary Canadian artists alongside well-known international artists, to those who dealt with relatively unknown local artists and also carried a variety of crafts. Gallery owners differed in background from the experienced art historian to the amateur hobbyist. In addition, individual gallery owners and directors saw their roles quite differently. Many galleries were interested in selling contemporary Canadian art in Canada, while some were interested in promoting contemporary Canadian art internationally.

The galleries interviewed varied widely in the price range of Canadian contemporary art sold. The range was from less than $500 to more than $20,000. Almost half the galleries (18) centred around $5,000 as the maximum price of art sold. Of 31 galleries who gave an average selling price for Canadian contemporary art, most noted an average selling price of less than $500. Typically, a gallery would represent between eleven and thirty Canadian contemporary artists.

Finding New Artists

A number of important points emerged concerning the way in which galleries find new artists and "acquire" their works. For the most part, galleries appear to find new artists through an informal network of people and events; for example, on the recommendation of the artists whom a gallery already represents; through friends; or by visiting other galleries, public art showings, and art schools. Many artists approach galleries for representation. Gallery operators indicated that, although they were open to considering these artists, this was not generally a successful means of making contact with "good" artists. Most of the galleries introduce one to four new "unknown" artists each year. The limitations to the number of new artists that a gallery can introduce each year is determined by a number of factors including the availability of "good" artists, the ability of the gallery to offer more exhibitions, and by the particular specializations or interests of the gallery or owner.

Artist/Dealer Relationships

Galleries reported making a variety of arrangements for carrying artists' works. These arrangements, whether written contracts or informal verbal agreements, concern whether the works of art are purchased by the gallery or taken on consignment; whether the gallery will be the only agent dealing with the works of the artist (exclusivity); what the commission will be; who will handle the costs of an exhibition; and whether any stipend will be paid. Of course, where the works are purchased outright, there was no commission and the galleries paid the full costs for exhibitions. However, some arrangements could be made with respect to exclusivity or stipends. Those galleries who purchase artists' works tend to be larger, more experienced dealers and with a large volume of sales.

Promotion and Sales

Without exception, gallery owners or directors attributed the ability of their galleries to sell art to the reputation of the gallery and/or owner. Reputation in the opinion of most gallery operators interviewed was related to the quality of the work carried. Generally, the longer a gallery had been in business, the more "established" it became in terms of the gallery's reputation and the reputation of the artists represented. The appearance of a gallery was reported by some to be important as a means of creating an "image" which was appropriate to the art being carried and the clientele a gallery was attempting to develop.

Gallery owners or directors found it difficult to respond to detailed questions which attempted to determine the relative importance of a variety of marketing factors, e.g., length of time in business, location, appearance of the gallery, advertising, exhibition, mailing lists, professional association, range of art carried, etc. Many pointed out that separating these factors, one from the other, was not very useful. All gallery owners or directors were in agreement however, that all of these were important factors in the promotion and sale of art.

Advertising (restricted mainly to newspapers and art magazines) was generally considered by gallery owners and directors to be expensive but necessary, yet of unknown effectiveness. Discussion with respect to advertising tended to centre on the need for improved press coverage of art and gallery exhibitions. This ranged from concerns about the quality of reviewers to the need for more reviews. All the galleries interviewed had mailing lists. However, at least partially due to the expense of printing and mailing, gallery operators reported a tendency to limit the size of their lists through regular updating. One gallery charged an annual fee for mailings. Most galleries restricted mailings to regular clients and indicated that announcements were kept as simple as possible.

Except for the few artists who maintain a high public profile, artists were said to play a very limited role in marketing. The one exception was with regard to pricing, where most gallery owners reported that most artists set the prices of their work. This, however, was generally done in consultation with the gallery operator. The major factor in pricing that was reported was the extent to which an artist is known. Other factors such as size and medium were reported to be less significant. In addition, the means of sales influenced price. In the artists' survey, all artists stated that prices were higher in "good" galleries. Geography also affects price and works are sold at different levels depending on the country and city where sold.

Of the two ways in which a gallery can realize a profit from the sale of art - a gallery can earn a percentage (commission) through the sale of works of art held on consignment, or a gallery may invest in a work of art (i.e. purchase) and realize a profit through an increase in value of the work over time - it was obvious that a number of galleries made profits as a result of investment, but very little discussion of this aspect of the art market took place.

The Views of Commercial Gallery Owners and Directors Regarding the Role of Government in the Marketing of Art

Gallery owners and directors were asked to comment generally on the role of government in the marketing of contemporary Canadian art and on current government programs and policies. Many issues were raised and a range of opinions regarding the various issues were expressed.

Of all the issues considered, the Art Bank was by far the most contentious. Most dealers agreed in principle with the Art Bank, indicating that it was more desirable for government to purchase the work of artists than to give them grants. It was also pointed out that the Art Bank purchases are good for an artist's reputation. However, almost all dealers interviewed were very critical of the Art Bank's policy of purchasing art directly from the artist. Dealers felt that it was reasonable to expect assistance to go to the artist but that it did not require the government to be in competition with galleries. In addition, some felt that the Art Bank was subverting the dealer system by going directly to the artists. Without a strong dealer system, they contended, it was impossible to have strong visual arts. Many felt that the Art Bank was destructive of the gallery/artist relationship. Concern was also expressed that the Art Bank skims off the best of an artist's work which then cannot be shown publically.

Other opinions were expressed concerning the proper role of government in the visual arts. These included the extent to which government should be involved in marketing, the approach the government should take, and the role of commercial galleries with respect to government actions. The comments varied widely and covered a great range of possible actions. However, one common theme emerged: dealers were primarily concerned with government interventions that they felt would improve the possibility of sales of Canadian contemporary artists. Four areas were seen as contributing to improved

45

sales.

First, dealers wished the government to take a more active role in educating the public about art. This educative function, they believed, could be achieved through government financial support for good art education in the schools. It could also be achieved through government aid toward better media coverage for the visual arts. For example, some dealers felt that the government could subsidize good books on contemporary Canadian art and subsidize art magazines. Second, particular emphasis was given to the possible role of government in establishing an international market for contemporary Canadian art. Many dealers felt that the Canada Council should support regular showings of Canadian art internationally. Third, dealers were concerned that purchases of art by government and public agencies should be more visible, both to Canadians and internationally. They believed there should be frequent public showings of the Art Bank and other government collections. Finally, a number of gallery owners believed that government could do more to aid in the development of new artists, for example, through a grant system whereby commercial galleries would be encouraged to show new artists.

SOME COMMENTS AND CONCLUSIONS

As a result of indications from the data in the study and analysis of policy implications for the marketing process, a number of observations seem warranted. There is consensus among both artists and dealers that there can be a useful and positive role for government intervention in the visual arts, a role aimed at helping the existing market to function more effectively and to develop further. There is clear agreement that such positive intervention is the preferred role for government. In addition, the data from the survey of art buyers and non-buyers indicate clear opportunities for market growth, particularly if the government can take a more active role in the educative and communication functions in the market.

Some specific marketing actions aimed at development of a mode of positive intervention are suggested below:

1. There should be an expanded role for public galleries in providing information and promotion concerning contemporary Canadian art. The study indicates a strong desire for this role on the part of artists and the buyer survey strongly reinforced such expansion. Even more, an active role for public galleries in the direct facilitation of

sale of contemporary Canadian art should be fostered. Buyers and potential buyers, as indicated
in the art buyer survey, would react favourably
and likely increase purchases significantly if this
direct role was expanded. In encouraging such development, however, great care must be taken not to hurt
the normal channels for sale of contemporary art through
commercial galleries. The study indicates that the
public and artists feel the commercial galleries fill
a needed role. There is room for improvement, of
course, particularly in promoting artists and reaching
out to new markets and buyers.

2.   There are strong indications that government
agencies such as the Canada Council need to significantly
improve their interaction with the commercial dealers,
particularly to make more use of their expertise in
the visual arts. Such comments were widely reported in
the dealers' survey. However, it is more than just a
special interest claim from a group feeling left out.
The other interviews, surveys and observations also
strongly indicate the need for a very active and reinforced relationship between governments and dealers.

3.   The stronger and more active the dealers (not
just in the major centres) the more the market will
be expanded and developed, the more the public will
be exposed and educated, and the better the chance of
moving the contemporary Canadian art scene forward to
a major position nationally and internationally. It
is fundamental to a strong international marketing
activity that there be a large and complex commercial
dealer market for contemporary art in this country. In
order to attract buyers from other countries, the commercial market needs to be perceived as, and be, large,
active and dynamic.

4.   A contemporary Canadian presence needs to be
encouraged outside of the country more actively than
at present. This means continuation and stepping up
of current programs which encourage cultural and
aesthetic exposure. It also means much more stimulation and assistance for direct commercial activity
outside of the country, particularly in areas such as
sales representation, exhibition costs, information
and promotion.

5.   It appears preferable to increase artists'
income through sales rather than grants or even
direct government purchases. This observation is,

in part, a reflection of artists' feelings expressed in the survey. It is also logical as a move to strengthen further the buying process and the level of market activity, and keep artists actively in the market, all of which will enhance long-run sales possibilities. To the extent possible within fund limits, grant activity which aids the marketing and sales process would be appropriate (i.e. help for exhibitions, commercial tours, promotion, media coverage, international marketing activity, facilitation of exposure between artists and potential buyers).

6.   The quantity, quality and scope of media coverage for the visual arts needs to be substantially improved. This would have both short and long-run benefits. In the short run more adequate information about commercial exhibitions and more extensive and current review would undoubtedly increase sales. In the long-run, a major expansion in communication to the public is needed for significant impact on the growth of number of buyers. Some form of initial or perhaps even continuous support for well produced and distributed frequent publications giving full reportorial coverage is needed, at the very least.

7.   The consumer survey clearly indicated that any significant increase in the number of active buyers of contemporary Canadian art as opposed to more sales by current active buyers will only come through education which leads to increased cultural awareness and activity. The effect of education on buying outweighs but does not eliminate other influences such as income.

8.   The art buyers' survey indicated a high level of sales through direct contact with artists. Many buyers clearly enjoy the direct contact as an element important in their purchase of contemporary art. At the same time a major expansion of sales by this method would be inefficient and eventually troublesome and negative to the creative process. Dealers need to be encouraged to capitalize more on this desire of the public, particularly as it reflects a desire of the public to aid artists. However, it is expensive and time consuming for the dealers to initiate much activity in this area on their own. Governments might well play a role in helping the dealers extend this artist/buyer interface, although specific measures will have to be very carefully planned and executed.

9. Increased exposure of the Art Bank and other quasi public and public collectors would be helpful to the public. A few steps have been taken in this direction (for example, at Stratford, the National Arts Centre and Harborfront in Toronto) but much more would be beneficial. In this way the public would get a much enhanced sense of the contemporary art scene in Canada, within a framework of expert selection and approval. This would substantially enhance the process of public education and would improve confidence and knowledge necessary for more buyers to enter the market.

10. To augment the process indicated in the last recommendation, corporations and other major private collectors of Canadian art should be encouraged and perhaps assisted to display their collections publicly. **Such activity would reinforce the process of** positive education of the public to the purchase of contemporary Canadian art. It would provide additional reinforcement by example, of the validity and desirability of purchasing. Every encouragement should be given to continued and expanded corporate art collecting. Active purchases by corporations further strengthens the commercial market and provides a major supplement to the limited possibilities for significant private patronage.

These conclusions and the study itself delineate a role for government which is essentially supportive rather than competitive with regular commercial channels. Given the continued need for patronage, this will be a difficult line to hold and will require constant surveillance both by government and its agencies and by other members of the contemporary art market.

REFERENCES

20th Annual Report, Canada Council 1976-77 (1977), Ottawa: Government of Canada.

THE POST OFFICE IN THE MARKET PLACE: A TEN YEAR RETROSPECTIVE

Stanley J. Shapiro, McGill University
J.A. Barnhill, Carleton University

ABSTRACT

Marketing, viewed both as a distinguishable function and recognized unit of the Canada Post Office, has just celebrated its tenth birthday. Three separate stages - establishment, development and maturity - into which the past decade can be divided are identified. The governing orientation, new programs and activities and the organizational structure of CPO-marketing during each of these stages is discussed at some length. Particular attention is paid to market planning activities, research programs, efforts at environmental forecasting, new product launches and intra-organizational difficulties. How the objectives of CPO-marketing were redefined in light of the cost structure and the public sector context of CPO-marketing is also examined. An attempt is made in closing to show that CPO-marketing differs appreciably from private sector marketing in terms of how it is affected by the traditional "uncontrollable elements" of marketing management. It is further suggested that marketing's major contribution - to the Canada Post Office in particular and, more generally, to most not-for-profit entities - may be its role as a future-oriented unit and proponent for change in organizations that would otherwise become preoccupied with immediate problems and concerns.

Le marketing, doublement considéré comme une fonction distinctive et un complément reconnu par le Bureau des Postes Canadiennes, vient de célébrer son dixième anniversaire. Les trois étapes distinctes dans lesquelles ces dix dernerières années peuvent se diviser sont identifiées comme suit: l'instauration, le développement et la maturité. L'orientation dirigeante, les nouveaux programmes et activités, et la structure d'organisation du marketing du B.P.C. durant chacune de ces étapes sont discutés assez longuement. Une attention toute particulière est portée sur les activités de planification du marché, sur les programmes de recherches, sur les efforts de prévisions écologiques, sur le lancement de nouveau produits et

et sur les difficultés intra-organisationnelles. Il est aussi
discuté comment les objectifs de marketing du B.P.C. ont été
redéfinis à la vue du cout de la structure; le contexte du
secteur public du marketing au B.P.C. est aussi examiné. Enfin,
un essai tente de démontrer que le marketing au B.P.C. diffère
sensiblement du marketing en secteur privé, dans le sens qu'il
est affecté par les traditionnels "éléments incontrolables" de
l'administration du marketing. De plus, il est suggéré que la
contribution majeure du marketing - en particulier au Bureau
des Postes Canadiennes et, de facon plus générale, à la plus
grande partie des entités sans but lucratif - peut etre son
rôle en tant qu'unité s'orientant davantage vers le futur et
proposant de nouveaux changements à ces organisations qui,
autrement, auraient tendance à ne se préoccuper que d'affaires
et de problèmes immédiats.

INTRODUCTION

A few agencies of government and many crown corporations operate under the twin disciplines of profits and the
public interest. However, the Canada Post Office (CPO) is by
far the largest government department in this category and probably has the most profound impact on Canadians and Canadian
society. Consequently, a study of marketing in the CPO with
particular reference to the social, political and economic
context within which that marketing takes place seems an appropriate contribution to a Canadian publication on macro-marketing.

Two other factors have made this investigation an
especially timely one. The first study of how the Canada Post
Office might develop a marketing capability and of what priority CPO marketing concerns should be was commissioned in early
April of 1969 (Mintzberg 1969). Although the decade that
followed has been one of sustained marketing activity, ten
years is still a short enough period to review relevant developments in some depth. A marketing retrospective also seems
appropriate at a time when the Canada Post Office may be making the very important transition from a Department of Government to a Crown Corporation. Such a review provides some
basis for comparing what has been accomplished to date under
the present structure with the likely future impact on CPO
marketing of crown corporation status.

Marketing within government is often justified as
a method for furthering the public interest and/or better
serving the public. Emphasis is also placed on the importance
of a pervasive change in attitude: "Patrons are, too often,
people we patronize; customers, in contrast, are people whose

custom we strive to deserve." However, a marketing orientation, marketing programs and a marketing organization are not easily introduced within the public sector.

This paper reviews at length both the problems that existed and the degree of marketing progress made by the Canada Post Office. Receiving particular attention is the fact that CPO-marketing differs appreciably from private sector marketing in terms of how it is affected by the "uncontrollable" elements of marketing management. The concluding paragraphs suggest that marketing may have an important and as yet only partially appreciated role to play, specifically in a CPO that is either a crown corporation or a government department, and more generally in any not-for-profit entity. The role in question is that of a future-oriented unit **and chief** advocate of organizational change.

STAGES OF MARKETING MATURATION: THE ESTABLISHMENT STAGE

Eric Kierans became Canada's Postmaster General on July 7, 1968. The appointment of Mr. Kierans was an important event, an impetus for change in the CPO at a time when change was generally believed to be in order. Problems confronting Mr. Kierans included labour unrest, mounting deficits, fluctuating standards of service and adverse public reaction to the first postal rate increase in many years. Given such conditions, the Kierans appointment was widely hailed as an especially appropriate one. More specifically, the new Postmaster General was viewed as a "problem solver, a doer," a man with a business background who would make changes: for example, bring in new management, develop a new organization, guarantee employees an opportunity to make meaningful contributions, and more generally, provide the CPO with a new sense of purpose.

Mr. Kierans soon acted in a manner consistent with his reputation. By September of 1968, he had directed the CPO to retain outside consultants to work with Post Office employees in carrying out a detailed evaluation of every aspect of Postal operations. By November, 1969 one of Canada's leading management consulting firms, in a baseline report intended as an overview of the Post Office and its management, had reached the following conclusion:

Officers in the Department lack the marketing orientatation essential for an efficient service. They see the market as users of mail rather than of communications, transportation and banking services. The services that the Department is permitted to provide under the Post

Office Act have been interpreted precisely and have been offered in an administrative and unimaginative manner. (Canada Post Office 1969, p. 41)

Kates, Peat, Marwick & Company also chose to emphasize the need for a consumer or user-orientation. Particular stress was placed on user expectations of postal service:

Economic trends, technological advances and social factors have all influenced the changing expectations of the user in respect to mail service. In the context of improvement and dramatic advances in all elements of the economy, they rightfully anticipate greater reliability and speed in mail delivery. (Canada Post Office 1969, p. 11)

Although the Kates, Peat, Marwick report was a landmark study of CPO organization and administration, another of the 15 investigations dealt specifically and at much greater length with marketing issues. That study, The Post Office in the Market Place, launched the first stage of marketing development in the CPO and made four major conceptual contributions:[1]

1.   The Post Office was presented as a marketing system consisting of an input sub-system, process sub-systems and an output sub-system;

2.   The concept of market segmentation, both by customer and by content, was introduced;

3.   Marketing strategies reflecting a consumer orientation, clearly formulated marketing objectives and a series of operating premises were formulated; and

4.   The influence of environmental restraints, notably competition, technological developments, and socio-economic trends were discussed at length.

In addition, the Marketing Task Force made specific recommentations as to the nature of the marketing information system that was deemed necessary and the type of marketing organization being recommended. A detailed study of Parcel Post was

[1] An expanded treatment of the establishment stage is found in J.A. Barnhill, "Developing a Marketing Orientation - A Case Study of the Canada Post Office" in Ronald C. Curhan, (ed.) 1974 Combined Proceedings (Chicago: American Marketing Association, 1975), pp. 293-298. In contrast, the remainder of this historical review draws heavily upon internal CPO marketing

presented as an illustration of how marketing might be applied to an existing CPO program.

Implementation

Although the report of the Task Force introduced several new concepts that were to prove useful in establishing a Post Office Marketing presence, the marketing executives subsequently hired from "outside" still had their work cut out for them in operationalizing its recommendations. By May, 1970 the direction CPO marketing would take in this initial stage was becoming clear. The approach, a rather fundamental one by commercial standards, was nevertheless new and different to a government department.

CPO management began one report with a discussion of "purpose," much of which revolved around Peter Drucker's classic question "What is our business?" Conventional marketing thought is also reflected in the following statement of marketing policy approved in 1970 by the CPO.

> It is the policy of the Canada Post Office to become marketing oriented, through development of a marketing capability and organization, comparable to the best examples in private industry. In our view, the Post Office exists to serve the people of Canada, in pursuit of their social and economic objectives.

> Marketing orientation therefore means an organized concern for the needs of our customers, and a recognition that we exist to serve them. Services must be planned, and priced so as to meet the greatest degree of customer need, while achieving a much more satisfactory financial result. The aim is to bring every service provided by the Post Office as close a possible to financial self-sufficiency, thereby relieving the burden on all other services, and on the tax-paying public.

On the strength of this policy statement, six basic marketing objectives each one corresponding to a principal area of CPO marketing activity, were formulated:

> 1.   Maintain a direct and continuous channel of communication with major customers, to ensure servicing of their total needs in the most profitable way and to provide essential customer contact.

----

documents that have not been publicly disseminated and, consequently, will not be referenced.

2.   Maintain a comprehensive appreciation of all factors
having a significant effect on present or future market
conditions, including customer needs, competition, technological changes, mailing and distribution patterns and
business trends.

3.   Investigate, evaluate and develop product and
pricing changes and new service concepts which may
enhance the profitability of existing services and
identify new lines of profitable endeavor for the Canada
Post Office.

4.   Simplify and refine methods of doing business to
the mutual advantage of both customers and the Post
Office.

5.   Develop a selling capability which will ensure
achievement of full market potential for each product
and service of the Canada Post Office.

6.   Improve and maintain Post Office public offices
to the best contemporary standards of appearance and
decor, and recruit, train and motivate counter sales
and service staffs to serve customers in the most
efficient and friendly way.

Strategies

Based on the direction provided by these objectives, an
analysis of eleven major marketing problems and eight major
marketing opportunities was then conducted. A Marketing Plan
that included a set of market **and product** strategies evolved
from this analysis. Thus, by mid-1971, planning was an integral part of CPO marketing. The role of marketing in the CPO
was discussed at some length in the first formal marketing plan.
More specifically, consumer acceptance and competition were
revealed as two major concerns:

To a large extent..., the challenge of the future for
the Post Office is a Marketing challenge. The need
to provide services and products which meet with
customer acceptance and which contribute to overall
profit is obvious. The ability to deal effectively
with customers and to explain how the P.O. can meet
their service needs will be of increasing importance
in an environment of growing competitiveness.

Since market planning required information on products,
markets, customers and competitive conditions, a marketing
research program was launched in 1971. (Prior to the initiation

of that program, no marketing-oriented research other than the studies conducted in 1969 by the Marketing Task Force had been undertaken.) The research program was introduced with two objectives in mind: (1) to provide a substantive base for analyzing market conditions, public attitudes, the image of the Post Office, the manner in which business uses the mail, etc. and (2) to reveal specific user needs, suggestions, ideas and concepts regarding the market - the need for courier service, householder perceptions of advertising mail and business suggestions regarding postal service standards and the proposed postal code.

A concern with the future and its impact on the CPO was reflected in the commissioning of an environmental forecast. The resulting report, released in March of 1971, explored the likely impact of environmental change on the CPO and its marketing activities. Particular attention was paid to socio-economic trends, apparent changes in life styles and expected technological breakthroughs.

Organization

The new marketing organization was being established during that time when the CPO as a whole was moving toward a decentralized structure, a change that had been recommended by Kates, Peat, Marwick & Co. The marketing structure, formally introduced in 1971 at the Headquarters level, is set out in Exhibit I. That structure reflected a mix of the functional (Philatelic and Retail and Postal Rates & Classification) and market or user oriented units (Service Development and Customer Sales & Service). When the marketing branch was first established, it was headed up by a Director-General. This position was later up-graded to Assistant Deputy Postmaster General-Marketing.

Later in 1971, a marketing organization was developed for Ontario's "pilot" autonomous region and Directors appointed for the four marketing sections of the Headquarters Branch. A Coordinating Marketing Council was also established at approximately the same time. Marketing personnel throughout the CPO organization were expected to use the Council as a vehicle for integrating their efforts and exchanging information. The emphasis was on cooperation and coordination since Headquarter's Marketing personnel had no line authority over regional marketers who reported, instead, to the Assistant Deputy Postmaster General responsible for that region's overall operations.

By mid-1971, marketing had established a fundamental presence in the CPO. Flowing from this commitment to marketing were efforts to develop new services, market information and

EXHIBIT I

HEADQUARTERS MARKETING ORGANIZATION (CIRCA 1971)

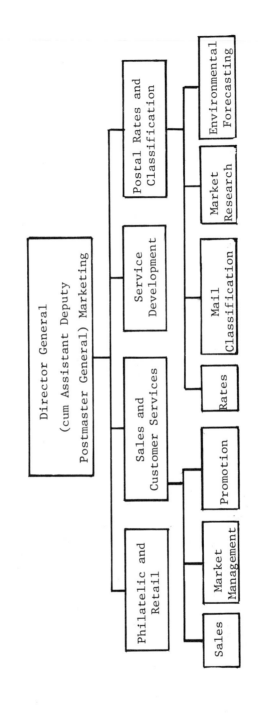

higher postal rates.

THE DEVELOPMENT STAGE (MID-1971 - MID-1974)

A "commercial" orientation was a fundamental part of CPO marketing management philosophy throughout its second or developmental stage. Seeking profits for the CPO, still viewed as an organization likely to become a crown corporation, was an objective consistent with that commercial orientation. An ongoing commitment was also made to the formulation of market-oriented policies, objectives and goals. Assured Mail was introduced, in part, as a "brave attempt to set standards for service." This program was oriented toward first in, first out service rather than the random mail handling - occasionally involving last in, first out postal service - that previously took place.

Development of the postal code was another major effort by the CPO to set and meet delivery standards. Marketing and Operations worked together in developing, implementing and modifying the Postal Code. Indeed, marketing was then being viewed by the CPO, according to the former Assistant Deputy Postmaster General - Marketing, as an "extension of Operations" whose role was "to sell the code" and provide market intelligence through Postal User Conferences and its sales representatives.

The first of these Postal Users Conferences, held in Ottawa in October of 1972 with 360 people in attendance, was noteworthy primarily for the opportunity afforded CPO executives to meet the organization's major customers. In 1973, the Second Canadian Postal Users Conference was held in Winnipeg with the major focus at that time being on Assured Mail performance. Reports of service tests, conducted across Canada between April and July, 1973, indicated that 89 percent of the 250,000 test pieces mailed from 150 locations to 22 destinations had been received on time, 10 percent were one day late and only 1/10 of 1 percent were more than three days late. Other major market-related topics discussed during the second Postal Users Conference included postal coding and the provision of free list coding for users, postal service improvements, customer relations and changing concepts in goods distribution.

CPO management continued to have a keen interest in the environment of its marketing program. A second Environmental Forecast had been produced by January of 1972. An overall review of economic, social, business and technological trends was again provided. In addition, special studies were made of specific environmental factors such as the shortened work week, general labor force attitudes and characteristics, electronic funds transfer systems, centralized credit transfer systems, direct mail advertising and transportation.

A management "Delphi" on the future of the CPO was also conducted during the summer of 1973.

Strategies

CPO marketing personnel were also devoting considerable thought and effort to planning and strategy formulation. The end product of these deliverations can be considered the four major strategic thrusts reflected in the new programs discussed below.

Postpak. This new service was a response to the fact that the CPO's traditional parcel post business was declining. In Nova Scotia, for example, a new internal distribution system for catalogue customers was being used by Simpson Sears. The CPO responded by conducting, in collaboration with Eatons, a feasilibity study of a new form of Parcel Post Service. Based on this study, management concluded that the CPO was capable of competitively distributing consolidated parcels weighing up to 66 pounds, the traditional limit for Fourth Class mail packages. Once the consolidated packages reached their destination point, individual items would be distributed by the recipient.

In 1971, Postpak service was established in five major centers (Halifax, Montreal, Toronto, Winnipeg and Regina) with a limited number of destinations (approximately 60), most of which were catalogue sales offices operated by Eatons and Simpson Sears. Competitive pricing and the absence of paper-work for users (such as the weigh bills required by "common carriers") were strategic aspects of Postpak that generated a growing demand. Consequently, this new service went "national" in 1972. Nevertheless, Postpak was not without its problems. The program achieved varying degrees of acceptance in the increasingly decentralized CPO. More specifically, doubt was expressed as to whether or not Postpak was making a "net contribution" (CPO terminology for profit).

Telepost. This new CPO service was launched in late 1972. The United States Post Office reported that its new Mailgram service had proven successful. Contrastingly, Canadian tele-communications companies were having their difficulties deliver-ing telegrams. Consequently with the help of a few "non-scientific" studies, Telepost was developed, with the telecom-munications companies provided te "hardware" and the CPO its extensive delivery service.

Telepost initially required senders to have Telex machines
However, this service was subsequently expanded to over-the-
counter and "phone-in" services at CN/CP offices. Telepost
strategy was based on competitive pricing (i.e., less than
night letter), use of special envelopes, targetting promotion
and a selective distribution network. Telepost was expected to
have expanded to 55 centres by 1979 serving a very large proportion of the total Canadian market.

Telepost generated a certain degree of conflict within the
CPO organization even though this service had been reasonably
well received in the market place. Once again, contributing
difficulties included organization confusion as to objectives,
internal communication problems and varying degrees of regional
acceptance.

Certified Mail. In late 1972 and early 1973, Certified
Mail was launched to meet the need by government, law firms
and financial institutions for a signature acknowledgement
receipt type of service that did not involve the hand-to-hand
delivery associated with Registered Mail. (The latter service
had been a money loser for some time.) Certified Mail was
tested for market potential and its contribution to the service
mix of the CPO. Study results, both in their own right and in
comparison with a similar U.S. service, led to a national
launch.

Certified Mail was far from an immediate success. The
expected shift in demand from Registered Mail did not initially
occur. The major barriers were legal stipulations and statutes
which stated that, under specified circumstances, official
notice and other legal documents could only be delivered by
Registered Mail. With the gradual modifications of such provisions, Certified Mail has grown steadily in popularity.

Unlike the situation with Postpak and Telepost, relatively
few problems were encountered in launching Certified Mail. CPO
personnel, both at Headquarters and "in the field", (Regional
and District offices), viewed Certified Mail as an "appropriate"
new service that had been logically developed and properly
launched. Consequently, the desired degree of internal cooperation and regional support was obtained without undue difficulty.

Philatelic. The Philatelic program of the Retail Marketing Branch also achieved considerable success. Until 1973,
the Philatelic program was a responsibility of the Financial
Administration Branch. This followed from the fact that stamp
collecting was viewed essentially as a prepayment for the
delivery of mail by those who subsequently retained stamps for

60

their own purposes. Consequently, there was no Philatelic marketing organization and no particular concern with the needs of stamp collectors. In early 1973, however, a decision was made to develop a market-oriented Philatelic program. By 1975, the Philatelic Program was viewed as an integral and successful part of CPO Marketing. Revenues were up nearly six-fold from $2,500,000 in 1973 to $13,500,000 in fiscal 1975. Not only had a source of high contribution revenue been exploited, but new markets had been developed, public needs were being better satisfied and higher standards for postage products had been established.

Other marketing initiatives between 1971 and 1975 deserve at least brief mention. A study of electronic mail was under-taken and Phase I (involving 13 case studies of major mail users) of the CPO's Busines Market Analysis was completed. A formal management information service was also developed. In addition, the first market demand model for Canadian postal products (MADAM) became operational in 1974. MADAM was expect-ed to provide CPO management with a capability for assessing the impact of alternate rate structures and changes in the level of economic activity on mail volumes and revenue.

Marketing Organization

By 1974, the Marketing organization at CPO headquarters had been modified to reflect the marketing developments of the period. The organization, as then constituted, is presented in Exhibit II. At the Branch level, the Postal Rates and Classification Branch became, after some modification, the Marketing Services Branch. Mail Classification was assigned to an expanded Service Development Branch. Marketing Admin-istration and Sales Analysis were both included in new Market-ing Services Branch. A comparison of this chart with Exhibit I also reveals that a number of units, called divisions in Post Office parlance, had been transferred from one branch to another.

This period, however, should also be noted as one of org-anizational unrest within CPO-marketing. The marketing executives who had joined the CPO from the "outside", i.e. from the Canadian National Railway and the private sector, were becoming increasingly frustrated. Difficulties were experienced with the decentralized organization, the production (operations) orientation of the CPo and the federal bureaucracy of which the Post Office was a part. The organization environ-ment, along with the absence of an overriding profit objective and a reluctance to be held to service standards, was perceived as inhibiting the development of a truly market-oriented Postal Service. According to Mr. G.C. Campbell, the first Assistant

EXHIBIT II

CPO Marketing Organization – Headquarters, 1974

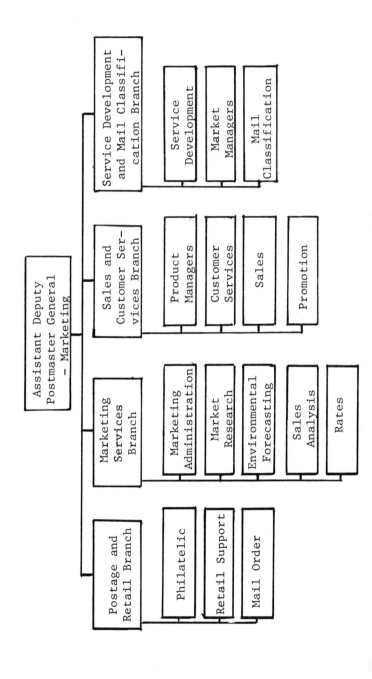

Deputy Postmaster General-Marketing, CPO-Marketing was, instead, being pressured to function as an "old line" sales department charged with selling whatever its production-oriented organization chose to produce. He also believed marketing was being viewed by other units as essentially a public relations function. By painting mailboxes, setting up boutiques and using other "cosmetic" techniques, the public could be kept happy. By mid-1974, Mr. Campbell had concluded that his expectations for CPO-Marketing were incompatible with existing organizational pressures and practices.[2]

THE MATURITY STAGE (MID-1974-MID-1979)

By late 1974, CPO Marketing had become more oriented toward internal conditions, particularly the overall financial situation of the CPO. In early 1976, the importance of profitable **marketing** (and operations) was emphasized in an address by the new Assistant Deputy Postmaster General - Marketing in which he stated: "...the job of Marketing can be summarized in six words, to improve the net financial position."

Both formal market research and periodic meetings with customers revealed that real or perceived service failures, most notably unreliability and inconsistency of service, were regarded as the most serious CPO deficiency. More specifically, strife-ridden labour-management relations, the unrealized expectations associated with mechanization and other operational dislocations had to be solved if CPO Marketing was to gain credibility with its customers and compete successfully in the market place.

A review of principal marketing functions, conducted in September of 1974, reached the following conclusions:

- product/service offerings to the market were expected to gain acceptance and prove sufficiently attractive to maximize net financial results;

- the product/service offerings of the CPO were expected to realize maximum possible revenues even if such offerings failed to meet all the expectations of the market place;

- CPO marketing administrators, especially those directing sales functions, were to achieve the

---

[2]Impressions gathered by the authors during an interview with Mr. Campbell in late January, 1979.

optimum balance of sales, costs, service quality
and customer attitudes;

- the best possible relations were to be established
with major customers, customer associations, special
interest groups and other influential bodies whose
attitudes toward and opinion of the CPO were of great
importance;

- the operational side of the CPO was to be supported
by CPO-Marketing's achieving cooperation and assistance
from customers;

- the Personnel/Labour Relations functions were to be
supported in a manner consistent with the marketing
progress of the CPO.

The increasing internal and financial orientation of CPO-
Marketing was clearly reflected in Marketing objectives for the
period 1975-77. These objectives included: a) specified
revenue and volume targets; b) a required degree of code acceptance and mail standardization; c) selective new services (e.
g., Courierpost and Urban Parcel Delivery); d) effective
communications with customers, customer associations and other
influential groups; and e) understanding of and commitment to
the Marketing role and objectives by all employees of the
organization, both front-line and managerial.

Productivity Selling. One of the priority thrusts of the
middle 70's was "productivity selling." In July of 1975, the
Marketing Branch of the Manitoba Postal District outlined the
concept in a report referred as a "Productivity Selling Pack-
age."

A concise definition of Productivity Selling is
practically impossible as it covers such a wide
range of activities, and can take so many varying
approaches. The objective, however, is clear:
THAT PLANT EFFICIENCY IS MAXIMIZED BY THE MAILING
PROCEDURES OF THE CUSTOMER.

CPO sales people were expected to convince major mail
users that - by adopting productivity maximizing procedures in
their plants - they would benefit from "better mail service."
Customer resistance to productivity selling was expected since,
in many cases, the benefits associated with this program: a)
were perceived as, in fact, part of "normal" postal service;
b) tended to be intangible and hard to document; and c) would
result in additional activities and costs being incurred by
the customer. Such resistance was to be overcome by "aggres-

64

sive and continuing sales effort."

The expected benefits to the CPO of productivity selling were believed to justify a major effort along these lines.

1. through productivity selling activity, and results, Marketing can firmly establish its value in the organization with line management;

2. by ensuring the customer follows proper mailing procedures through productivity selling, there is an increased probability of satisfactory service performance, and in turn, customer satisfaction and repeat business revenue; and

3. through productivity selling, there is opportunity to identify new applications for postal services and generate new business revenue. It provides an excellent opportunity to acquire a thorough knowledge of the customer's operation and establish a sound business relationship with management contacts.

Revenue Generation. In an effort to increase its revenue, the CPO undertook to increase both postal rates and the volume of mail being handled. Subsequently, rate increases were scheduled, the Secretary of State started to pay a subsidy that covered the full costs of Second Class mail and the volume of certain classes of mail actually increased. The Marketing Plan for 1975-6 and to 1979-80 postulated increased revenues of 7 to 8 percent for each of the five years covered by that plan.

Corporate marketing strategies for 1975-6 to 1979-80 included:

1. expanded sales of existing services;

2. complementing existing services with feasible new services;

3. pricing all services competitively and in proper relation to each other; and

4. encouraging customers to "trade up" to services which are more profitable to the CPO.

These general strategies, in turn, were translated into market and product line strategies. In the correspondence and communications market, the strategy emphasized services related to the rapidly growing electronics communication segment. In addition, flexibility in pricing such services was recognized as necessary to retain the business of large volume users. In the direct mail segment, considered to have the largest growth potential for the CPO, the strategy involved working in cooperation with the direct marketing industry and being price and service competitive with private distributors. Marketing strategies for parcel distribution, identified as another promising growth market, included promotion of Courierpost as a competitively priced delivery service providing distribution between major urban centers.

As far as product line strategies were concerned, Premium Mail was to be hard-sell oriented. A direct sales effort stressing the speed and reliability of hard copy mail was to be aimed at selected identifiable targets. This sales effort was to be augmented by a direct mail campaign and advertising in the busines press. Strategies for Assured Mail involved improving public awareness of what the term meant through direct mail and media advertising, sales contact with large volume mailers stressing the potential cost savings and, of course, improved performance. Third class (direct) mail was scheduled to grow significantly because of a strategy based primarily on close sales reprsentative contact with direct mail users, associations and large retailers. Direct selling and advertising were to be used primarily for promoting parcel sales to large volume urban and inter-city users. In 1976, the rates for Parcel Post were based, for the first time, on the distance each parcel was to travel.

These strategic thrusts were supported by an extensive set of tactical marketing programs and work plans. New programs were required for the achievement of satisfactory service levels, the securing of customer support of mechanization and the training of operational, sales and managerial personnel. Consequently, sales performance measurements, a national sales plan, distribution guides and similar activities facilitating rationalization were introduced. The Standards and Code Task Force, established in January of 1976, continued its work through 1977 and 1978, completing a major postal codes and standards research project along the way. Selective new products and services were developed and launched but only after careful research, analysis and testing. A parcel post strategy aimed at competing effectively with UPS, Canpar and Air Canada was approved in early 1977. Field testing of this new service, Priority Post, started in January, 1978. The decision to move to national implementation was made late that same year.

Organizational Issues

The period began with CPO-Marketing suffering from considerable organizational turmoil. In early 1974, the first Assistant Deputy Postmaster General-Marketing (ADPMG-Marketing) went on full-time French language training for a year. Subsequently, Mr. Campbell decided, for reasons previously mentioned, to leave the CPO. After an 18 month period of "acting" replacements, Mr. Larry Sperling, formerly of IBM and Consumers Distributing, was appointed ADPMG-Marketing in October, 1975.

The organization Mr. Sperling inherited was not in the best of health. Despite some very competent people in such units as Rates and Classification, Market Research and Philatelic, CPO-Marketing - perhaps understandably - lacked cohesiveness and a sense of direction. An internal "climate" report which had severely criticized the Marketing Branch to the point of suggesting that CPO Marketing be abandoned further complicated matters.

What had prompted such severe criticism of CPO-Marketing? The most likely explanation is the way new products and services had been launched in the past. CPO-Marketing, in its zeal to introduce Postpak and Telepost, failed to coordinate effectively with the operating units of the CPO organization. (On the other hand, the decentralized organization and a production bias made such efforts at communication and coordination far more difficult than is usually the case.)

Problems with the Assured Mail program had a still more serious effect. Even the name of the service, both in French and in English, posed difficulties. There was a failure to inform the public that the program was intended to be merely a scheduled service based on times of mailing and normal operating conditions. Delivery, however, was not "assured" in the customary sense of the word. Also, poor communication and coordination with the Operations unit of the Post Office once more resulted in a lack of cooperation and support for "Assured Mail."

Given these and other adverse organization conditions, the new ADPMG-Marketing had to move quickly to rectify the situation. Primary attention was devoted to the support of effective individuals and contributing components. These executives were to be shielded from the on-going organizational criticism associated with real and alleged CPO-Marketing mistakes. A major effort was made to develop credibility for CPO-Marketing with other parts of the postal organization, especially with Operations. Initially, there were some modest shifts in the organizational structure with more major organizational changes subsequently occuring. (Basic organizational areas of responsibility are identified in Exhibit III).

An effort was next made to develop roles for marketing appropriate to the expected performance of the entire organization. One such role involved CPO-Marketing supporting financial and **operational** aims, for example, through productivity selling, revenue generation, the promotion of the postal code - of standards and related procedures facilitating mechanization. A more traditional marketing role involved showing the "marketing concept" in action. Useful linkages were to be provided between major mail users (and their associations) and the operating units of the CPO organization. A third role involved leadership in the CPO's overall planning process. Marketing studies and marketing strategies were expected to serve as the point of departure for overall departmental planning. To the extent that it was possible, emphasis was placed on total "organizational marketing," not merely by a Branch at Headquarters or by a limited number of District or Regional marketing specialists.

THE CONTEXT OF CPO MARKETING

The essential task of marketing was defined over twenty years ago as creatively adapting to external factors that are both uncontrollable and constantly changing. What constitutes significant external factors or uncontrollable elements will differ somewhat from organization to organization. In most cases, however, Howard's classification of marketing management uncontrollables into demand, competition, distribution systems, public policy and organization is a useful starting point (1973).

The environmental constraints confronting Post Office marketers differ, but only in degree, from those facing their corporate counterparts. The paragraphs that follow will document the fact that existing similarities are often far more striking than any differences. CPO marketing has obviously recognized the importance of environmental factors and organizational constraints. It has used the results of its studies of the external environment as a framework for marketing planning. After some painful lessons, the CPO's marketing unit has also learned to function effectively within the larger organization.

Demand for Market Analysis

A great deal of CPO-Marketing effort and attention has been devoted to studying existing patterns of demand and fore-

EXHIBIT III

AREAS OF CPO MARKETING RESPONSIBILITY - CIRCA 1979

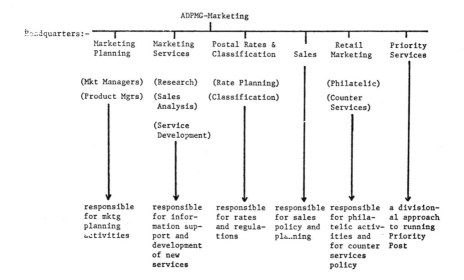

Headquarters:-

ADPMG-Marketing

Marketing Planning	Marketing Services	Postal Rates & Classification	Sales	Retail Marketing	Priority Services
(Mkt Managers) (Product Mgrs)	(Research) (Sales Analysis) (Service Development)	(Rate Planning) (Classification)		(Philatelic) (Counter Services)	
responsible for mktg planning activities	responsible for information support and development of new services	responsible for rates and regulations	responsible for sales policy and planning	responsible for philatelic activities and for counter services policy	a divisional approach to running Priority Post

Regions:-   4 Regional Sales Directors

responsible for coordinating
Regional and District activities

Districts:-   14 District Sales Managers

responsible for:

a) direct sales programs (execution)
b) customer service (complaints,
   claims and enquiries)

69

casting how such patterns are likely to change in the foreseeable future. One major aspect of this effort was the aforementioned sustained commitment to the monitoring of environmental changes likely to affect CPO markets.

As the decade passed, successive efforts at environmental scanning became progressively more action-oriented. Such efforts tended to be combined with forecasts as to the likely effect of externalities on existing post office markets and the likely volume of mail. Efforts at environmental analysis were also accompanied by a pronounced emphasis on identifying, segmenting and studying markets and/or customer groups.

Given the wealth of data that is now available, it is hard to believe that the first list of the Post Office's large customers was a by-product of the 1969 Marketing Task Force. Subsequent investigations have far more carefully documented the fact that a relatively small number of customers generate most of the mail carried by the Canada Post Office. In addition, every important Post Office Customer segment has been studied in considerable detail one or more times over the last decade. Periodic Postal Users Conferences and regular meetings with interested trade associations have also provided valuable market place feedback.

Competition

The Canada Post Office, circa 1969, was not permeated with a concern for what competition might do to established markets. Exceptions did exist such as the determination at the time to preserve the statutory monopoly on the handling of first class mail. However, that a substantial amount of potential business was being lost by artificial restraints on the types of third and fourth class mail the Post Office would deliver was not a matter of major concern. After all, catalogues, parcels and samples were not realy what most operating executives wanted to move!

The aforementioned efforts at market analysis in particular and , more generally, the existence of a marketing unit appears to have greatly altered the previously prevailing ethos. The same sort of business treated with indifference, if not disdain, a decade ago constitute the target markets being cultivated with increasing frequency and, in the case of third class or "advertising mail," with considerable success.

The competitive impact of new technological breakthroughs in traditional Post Office markets has also been closely monitored by CPO marketing. Long distance data transmission,

facsimile transfer of written material, text editing type-
writers which can send to and receive from similar machines
elsewhere, electronic funds transfer systems and corresponding
developments in the parcel market are now recognized as being
likely to have a major effect on the Post Office. Awareness
of these factors and corresponding developments in the parcel
market is reflected in the following extract from a CPO planning document:

> If the Post Office continues to react to
> competitive threats with inaction or slow-motion
> reaction, it will find itself handling the expensive
> volumes. In the communications/funds transfer market
> the volumes we will lose are those that are best
> suited to machine processing (standard size and
> coded). In the goods market, Canada Post will lose
> the more profitable business to business transfers
> in and between major centres and Canada Post will
> be left with the more expensive deliveries to house-
> holds, smaller more remote centres and rural areas.
> In the advertising mail area, it will also be the
> more expensive deliveries to rural points which the
> Post Office will retain.

Distribution System

The CPO analogy with commercial marketing breaks down in
the area of distribution systems. The corporate emphasis is on
selecting from among the existing network of marketing institutions those particular units which will become part of a given
manufacturer's own channels of distribution. Appropriate
physical distribution decisions are then made. CPO marketers,
however, lack the options and flexibility of their counterparts in industry. Except for possible improvements in the
sale of stamps, existing distribution systems are not likely to
change appreciably in the foreseeable future. Mail kiosks at
the corner of the street from which all householders must
obtain their mail or home delivery every other day with letters
being picked up as well as dropped off may be economically
desirable but such modifications seem politically impossible,
at least for the foreseeable future. Political considerations
also reduce CPO control over the number and location of Post
Offices.

The Post Office is, by far, the most extensive collecting,
sorting and disbursing mechanism in the nation. In some
respects, the obligation to deliver mail to all Canadians,
however remote their location, is a great disadvantage. Competitors can and do attempt to "skim off the cream" from
heavily travelled routes leaving the Post Office compelled to

service other locations where private enterprise sees no liklihood of making a profit. On the other hand, no other Canadian
organization or institution has the capability of calling on
every Canadian home. There are also more individual Post
Offices than all the Canadian chartered banks collectively
have branches.

Universal home delivery capability has been successfully
marketed to advertisers sending either addressed or unaddress-
ed third class mail. This fact suggests that the CPO may be
able to capitalize upon the advantage of a universal distribution system which it must, in any case, operate.

Cost

The cost structure of the Post Office has a very pronounced effect both on what can be accomplished and what should
even be attempted by CPO marketing executives. Most service
institutions, be they profit-oriented or otherwise directed,
are labour intensive organizations that do not lend themselves
to economies of scale in production. Opportunities for
mechanization or automation may exist but these are limited.
More business usually means, at least in a period of inflation,
that total costs - of which labour is the major component -
will go up at least as rapidly as revenues.

This service industry "fact of life" has had a very pronounced impact on CPO marketing. Personnel costs in recent
years have averaged 70% of total costs and have exceeded, by
a considerable margin, total Post Office revenues. **Phrased**
another way, the Post Office would still have operated at a
$200,000,000 deficit in both the 1976-77 and 1977-78 fiscal
years had its only costs been labour costs! Since there are
few economies of scale, marketing could not make the same
contribution rightfully expected of it in a capital intensive
organization.

High labour costs notwithstanding, the existing picture
would have been even more disturbing had the Post Office not
appreciably mechanized its operations over the last decade.
That the new Postal Code gained a high degree of acceptance,
especially from Canada's large scale corporate mailers, also
helped to control costs. As was indicated earlier, a considerable proportion of total CPO marketing effort and energy has
been devoted to facilitating these related efforts at cost
reduction.

Facilitating cost reduction through customer cultivation
rather than generating additional revenues may appear at first
glance to be a marketing objective unique to the CPO. Subse-

72

quent reflection indicates, however, that such action is an organizationally appropriate parallel to Ontario Hydro's efforts to demarket electricity or Bell Canada's emphasis on curtailing peak period use of telephones.[3] That Ontario Hydro and Bell Canada wished to reduce their capital requirements while the CPO's concern was with direct labour costs is irrelevant. All three cases demonstrate the need for an organization's marketing effort to adapt itself to the realities of its particular cost structure.

Public Policy

The very existence of the CPO reflects a recognition by government that provididng a postal system is a major public responsibility. At the same time, it is believed that such a service should be provided as economically as possible while minimizing the demands made on the public purse. Allegiance to these twin responsibilities is even found embodied in the approved objective of the organization.

> "To provide postal service to the people of
> Canada at rates which will provide a standard of
> service adequate to meet their needs without incur-
> ring subsidization from general taxation other than
> that required to cover losses specifically identified
> in relation to other government objectives."

The existence of an inherent contradiction between the Post Office as public service and as business enterprise has long been recognized both in this country and elsewhere. The public service nature of the Post Office requires it to engage in activities it might not otherwise carry out and to provide an all pervasive input, processing and distrubtion network. The CPO must also sell to all Canadians at essentially the same price despite the very real differences in the cost of serving different markets. Finally, the public service mission makes the Canada Post Office a prime target for requests that the network be used without appropriate compensation by other government departments to achieve their objectives. For example, Members of Parliament send out their mail without paying postage. Income tax forms are distributed for National

---

[3]For a discussion of Ontario Hydro's "demarketing" efforts, see J.A. Barnhill, "Environmental Forces and the Evaluation of Demarketing by Ontario Hydro" in George Fisk and Robert W. Nason, Macro-Marketing: New Steps on the Learning Curve (Boulder: Business Research Division, University of Colorado, 1979), pp. 335-355.

Revenue without payment ot the CPO and mail to and from Nouveau Quebec moves at preferential rates.

The problem of second class mail brings all the conflicting pressures and issues into perspective. Newspapers and magazines have been distributed for decades by the CPO at a fraction of the true costs of handling that material. Such publications contribute to a sense of Canadian identity and even to the cultural health and well being of the nation. However, does this fact entitle the publications in question to be distributed at a loss? If so, how much of a subsidy should be provided and by whom?

Only recently has it been agreed that the Ministry of State for Cultural Affairs should make a $125,000,000 transfer payment to the Post Office to cover the real distribution costs of second class mail. Such a transfer payment is consistent with the aforementioned objective of the Post Office - providing postal service at cost except when unprofitable activities are in the public interest. If any subsidy is required, it should be paid by the Department charged with that particular public interest responsibility.

The marketing impact of the Post Office become a crown corporation will be discussed more fully in the next section. However, a change in organizational form will not, in and of itself, eliminate the dichotomy between the public service and the business aspects of Post Office operations. Canadian Crown Corporations are not now entirely immune from political pressure and other Postal Administrations operating in a fashion analogous to a crown corporation still do not have "private sector" freedom of action.

Organizational Structure

The original Post Office marketing task force carried out its assignment in the expectation that the Canada Post Office would be a crown corporation no later than the early 1970's. Though the logic supporting crown corporation status was generally accepted and widely endorsed by Post Office management, no immediate action was taken to bring about such a change. In the early and mid 1970's, CPO management turned most of its attention to other problems that would have to be resolved whether the Canada Post Office remained a department of government or became a crown corporation.

Delay in the CPO becoming a crown corporation does not appear to have placed major restrictions on the activities of the marketing unit. Admittedly, the "one price" policy of the CPO as Department of Government made it impossible to introduce a quantity discount structure that would provide large customers with a real inducement for cooperating with CPO efforts at mechanization and coding. However, much of the desired degree of customer cooperation was obtained without such a direct financial inducement.

CPO marketing, of course, has been adversely affected by the many problems which crown corporation status might solve. A Post Office that was a crown corporation would have a greater degree of control over its own labour relations and its own physical facilities. It would no longer be forced to operate within a constricting governmental mold even though its rates would be set in a manner similar to that of Air Canada or Bell Canada. (Under the Crown Corporation legislation tabled in November of 1978, future rate increases would require the approval of a regulatory body established to determine the justification and reasonableness of all such requests.)

The likely impact of Crown Corporation status on CPO labour relations remains to be determined. Obviously, any strike reduces the Post Office's volume not only during the period of that strike - but to a lesser and more difficult to measure degree - in the months and years that follow. Perhaps most of the volume that could be lost to competing organizations because of a strike has, in fact, already been lost. The volume of first class mail handled by the Post Office in the future is more likely to be affected by technological breakthroughs in information transfer than by labour unrest. However, maintaining a profitable share of the total parcel (fourth class) and advertising mail (third class) markets would appear to depend on the ability of the CPO to provide a reliable, competitively priced operation. Any benefits associated with the introduction, under CPO marketing guidance, of new services and improved programs in these areas would be more than offset by continued labour unrest.

INSIGHTS FROM A RETROSPECTIVE

The investigation that was conducted as part of this historical review suggests that an efficient CPO marketing capability has existed for some time. Marketing studies, plans and programs have been both carefully designed and professionally implemented. Success in revenue selling, in winning acceptance for the Postal Code and in encouraging commercial customers to behave in a manner facilitating mechanization finally appears to have gained marketing a considerable degree of internal organizational acceptance. The organizational problems of earlier years reflecting an initial naivete as to how much marketing could accomplish and how fast it could move

75

in a decentralized, production-oriented government department are on their way to being resolved.

That CPO-Marketing is emerging as the primary future-oriented unit and the chief advocate for organizational change in a Department otherwise overwhelmed with present practices, immediate problems and past procedures may be this study's most significant finding.[4] The "change agent" role might have been anticipated from a unit charged wtih monitoring the environment and tracking competition but it is, nonetheless, a role whose crucial importance is only now being fully appreciated. Marketing's real value in its second decade may depend on its degree of success in converting the entire Canada Post Office into a market responsive organization. The status of that organization, be it Government Department or Crown Corporation, may not be as important as a willingness and an ability to make necessary changes in behaviour and performance. More generally, the real contribution of marketing to both government agencies and not-for-profit organizations may be the futures orientation and the impetus to market-responsive-change that must inevitably be provided.

REFERENCES

Canada Post Office Department (1969), A Blueprint for Change, Ottawa: (a study done by Kates, Peat, Marwick and Co.), 41.

Howard, John A. (1973), Marketing Management: Operating, Strategic and Administrative, Homewood, Illinois: Richard D. Irwin, Inc.

Mintzberg, Henry et al. (1969), The Post Office in the Market Place - Report of the Marketing Task Force, Montreal: Stanley J. Shapiro, Ltd.

MARKETING ASPECTS OF
CANADIAN MERGER POLICY

George S. Day, University of Toronto
Douglas J. Tigert, University of Toronto

ABSTRACT

The lack of a viable merger or combines law has become a
significant national issue. Whatever policy is eventually adopted toward the restriction or encouragement of combination, a
central issue will be the identification of the relevant market.
Only after this is established can possible anticompetitive effects be evaluated. Marketing concepts and approaches can make
an important contribution to market definition questions, especially if there is acceptance of a demand perspective rather
than a supply perspective based on production processes and inputs or operations. The different implications of these two
perspectives were illustrated with an analysis of the takeover
of Simpsons by the Hudson's Bay Co. Potential anticompetitive
effects were identified as a consequence of the Bay having substantial market share in a number of product classes and close
to complete control over shopping centre development in
Eastern Canada.

Le manque de lois viables sur les corporations ou les
amalgamations est devenu une question nationale importante.
Peu importe quelle politique est éventuellement adoptée vis-à-
vis des restrictions ou des encouragements aux coalitions, la
question principale restera l'identification du marché appro-
prié. Il ne sera possible d'évaluer les effets anti-compé-
titifs que lorsque ces lois auront été établies. Les concepts
et méthodes de marketing peuvent un apporter une contribution
importante aux questions de définition du marché, surtout s'il
y a acception d'une perspective de demande plutôt qu'une perspective d'approvisionnement basée sur des procédés de production et de données ou d'opérations. Les implications dif-
férentes de ces deux perspectives furent illustrées par une
analyse effectuée lors de l'achat de Simpson's par la compagnie de la Baie d'Hudson. Les effets potentiels d'anti-com-
pétition ont eur pour conséquence de donner à la Baie un sub-
stanciel montant des parts du marché d'un nombre de produits et
un contrôle presque complet du développement des centre d'achats de l'est canadien.

INTRODUCTION

This is a crucial period in the evolution of a Canadian merger policy. After years of extended but fruitless discussion, there is a distinct possibility that a more restrictive policy will be adopted. It is this possibility that will expand the role of marketing analysis in the evaluation of merger cases.

There are two features of the current environment which support a forecast of a policy change. First, a series of high profile mergers has brought the issue of potential anti-competitive effects of mergers into the public arena - and vividly demonstrated the impotence of the present Combines Investigation Act. Second, there is now a wide range of alternative merger policies to choose from, whose strengths and weaknesses are reasonably well understood.

The purpose of this paper is to contribute to the process of choice among the alternative policies by clarifying a crucial element of each of the alternatives, the definition of the relevant product-market. This determines the arena within which a determination of possible anti-competitive effects of merger is made. Marketing has a body of theory and methods to contribute to this issue, albeit with considerable adaptation. To set the stage for this analysis we will first compare and contrast the major alternatives to the existing law. This will be followed by a discussion of the conceptual issues underlying the relevant market question. The issues and some solutions will be illustrated with an application to the recent merger of the Hudson's Bay Company and Simpsons Limited.

ALTERNATIVE APPROACHES TO MERGER POLICY

The variety of legal approaches to anti-competitive mergers can be roughly classified along a continuum; anchored at one end with the U.S. Clayton Act and at the other end by the present Combines Investigation Act. A number of specific dimensions underlie this continuum, each contributing to increasing rigor in restricting mergers, when moving from right to left.

Combines Investigation Act

Mergers in Canada are presently governed by Section 33 of this Act. It is an indictable offence to form a merger (or a monopoly) by which competition in an industry is lessened, or is likely to be lessened, to the detriment of or against the interests of the public, i.e. consumers, producers, or others.

CONTINUUM OF APPROACHES TO MERGER POLICY[1]

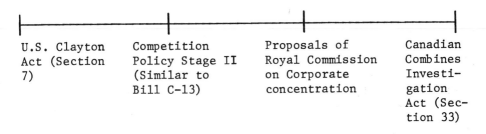

U.S. Clayton Act (Section 7)	Competition Policy Stage II (Similar to Bill C-13)	Proposals of Royal Commission on Corporate concentration	Canadian Combines Investi- gation Act (Sec- tion 33)

While the act is very clear and quite broad, the courts have chosen to interpret the act in a very narrow sense, by seeking overwhelming evidence that competition will be lessened to the public detriment. Only four cases have ever reached criminal trial.[2] The first two, Canadian Breweries, in 1959, and Western Sugar, shortly thereafter, both ended in acquittal. The Electric Reduction Company in 1970 pleaded guilty to a merger charge. In 1974, K.C. Irving Limited was found guilty by the trial court but the decision was reversed on appeal. Canadian Breweries had acquired about 65 percent of the Ontario Beer market at the time of its trial. K.C. Irving had acquired the last remaining English language newspaper in Nova Scotia when it was charged. Nonetheless the courts concluded in these cases that, despite the dominant market shares, there was no proof of specific instances of public detriment.

For constitutional reasons it was thought in the past that Parliament could legislate in this field only by using criminal law. This requires cases to be tried in the courts and that charges by proven beyond a reasonable doubt under strict rules of evidence. With mergers, current case precedents require conclusive proof that competition is likely to be lessened "in the future" and that there will be detriment to the public interest. It is virtually impossible to demonstrate beyond a reasonable doubt that detriment will occur in the future. This present law effectively allows any merger unless it creates a virtual monopoly, with no competition from imports. And as time passes after a merger, a conviction is less and less likely because higher prices or other adverse consequences could be

---

1 Although it is helpful to think of a continuum, we are actually dealing with an ordinal scale where distance have no meaning. Some proposals have not been portrayed on the continuum, even though they represent other points of view. A good example is the Skeoch–McDonald report (1976).

2 For analyses of these cases see G.B. Reschenthaler and W.T. Stanbury (1977), McFetridge (1974) and Jones (1967).

attributed to the other intervening factors (Cheveldayoff 1979).

Because of the lack of cases there are virtually no pre-cedents to guide the definition of the relevant markets. The law is limited to defining monopoly as substantial control of "the class of business" in which they are engaged "in any area of Canada." Accordingly, only strict product definitions have been accepted, without consideration of even close substitutes:

> "Thus in the Canadian Breweries merger case of a few years ago, the defense argued that the relevant market was not beer, but as a minimum was all alcoholic beverages, in-cluding wine and hard liquor, and probably should be seen as all beverages, including soft drinks and milk. The prosecution argued that the market was beer, that was what the charge read, and that's what it was, beer and nothing else - and the court agreed. In the Eddy Match case, the court agreed that a monopolized product was wooden matches and that substitute products such as paper matches and cigarette lighters were irrelevant; it was a defined pro-duct that one monopolized, nothing else." (Thompson 1978)

U.S. Antitrust Law

With Section 7 of the Clayton Act we move to the other ex-treme in merger policy. This is a civil statute, requiring only that the effect of a merger "may be substantially to les-sen competition, or to tend to create a monopoly." In fact, it is not necessary for a merger to actually reduce competi-tion; there need be only a reasonable possibility that it do so in the future.

The enforcement policies of the Justice Department have made this statute even more rigorous. The avowed emphasis of enforcement is the preservation and promotion of market struc-tures conducive to competition. The arguments in favor of this emphasis are: (1) that the conduct of firms in a market tends to be controlled by the structure; and (2) that an emphasis on a few structural factors facilitates both enforcement decision-making and business planning which involves anticipation of likely government action. Indeed the Department issues spec-ific guidelines as to the mergers they will probably challenge. In a highly concentrated market, for example, a merger of a firm having a four percent share with another firm of the same size would be challenged.

There may be extenuating circumstances which would over-ride the guidelines - notably a failing firm argument. However, the Department specifically will not accept claims that a merger

will produce improvements in efficiency on the grounds that:
(a) adherence to the standards will mean that mergers of firms
operating below efficient scale would not be challenged anyway;
(b) substantial economies can normally be realized through internal expansion; and (c) there are severe difficulties in ac-
curately measuring the claimed economies (Note on U.S. Antitrust Merger Guidelines 1978).

The heavy structural orientation of U.S. antitrust laws
means that the definition of the relevant product and geographic market is normally the major issue (Kintner 1973). Until
the early sixties the primary basis for defining market boun-
daries was flexibility of production capabilities; a company
was argued to be a potential competitor in a market if it had
the technology available to compete (Werth 1965). Since that
time the courts have adopted a more eclectic, multiple criteria approach.

One of the pivotal decisions which signaled the more comprehensive view was handed down in the Brown Shoe case (1962).
Indeed, all subsequent merger decisions have been within the
criteria established by that case. According to the court in
the Brown Shoe case:

> The boundaries of a product market are determined by the
> reasonable interchangeability of use or the cross-elas-
> ticity of demand between the product itself and substi-
> tutes for it. However within this broad market, well-de-
> fined submarkets may exist which, in themselves consti-
> tute product markets for antitrust purposes. The boun-
> daries of such a submarket may be determined by examining
> such practical indicia as industry or public recognition
> of the submarket as a separate economic entity, the pro-
> duct's particular characteristics and uses, unique pro-
> duction facilities, distinct customers, distinct prices,
> sensitivity to price changes, and specialized vendors.

Submarket criteria are not separate and distinct from the
over-riding criteria. With one exception (dealing with supply-
side flexibility), they are indirect or proxy evidence of interchangeability or cross-elasticity. They are used because
they are generally more specific, and hence more workable in
most situations. Especially in the preliminary stages of the
case, government attorneys use them almost in a check-list
fashion to assess the probability of success according to the
number of criteria that are indicative of competitive overlap.
It is a case of the more the better, because the presence of
one or even a combination of sub-market factors is not necessarily determinative.

A Revised Competition Act

Sporadic efforts have been made to reform Canadian merger policy to overcome the present impasse. A common feature of all proposals is that mergers become civil matters. Otherwise they have departed significantly from the U.S. emphasis on a limited number of structural variables. The most recent proposal, Bill C-13 (Stage II Amendments to the Combines Investigation Act), which died on the order paper in April 1978, illustrates these differences.

Only mergers with a combined market share above a threshold value of 20 percent would come under the purview of the Stage II proposal. It is not clear why this threshold level was chosen, or how the market is to be defined for testing the threshold. Answers to these questions would become very important in light of the all-embracing criteria to be used to assess whether those mergers that are challenged are "likely to lessen substantially, actual or potential competition." The full list of evaluative criteria is shown in Table 1. With this list, one could explore virtually any structural, conduct or performance implication of a merger. This doesn't mean that the list will make it any easier to determine anticompetitive effects. First, the potential for conflicting judgments is enormous given the arguable nature of such terms as "acceptable substitutes," "barriers to entry" or "intent to control." Second, an overall judgment would require an assessment of the relative importance of each of the criteria in the particular proceeding. Such a weighting is doubly important in order to put some of the criteria with very restrictive language (i.e. "any" evidence, "any" history and "any" likelihood) into perspective. Failing such a perspective, the criteria provide an abundance of opportunities to argue that a proposed merger is anticompetitive.

Even if a merger was judged to be above the 20 percent market share threshold, and to lessen competition, it would still be permitted if there was a "clear probability that it (would) bring about substantial gains in efficiency." This is a further departure from the Clayton Act, as it recognizes the endemic weakness of much of Canadian industry operating below scale thresholds. In effect the government is willing to trade the possible consequences of lessened competition for efficiency gains (MacCrimmon and Stanbury 1978). Some amendments would have the desired effect given the lack of predefined criteria of efficiency and the severe measurement problems which U.S. antitrust authorities have cited as a reason for not considering the possibility of efficiency gains. A more serious criticism is that all the proposed amendments miss the point by not distinguishing between industries where mergers should be

TABLE 1

CRITERIA FOR EVALUATING WHETHER
A MERGER WILL LESSEN COMPETITION
(PROPOSED IN STAGE II AMENDMENT)

a) the degree to which acceptable substitutes for products supplied by the parties to the merger are or are likely to be available........

b) the degree to which imports offer or are likely to offer effective competition in respect of products supplied by parties to the merger.

c) the trend of concentration among producers, suppliers and purchasers of products supplied by parties to the merger......................

d) the size differentials between the businesses of the parties to the merger and any remaining competitors (relative market share)........

e) barriers to entry into the market and the affect of such merger on those barriers...

f) any history of growth by merger on the part of the parties to the merger...

g) any history of anti-competitive behaviour by the parties to the merger...

h) any likelihood that the merger would result in the removal of a vigorous and effective competitor as an independent force in a market..

i) any evidence of intent on the part of the merger parties to reduce competition or control a market..

j) any likelihoood that the merger would result in foreclosure of sources from which a trade, industry or profession obtains a product or outlet through which a trade, industry or profession disposes of a product...

k) any likelihood, where a party to the merger is or would be entering a new market by means of a merger, that such person would, without the merger have entered that market in a manner less restrictive of competition...

l) the nature and extent of change and innovation in a market..........

m) any likelihood that the merger will or would not stimulate competition.

encouraged, in order to improve Canada's competitive position in world-class industries, versus "low trade", geographically protected industries such as cement, retailing and services, where a dominant market position can be abused to the public detriment (Fleck 1978).

Royal Commission on Corporate Concentration

The Report by this Commission appeared in 1978 after a three year gestation period. The terms of reference were broad so merger policy was only one of a number of topics. A pervasive feature of the discussion of mergers was needed for a policy to reflect Canada's dilemma of underspecialized companies making short production-run products for a small and geographically dispersed market. Generally, the Commissioners opted for more competitive efficiency and the use of devices such as tariff reductions to reduce concentration (as measured in a global market) by expanding the market rather than by diminishing the firm (Jacoby 1978). In this respect they support the critique of Bill C-13 by James Fleck.

The specific recommendations about merger policy are based on the conclusion that mergers in the period following World War II "(do) not appear to have given rise to (serious) anti-competitive consequences." (Report 1978, p. 158). While they propose that mergers should be in civil law, the focus of the law should be "on the misuse of dominant market power or the attempt to increase of entrench a dominant position by anti-competitive means." (Report 1978, p. 159). Further, the anti-competitive consequences of mergers should be evaluated after the merger has occurred, rather than before as is proposed in Bill C-13.

The fundamental criticism of these recommendations is that they are based on dubious statistics and analytical premises and would virtually mean a continuation of the status quo. As Stanton and Waverman (1978) note, "The willingness of Canadians to trust the possessors of economic power until undue abuse is conclusively established apparently remains unchanged."

In light of the analysis of the Bay-Simpson's merger to follow, it is worth noting the criticism of the Staff of the Bureau of Competition Policy (1978):

"It seems clear that in reaching the conclusions it did, the Commission was concerned mainly with mergers in the manufacturing sector, where, in many cases at least, the possibility of import competition or the need to be competitive in foreign markets can be relied upon to influence the performance of Canadian firms. It is much more difficult to understand a complacent attitude about mergers in other sectors, such as food distribution. Concentration in food distribution, which came about in significant part by the elimination of local or regional chains, has reached such a point that some critics believe governments may be hard put to resist direct regulation."

This comment was written before the "Store Wars" broke out, but represents an advocacy of the ex ante merger review procedure embodied in Bill C-13. Before we can assess whether their concerns are justified we need a clear understanding of the concept of relevant market.

THE CONCEPTUAL ISSUES

Other things being equal, the greater the percentage of the "relevant market" controlled by a given firm, the more downward sloping the demand curve for that firms' products. If a firm enjoys 100 percent of "the market" it need not concern itself with the effects of changing its price on switching of demand to its direct competititors. Only the slope of the "market" or "primary" demand curve is relevant, and this will always be more steeply sloping than the demand curve faced by a particular firm in a competitive market. Thus, "share of relevant market" has become one of the indicators of monopoly power.

This analysis still leaves us with the question of how to determine the relevant market. The usual answer implied by the "share" argument is that the determining factor should be the size of the cross-elasticity of demand. This, in fact, has been the position of the U.S. antitrust enforcement agencies. However, the difficulty and expense of collecting data on sales and prices and controlling for the effects of other variables on sales usually precludes the use of cross-elasticity measure. Thus, it is necessary to look for a surrogate measure. Usually this is some variant on the concept of "interchangeability in use." Not only has this position been accepted by the U.S. courts, but it can also be shown to be consistent with two basic premises derived from consumer behaviour.

The first premise is that people seek the benefits from products and services, rather than the product or services per se. The economic value of these alternatives depends on the extent to which they provide benefits to potential patrons, or represent satisfactory solutions to specific problems.

The second premise is that buyers evaluate the available product or service alternatives from the vantage point of their usage situation (or application, on purchase requirement). It is this situation that dictates the benefits being sought.

From these two premises we can define a relevant market as the set of alternatives judged by customers to be competitive within those situations in which similar patterns of benefits are sought. This definition is based on a demand or customer orientation. Customer needs and requirements have primacy. The alternative is to take a supply perspective, and define markets according to criteria such as similarity or production process, physical appearance, function or operation. These are the criteria which are the basis of the Standard Industrial Classification system, and most of the market definitions employed by Statistics Canada. While they are easy to implement they will not necessarily yield market definitions which correspond to those used by customers. Whereas the competitive arena is constantly evolving, the government reporting categories are held constant to ensure comparability of data series across time, to permit trend analysis.

A MERGER CASE STUDY: THE BAY TAKE-OVER OF SIMPSONS

The so-called "Store Wars" binge that started in 1978 and continued into 1979 involved mergers that could have created a giant retailing/wholesaling conglomerate with revenues of more than eight billion dollars, had George Weston been the successful purchaser of The Bay. The actual series of mergers involving The Bay started two years earlier, in 1976, when Fields in British Columbia acquired control of Zellers, a Canadian subsidiary of the bankrupt U.S. chain, W.T. Grant.

A year later, the Bay acquired control of Zellers and Fields and Joseph Siegel, president of Fields became one of the largest stockholders in the Bay. Subsequently, in 1978, The Bay challenged Sears for control of Simpsons after Sears and Simpsons announced their own internal merger. By January 2, 1979, The Bay controlled over 60 percent of Simpsons stock and by March, it had acquired most of the remainder. The Bay also acquired control of 37 percent of Sears stock as well and became the second largest, but not controlling stockholder in Sears. The final round was completed in late April, 1979, when the Thompson Newspapers group successfully challenged the George Weston group for control of the Bay/Simpsons/Zellers retailing combination.

Rationale for the Mergers

There were many reasons for the rash of mergers in the retail sector in both the U.S. and Canada. First, with economies slowing in both countries, merger became an attractive vehicle

for continued growth. Second, the shares of many retailers
were selling at attractive market prices, sometimes below book
value. In many cases book value did not reflect the market
value of assets such as land and buildings which had appreciated substantially. Third, the results of the PIMS (Profit
Impact of Marketing Strategies 1977) project in the U.S. were
persuasive evidence that market share was an important determinant of profitability. In this regard, it was believed that
The Bay was losing money in Eastern Canada in its department
store division and that the chain held a weak third place in
market share behind Eaton's and Simpsons. Furthermore, The Bay
occupied many weak, secondary malls compared to the major malls
that were controlled by Eaton's and Simpsons. Finally, there
was the feeling that Simpsons' profit performance was weak in
spite of very high sales per square foot and that new management might accomplish fairly rapid profit improvement with no
improvement in sales productivity. At the time of the take-
over, Simpsons' annual sales per square foot of gross leasable
space were about $155.00, compared to less than $100 per square
foot for The Bay (Burns/Fry Co. 1978).

A Systematic Appraisal of the Mergers

An investigation of the Bay-Simpsons' merger by the Director of Combines Investigation was suspended when The Bay
signed an agreement that they would hold the Simpsons-Sears
shares as a "passive investment, and intended to keep Bay-
Simpsons management and operations completely separate and in
competition with Simpsons'-Sears." However, the Director of
Combines Investigation was on record as stating that even with
The Bay's undertaking, the merger was not in the best interest
of the consumer. The question here is whether the same outcome
would have occurred had the Bill C-13 amendments to the Competition Act been in effect. This raises three questions: what
is the relevant market? would competition have been found to
have been substantially lessened? and would efficiency gains
have offset the reduction in competition? Our purpose in this
case analysis is to indicate how these questions should be approached in this context. We lack sufficient data to reach a
judgment on the merits of the merger.

The first question to be resolved is the definition of the
relevant market. It has primacy because the bill specifies
that action will be taken against a merger if the combined
shares exceed a threshold limit of 20 percent. The combination
of The Bay + Zellers + Fields + Robinsons + Simpsons has 7 percent share of the market for department store type merchandise
(DSTM). On the other hand, if the market is defined as department stores (DSM) the combination would have 23 percent of the
market and be subject to investigation. This figure is for the

total Canadian market, which raises the question of whether markets should be defined for specific geographic areas, such as a Census Metropolitan Area. Neither definition of the market is necessarily compatible with the conceptual approach discussed in the previous section.

What is the Relevant Market?

Are Department Stores a defineable market? There is considerable evidence that Department Stores are viewed by developers and consumers as a distinct market within the broader DSTM (Department Store Type Merchandise) retailing environment.

First, shopping centre developers define department store chains as the "anchor tenants" in a major regional mall. Department stores provide "value" and attractiveness to a major mall. They "pull" customers to the mall and the remaining tenants depend on that pulling power for their customer traffic generation. Department stores frequently take a financial position in the mall, often as a major financial partner with the developer. The Bay, through its own Markborough Properties, is also a shopping centre developer itself. The department stores often participate in the cash flow generated from malls. They often construct their own buildings. Their annual net rents in terms of rent per square foot are usually much lower than the rents for other mall tenants. In short, the smaller chains and independent retailers are prepared to pay a much higher price than the department stores to piggy-back onto this distinct attractiveness generated by the regional mall. Without two and often three major anchor department stores, there would be no mall.

There is considerable evidence that consumers perceive department stores to be different from "discount" or promotional department stores: Table 2A and 2B examine this difference using consumer survey data collected in Toronto over the period 1974-77. When consumers are asked where they shop "most often" between 84 and 88 percent of mentions are captured by the four large department store chains. The combination of The Bay, Simpsons/Sears has been steadily moving up, from 53 to 65 percent of the total mentions. Two of the discount chains, Horizons and Sayvette, had disappeared by the end of 1978. From Table 2B it is clear that the department stores are perceived to dominate the market on "best value." It is this unique position for the major department stores that gives them their strength in shopping centre developments.

The perceptual map, Figure 1, which portrays the positions of all the mass merchandisers on price, quality and value, shows Eaton's, Simpsons' and The Bay to be clustered in the

Table 2A

CHAIN MENTIONED	Outlet Shopped Most Often			
	1974	1975	1976	1977
1. The Bay/Simpsons/Sears	53%	58%	61%	65%
2. Eatons	35	26	24	21
3. Woolco	5	5	6	5
4. Horizon/Towers/Zellers/ K-Mart/Sayvette.	7	11	9	9
	100%	100%	100%	100%

Table 2B

TORONTO, 1974-77: CONSUMER PERCEPTIONS OF DEPARTMENT STORES AND DISCOUNT STORES ON VALUE FOR THE MONEY

	Department Store[a]	Discount Store[b]	TOTALS
Best Value For The Money			
1974.	80%	20%	100%
1975.	75%	25%	100%
1976.	76%	24%	100%
1977.	77%	23%	100%

[a]Department Stores: The Bay, Eaton's, Simpsons, Sears

[b]Discount Stores: Horizon, Towers, Woolco, Zellers, K-Mart, Sayvette.

Source: Psychographics International of Canada, Limited. Anuual survey of 1,000 female household heads, probability sample, projectible to the total population of Census Metropolitan Toronto.

FIGURE 1

TORONTO: 1975 Mass Merchandisers Study:
A Perceptual Map

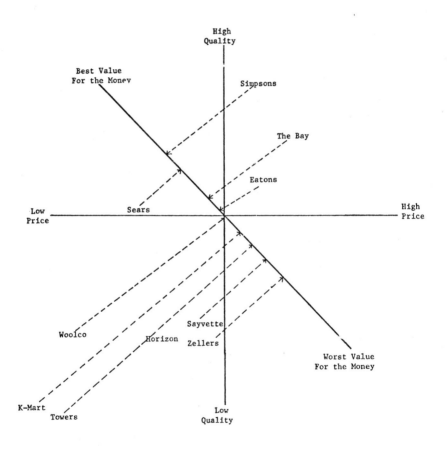

"Where Would You Be Most

Likely to Shop For Major

Mentioned	Appliances?"			
	1974	1975	1976	1977
mpson/Sears[3]	36%	40%	41%	46%
	33	28	26	26
epartment Stores	1	1	1	1
stores	30	31	32	27
	100%	100%	100%	100%

rom the above that The Bay group would control al-
total business and that the department stores
dominant retail outlets for this product class.
r" category would include the independent retail
ppliances such as Leon's, Tasco Distributor, Cap-

has not historically been a strong chain in appli-
therefore reasonable to assume that The Bay would
in the Simpsons/Sears buying group for major ap-
initiate centralized buying in this product cate-
r to achieve maximum volume rebates from suppliers.
ucers who could not meet the volume requirements
ected to be shut out from supplying the new Bay
ddition, a significant reduction in competition
higher prices as The Bay group forms the "umbrel-
vel for the total market. It is also possible that
w GATT agreement, The Bay group could begin shifting of major commodity classes such as appliances to
utside Canada, in a search for large volumes at the
tive prices.

product classes do not show the same concentration o
e hands of The Bay group of stores. For example, th
res only about 30 percent of a metro market in
shion items. In this product category, the indepen-
ques are quite powerful, as are the national specialt
shion chains. In addition, the national specialty
grown much faster than the department stores in thi

ars has announced its intention to go alone in major
, The Bay's 37% stock interest in Sears suggests tha
not likely to jeopardize the overall appliance

upper righthand quadrant, a position reflecting strength on
high price, high quality and good value for the money. The discounters are all clustered in the lower lefthand quadrant.
Woolco is clearly in the discount camp. It is not considered
to be as strong a candidate as an anchor chain by most shopping
centre developers. Sears in somewhere in between. While it
has an image of being lower price and carrying lower quality
merchandise compared to the department stores, it has a very
strong image on value. Consequently, it is considered to be a
stronger contender for shopping centres than is Woolco.

If the argument that department stores are a distinct market is valid, what is the current situation in Canada? Tables
3 and 4 shows that the combination of The Bay/Simpsons'/Sears/
Robinsons accounted for 64 percent of all department stores, 58
percent of total gross leasable space and 61 percent of dollar
sales in Canada in 1977. Even the elimination of Sears as a
non-controlled entity, still leaves The Bay group with 36 percent of dollar sales in 1977. This is well above the 20 percent threshold share. In addition, Table 4 suggests that the
degree of concentration will rise steadily during the next few
years. The Bay group accounts for 89 percent of all new construction completed, under construction or committed of through
1981. Eliminating Sears lowers that figure to 72 percent.

What about an "interchangeability in use" approach? Rather
than classify stores according to similarity of operation, which
is the basis for Statistics Canada DSM and DSTM data, we could
apply the concepts developed in the previous section. This
leads to definition of a retail market as the set of retail outlets (including stores and catalogue) judged by customers to be
competitive within purchase situations in which similar patterns
of benefits are sought. In this context the benefits sought
might include convenience, type and selection of goods, level
of services and so forth. Pertinent evidence would be the degree to which each retail outlet was utilized or judged to be
suitable as a source for each distinct purchase requirement.

The output from this approach is not a single share estimate, but rather a large number of shares, one for each of the
distinct purchase situations. While this analysis has not been
undertaken, the following data from two separate product categories illustrates the approach and the findings that would be
encountered.

During the period 1974-1977 large scale consumer surveys
in Toronto have included a series of questions to respondents
about "where they would be likely to shop" for each of a number
of product classes. The responses to the major appliance question generated the following response pattern:

TABLE 3

POTENTIAL CONTROLLING SHARE
OF TRADITIONAL DEPARTMENT STORE MARKET
BY THE BAY

Name of Store	% of Total Stores	% of Total Sq. Ft. Gla.	% of 1977 $ Sales
The Bay [1]	18.9%	20.2% *	21.3% [5]
Simpsons	10.5%	12.3%	13.3%
Simpsons-Sears [2]	31.3%	23.5%	25.2%
Robinson's	3.0%	1.8%	1.3%
Sub-Total Bay Share	63.7%	57.8%	61.1%
Eaton's [3]	25.4%	29.8%	29.2%
Woodwards [4]	10.9%	12.4%	9.7%
Total	100.0%	100.0%	100.0%
Alternative Bay Share [6]	32.4%	34.3%	35.9%

SOURCE: Larry Smith & Associates Ltd.
1) Excludes wholesale and fur sales.
2) Excludes catalogue operation.
3) Excludes 14 Horizon stores.
4) Excludes food stores in the Woodwards stores.
5) Total retail sales including stores of less than 75,000 Sq. Ft.Gla.
6) Excluding Sears
* A recent publication by The Bay shows 10 downtown stores with a total of 4,094,000 Sq. Ft., and 28 suburban units with 3,485,000 Sq. Ft. for a grand total of 38 stores and 7,579,000 Sq. Ft.

92

NEW TRADITIONAL
COMPLETIONS, UNDER CO
197

STORE NAME	NUMB UN
The Bay	
Simpsons	
Simpsons-Sears	
Robinson's	
Eaton's	
Woodward's	1
TOTAL:	46
Potential Bay Share [1]	41
% of Total	89.1%
Alternative Bay Share [2]	33
% of Total	71.7%

SOURCE: Larry Smith & Associates Ltd.
1) Includes - The Bay, Simpsons,
2) Excluding Sears.

Chains N

1. The Bay/Si
2. Eaton's
3. Discount D
4. All other

Total

It is clear f
most half the
would be the
The "all othe
outlets for a
lans, etc.

The Bay
ances. It is
attempt to j
pliances and
gory in orde
Smaller prod
might be exp
group. In a
could lead t
la" price le
under the ne
ing the buy
suppliers o
most attrac

Other
sales in th
group captu
women's fas
dent bouti
women's fa
chains hav

3 While Se
appliances
The Bay is
business.

93

product category during the past decade. We would therefore
conclude that there is ample competition in the fashion arena
in the Canadian market.

"Where did you last buy....?"

CHAINS MENTIONED (1978)	Basic Blouse	Fashion Blouse	Skirt	Everyday Blouse
Bay/Sears/Simpsons	34%*	27%	27%	30%
Other Mass Merchandisers	14	14	11	12
Specialty Chains	20	22	22	19
Independent Boutiques	32	37	40	39
Total	100%	100%	100%	100%

An "interchangeability in use" approach provides much
clearer insights into patterns of retail competition. These
insights, unfortunately, do not come cost-free. There is the
direct cost of collecting acceptable data for each of 55 retail
commodity groups. Second, as the data for appliances and
women's fashions indicate, the results are likely to be quite
mixed: department stores will have large shares of some commodities and small shares of others such as hardware. What
then constitutes an aggregate share for purpose of invoking the
20 percent threshold? In the next section we will proceed on
the assumption that the combined shares were judged to be above
the trigger, and ask whether there would be anticompetitive effects.

Competitive Effects of the Merger

The question of impact can be approached from two directions. One is a straight-forward application of the criteria
of Bill C-13 for determining whether a merger will lessen competition. This approach would be based on examining the criterion listed in Table 1 from the perspective of a variety of
publics. Obviously not all criteria or publics are equally important. In particular, the impact of the merger on developers
emerges as an important facet.

In eastern Canada, shopping centre developers would have
to turn to The Bay for all future shopping centre developments.
Through control of Simpsons and some influence at Sears, The
Bay could effectively control shopping centre development. The
only alternative would be Eaton's. Given the perceived need

*Read: In a major metro market in 1978, 34 percent of a large
        sample of respondents reported last purchasing a basic
        blouse at The Bay, Sears or Simpsons.

for at least two "anchors" by the developers, The Bay could control and potentially dictate the terms of shopping centre entry by The Bay group (including Zellers, Robinsons, Simpsons, Shoprite catalogue). In fact, through its own development company, The Bay has all the necessary expertise and ingredients to develop its own centres. Eaton's does not. The reality would be a shift in relative power away from the developers and towards the new Bay group of stores.

One can easily forsee the possibility that fewer centres would be built unless The Bay saw an opportunity for high return in specific locations. In the absence of stronger department store competition, one can visualize a situation in eastern Canada where The Bay group would be the major participant in all new major regional malls. With a growing market share, The Bay group would then be in a position to also increasingly dominate the supply (vendors) side of the retailing environment, particularly for product classes where department stores already capture a fairly high market share. It should also be pointed out that Canada already experiences a very concentrated department store industry compared to the U.S. In most major markets, there are as many as 8 to 10 alternative chains available for shopping centre entry as "anchor chains." To take Chicago as an example, we find Sears, Wards and Penny's in the middle ground. Then three major department stores are available: Marshall Field, Carson Pirie Scott, and Wiebolts. Finally, chains such as Lord & Taylor, I. Magnin and Nieman Marcus, have achieved penetration. It is also unlikely that Canada will witness any new major market entry of U.S. or European department stores. A chain would require a major supply/distribution network system in Canada and would have to build such a system from scratch.

Given The Bay's current controlling interest in Zellers, the addition of Simpsons to the combined group would give The Bay considerable power over shopping centre development. However, in smaller centres, a mall might be built with one major anchor, one discount department store such as The Bay, Simpsons or Eaton's and a discount store such as Zellers, Woolco, K-Mart, etc.[4] Given the likelihood of increased power over shopping centre development, The Bay could being moving Zellers into these smaller centres at the expense of Woolco or K-Mart. Thus, in either major centres or smaller centres, The Bay could provide both major tenants whether they be two department stores (one of Bay, or Simpsons) or one department store and one discount department store. Again, we see here the possibility of substantially lessened competition across alternative chains.

---

4 Two Bay centres in Western Canada announced the addition of Zellers stores in April, 1979.

The Bay could effectively control rapid growth for all chains in its own combined groupd at the expense of other chains in the market. There would be little impediment to substantially increased market shares for all chains inside The Bay group.

What About Efficiency Gains?

Even if the case can be made for substantially lessening competition, there is still the question of efficiency gains. If the board finds that the merger will bring about substantial gains in efficiency that save resources for the Canadian economy, the board is specifically barred from disallowing the merger. The real issue is what is meant by "substantial gains in efficiency."

There is no doubt that some efficiencies could be realized by the merger. They include:

- elimination of overlap/duplication of warehousing and distribution facilities, if that function is to be merged
- joint buying functions for all stores and some joint merchandising programs
- financing of expansion and inventory management through joint financial packages with the banking institutions
- joint negotiations with developers
- common mail order catalogues (which do not currently exist)
- common financial services including trust branches, insurance, travel offices, credit card, etc.

However, the Bay does not have voting control of Sears and has publicly announced that it intends to operate Simpsons as a totally independent entity. In the absence of merged functions as outlined above, it is unclear whether any real efficiencies in operation would result from the merger. In fact, the very guarantees demanded by Consumer and Corporate Affairs thwart these benefits. Our conclusion is that the weight of judgment should come down heavily on the side of lessening of competition in the absence of any real gains in efficiencies and that there would be a strong case to be made for barring the merger under the proposed amendments to the Act.

SUMMARY

After years of extended, but fruitless discussion about the currently impotent Combines Investigation Act in Canada, there is some possibility that a more restrictive policy will be adopted. Two major phenomenon support such a policy change:

97

1) the recent rash of high profile mergers (including "Store Wars"); and 2) the wide range of alternative merger policies from which to choose.

The major purpose of this paper is to contribute to the process of choice among the alternative policies by clarifying the nature of the definition of the relevant market which is an integral part of the major proposals. This definition establishes the arena within which a determination of possible anticompetitive effects of a merger is made. The analysis focused on the utilization of marketing concepts and approached to define markets from a demand perspective, rather than the supply perspective which is adopted by industry statistics.

The Bay/Simpsons combination was explored in depth to point out the difficulties that are inherent in definition of markets for assessing anticompetitive effects. Not only are there many interest groups to be considered but a variety of ways to implement a marketing approach. As a result it is not clear whether the combined share of market controlled by the two retailers would exceed the 20 percent threshold suggested as part of the Stage II amendments to the Combines Investigation Act.

REFERENCES

Brown Shoe Co. v. U.S. (U.S. Supreme Court, 1962), 370 U.S. 294.

Burns/Fry Co. Annual Report, Toronto, 1978.

Cheveldayoff, Wayne (1979), "Merger Watchdog Contends Bay Merger Not Best for Public," Globe and Mail (January 5).

Clayton Antitrust Act (15 U.S.C. SS18 Section 7).

Fleck, James D. (1978), "A Personal Perspective on Stage II: The Views of a Provincial Deputy Minister" in I.W. Rowley and W.T. Stanbury, eds., Competition Policy in Canada: Stage II, Bill C-13, Institute for Research on Public Policy.

Gorecki, Paul K. and W.T. Stanbury, eds (1979), Perspectives on the Royal Commission on Corporate Concentration, Institute for Research on Public Policy.

Jacoby, Neil, "Corporate Concentration in Canada: An American Perspective," in P.K. Gorecki and W.T. Stanbury, op. cit.

Jones, J.C.H. (1967), "Mergers and Competition: The Brewing Case," Canadian Journal of Economics and Political Science, 33 (November).

Kinter, Earl W. (1973), An Antitrust Primer, 2nd ed., New York: The McMillan Co.

MacCrimmon and W.T. Stanbury (1978), "The Reform of Canada's Merger Law and The Provisions of Bill C-13," in J.W. Rowley and W.T. Stanbury, eds., Competition Policy in Canada: Stage II, Bill C-13, Institute for Research on Public Policy.

McFetridge, D.G. (1974), "The Emergence of a Canadian Merger Policy," Canadian Journal of Economics, 19.

Note on U.S. Antitrust Merger Guidelines (1978), Harvard Business School, 8.

Report of the Royal Commission on Corporate Concentration (1978) Ottawa: Supply and Services Canada.

Skeoch, L.A. and Bruce McDonald (1976), Dynamic Change and Accountability in a Canadian Market Economy, Ottawa: Supplies and Services Canada.

Staff of Bureau of Competition Policy, "The Royal Commission on Corporate Concentration - Recommendations and Comments Directly Relevant to Bill C-13," in P.K. Gorecki and W.T. Stanbury, eds., op. cit.

Strategic Planning Institute (1978), The PIMS Program, Cambridge, MA.

W.T. Stanbury and Leonard Waverman, "Merger Policy of the Royal Commission on Corporate Concentration: Conclusions Without Evidence," In P.K. Gorecki and W.T. Stanbury, eds., op. cit.

W.T. Stanbury and G.B. Reschenthaler (1977), "Benign Monopoly: Canadian Merger Policy and the K.C. Irving Case," Canadian Business Law Journal, 2 (August).

Thompson, Donald (1978), "Competition, Regulation and Market Structure," in John Cady, ed., Marketing and the Public Interest, Cambridge: Marketing Science Institute.

Werth, Robert W. (1965), "Determination of the Relevant Product Market," Ohio State Law Journal (Spring).

PRICING AND THE EXPERIENCE CURVE EFFECT[1]

Donald N. Thompson, York University

ABSTRACT

The experience curve effect refers to the decline in the inflation-adjusted unit cost of the value added in a production process of 20 to 30 percent each time accumulated production doubles. There is evidence from about 190 studies in 40 to 45 industries that the rate of decline is consistent from industry to industry, continues without apparent limit with every doubling of accumulated experience, and exists independently of the rate of growth of experience.

A number of managerial implications of the experience curve are discussed. An important one for Canadian companies operating under higher cost conditions than their U.S. competitors is that the relative growth of companies in an industry is more important than their absolute growth. That is, a company with a structural cost disadvantage from higher labour or tax rates, can compensate for it by a dynamic cost advantage, by accumulating experience faster than the competitor who enjoys the lower costs. It can be calculated by how much faster one must grow in order to overcome a given structural cost disadvantage.

This paper discusses some of the managerial implications of the experience curve, in particular those relating to pricing strategy designed to buy market share and position. The paper concludes with a discussion of public policy considerations in pricing under the experience curve effect, and the regulation of predatory pricing. Whether experience-curve based pricing by large firms constitutes predatory activity was a concern both of the Royal Commission on Corporate Concentration in its deliberations on size and scale, and of the 1977-78 meetings between officials of the federal Department

[1]Part of the work and analysis reported here was carried out in 1977 and 1978 as background to the Report of the Royal Commission on Corporate Concentration, of which the author was Director of Research. Contributions of a number of research personnel at the Commission are acknowledged with thanks. Some of the materials in this paper were earlier included in the 1978 Canada House Lecture at Canada House, London, England (March 9, 1978), and the 1979 E.T. Grether Lecture Series at the University of California, Berkeley, (March 29, 1979)

of Industry, Trade and Commerce and business leaders on the
implications of the Tokyo Round of tariff reductions.

L'effet de la courbe d'expérience réfère au déclin du
coût de l'unité ajusté à l'inflation, selon la valeur ajoutée
dans un procédé de production s'accumulant de 20 à 30 pourcent
à chaque double de production. Selon 190 études faites dans
40 à 45 industries, il est évident que le niveau de déclin
est le même d'une industrie à l'autre, qu'il continue sans
limite apparente avec chaque doublement d'expérience accumulée,
et qu'il existe indépendamment du degré de développement de
l'expérience.

Un certain nombre d'implications directoriales de la
courbe d'expérience y sont discutées. Une de ces implications, importante pour les compagnies canadiennes que doivent
fonctionner dans des conditions au coût plus élevé que leurs
compétiteurs américains, est que le développement relatif de
leur industrie est plus important que le développement absolu
de celle-ci. Ce que signifie qu'une compagnie ayant un désavantage structurel causé par un coût plus élevé de main-d'
ouvre ou de taxes, peut compenser par l'avantage d'un coût
dynamique, par l'accumulation d'expérience plus accélérée que
le compétiteur qui jouit d'une opération moins coûteuse. Il
est possible de calculer combien l'on doit accélérer le degré
de développement afin de pouvoir surmonter un désavantage de
coût structurel déterminé.

Cet article discute de quelques unes des implications
directoriales dans la courbe d'expérience, en particulier de
celles concernant la stratégie des taux désignés à l'achat
des parts et de leur position sur le marché. L'article se
termine sur une discussion de l'effet de la courbe d'experience sur les politiques de considération du public dans les
taux et sur les règlements sur les taux prédateurs. Que la
courbe d'expérience basée sur des taux établis par les grandes
compagnies constitue une activité prédatrice fut le souci de
la Commission Royale sur la Concentration des Corporations
lors de ses délibérations sur leur agrandissement et leur
envergure; il fut aussi le but de la rencontre entre les
représentants officiels du ministère de l'Industrie et du
Commerce avec des dirigeants en affaires concernant les implications de la Ronde de réductions des tarifs de Tokyo.

THE EXPERIENCE CURVE EFFECT

There is general agreement that four broad classes of
economies of size or scale exist in the industrial sector:

those that are product specific, those related to plant size, those related to operation of several plants simultaneously, and those related to aggregate firm size.[2] Product specific economies of scale occur because increasing the volume of production of a specific product or of closely related products, tends to decrease the average total cost per unit produced.

Although the phenomenon of steadily declining real unit costs with greater production experience is widely observed, the underlying factors are not completely understood. Certainly it is due in part to "learning by doing" for workers and management, in part to changes in the input mix, in part to more time spent by management on cost-cutting measures, in part to process automation, line-balancing to decrease idle machine time, greater use of standardized parts, and decreased inventory carrying costs and lower finance and procurement expenses as the "law of large numbers" comes into play. It is illustrated by the number of parts in one Canadian produced automobile door lock mechanism declining from 17 to 4 between 1954 and 1974, and the cost of the mechanism falling almost 75% in real dollars over that period.

Learning effects have been isolated from scale and technology effects in a number of studies, beginning with the U.S. aircraft industry where it was noted in 1936 that reductions in unit costs were related to cumulative output of particular aircraft (Wright 1936; Hirsch 1956; Nadler and Smith 1963). In 1956 the Boston Consulting Group, which had documented combined scale, technological and learning effects for many industries, proposed a general observation based on its consulting work. The characteristic decline in the unit cost of value added was consistently 20 to 30 percent each time accumulated production doubled, and that the rate of decline was consistent from industry to industry (BCG 1968).[3] They

---

[2]There are several possible definitions of economies of scale for any one industry, and the methodology for using data in measuring economies is dependent on which definition is being used. The implications of findings are certainly country-specific, and may be industry-specific. An outline of the analytics and measurement problems is given in Report (1978), pp. 46-67.

[3]In general, learning is highly significant in labor-intensive operations, and scale is most important in capital-intensive industries. However the interrelationships are apparently more complex than this. There is evidence for the plastic resin manufacturing industry that the rate of decline in unit cost of value added with a doubling of experience, increased with larger scale (and more capital-intensive operation).

further hypothesized that this decline in costs (in constant
dollars) would go on without limit with every doubling of
accumulated experience, and would exist independently of the
rate of growth of experience. Calculations over the past
decade, from about 190 studies in 40 to 45 industries, suggest
that, subject to some definitional and measurement problems,
there is no evidence so far to reject these general hypotheses.[4] They do not apply however if major elements of cost
or price are determined by patent or natural monopolies, or
by government regulation.

In a generalized form, the experience curve concept may
be stated as follows:

The experience curve concept: <u>Those costs related
to value added appear to decline at a fairly
constant rate, every time total production experience
doubles.</u>

Thus when costs are plotted against cumulative volume
on a linear scale, the resulting graph will take the form of
a characteristic hyperbolic cost function. If the relationship is shown on double logarithmic scale (which has the
property of showing percentage change as a constant distance
along either axis), the plotting of observed cost data will
show a characteristic straight line, reflecting the consistent
relationship between experience and costs.

Figures One through Five indicate examples of the experience curve phenomenon, from the production of heavy oil from
the Alberta Tar Sands, hydroelectric power generation, life
insurance operating expenses, production of float glass, and
long distanct telephone costs. (The latter seems an interesting exception of the general rule that the phenomenon likely
will not appear where either costs or price are subject to
government regulation).

---

[4]A major caveat must be stated, that much of the research and
literature on the experience curve has come from one source,
the Boston Consulting Group (BCG). The BCG is a private, prof-
it-making organization, and most of its work is proprietary.
Some of the BCG results have been replicated in the United
Kingdom, Franch, Sweden, West Germany, Japan, and Canada. The
majority of its material is descriptive and persuasive, but
neither well nor completely documented. In particular, little
is known about the characteristics of industries (particularly
in service sectors) to which the experience curve phenomenon
may not completely apply.

In the 190 studies mentioned, the rate of decline in value added with a doubling of production experience varied from 12% in automobile production (with this figure verified in three separate countries), 15% for color television set manufacture, and 20% for steel and related industries, to as high as 40-50% for semiconductors and integrated circuits. The result of the latter's high rate can be seen in operation with the step decline over a period of years in the price of calculators, digital watches and personal computers from firms like Texas Instruments. The majority of industries measured in BCG studies fall between 20% and 30%; those studied in Canada, West Germany, Japan and the United Kingdom have, for the most part, fallen between 15% and 25%.

FIGURE ONE

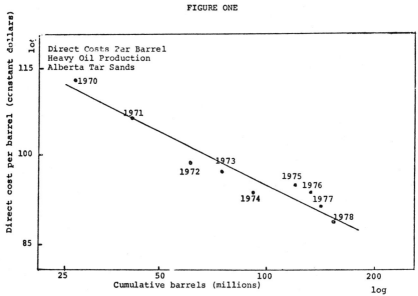

Source: Research Program, Royal Commission on Corporate
          Concentration, Government of Canada; updated
          through 1978 by author. Data compiled by
          Information Centre, Department of Energy,
          Mines, and Resources, Government of Canada

upper righthand quadrant, a position reflecting strength on high price, high quality and good value for the money. The discounters are all clustered in the lower lefthand quadrant. Woolco is clearly in the discount camp. It is not considered to be as strong a candidate as an anchor chain by most shopping centre developers. Sears in somewhere in between. While it has an image of being lower price and carrying lower quality merchandise compared to the department stores, it has a very strong image on value. Consequently, it is considered to be a stronger contender for shopping centres than is Woolco.

If the argument that department stores are a distinct market is valid, what is the current situation in Canada? Tables 3 and 4 shows that the combination of The Bay/Simpsons'/Sears/Robinsons accounted for 64 percent of all department stores, 58 percent of total gross leasable space and 61 percent of dollar sales in Canada in 1977. Even the elimination of Sears as a non-controlled entity, still leaves The Bay group with 36 percent of dollar sales in 1977. This is well above the 20 percent threshold share. In addition, Table 4 suggests that the degree of concentration will rise steadily during the next few years. The Bay group accounts for 89 percent of all new construction completed, under construction or committed of through 1981. Eliminating Sears lowers that figure to 72 percent.

What about an "interchangeability in use" approach? Rather than classify stores according to similarity of operation, which is the basis for Statistics Canada DSM and DSTM data, we could apply the concepts developed in the previous section. This leads to definition of a retail market as the set of retail outlets (including stores and catalogue) judged by customers to be competitive within purchase situations in which similar patterns of benefits are sought. In this context the benefits sought might include convenience, type and selection of goods, level of services and so forth. Pertinent evidence would be the degree to which each retail outlet was utilized or judged to be suitable as a source for each distinct purchase requirement.

The output from this approach is not a single share estimate, but rather a large number of shares, one for each of the distinct purchase situations. While this analysis has not been undertaken, the following data from two separate product categories illustrates the approach and the findings that would be encountered.

During the period 1974-1977 large scale consumer surveys in Toronto have included a series of questions to respondents about "where they would be likely to shop" for each of a number of product classes. The responses to the major appliance question generated the following response pattern:

TABLE 3

POTENTIAL CONTROLLING SHARE
OF TRADITIONAL DEPARTMENT STORE MARKET
BY THE BAY

Name of Store	% of Total Stores	% of Total Sq. Ft. Gla.	% of 1977 $ Sales
The Bay [1]	18.9%	20.2% *	21.3% [5]
Simpsons	10.5%	12.3%	13.3%
Simpsons-Sears [2]	31.3%	23.5%	25.2%
Robinson's	3.0%	1.8%	1.3%
Sub-Total Bay Share	63.7%	57.8%	61.1%
Eaton's [3]	25.4%	29.8%	29.2%
Woodwards [4]	10.9%	12.4%	9.7%
Total	100.0%	100.0%	100.0%
Alternative Bay Share [6]	32.4%	34.3%	35.9%

SOURCE: Larry Smith & Associates Ltd.
    1) Excludes wholesale and fur sales.
    2) Excludes catalogue operation.
    3) Excludes 14 Horizon stores.
    4) Excludes food stores in the Woodwards stores.
    5) Total retail sales including stores of less than 75,000 Sq. Ft.Gla.
    6) Excluding Sears
    * A recent publication by The Bay shows 10 downtown stores with a
      total of 4,094,000 Sq. Ft., and 28 suburban units with 3,485,000
      Sq. Ft. for a grand total of 38 stores and 7,579,000 Sq. Ft.

upper righthand quadrant, a position reflecting strength on
high price, high quality and good value for the money. The discounters are all clustered in the lower lefthand quadrant.
Woolco is clearly in the discount camp. It is not considered
to be as strong a candidate as an anchor chain by most shopping
centre developers. Sears in somewhere in between. While it
has an image of being lower price and carrying lower quality
merchandise compared to the department stores, it has a very
strong image on value. Consequently, it is considered to be a
stronger contender for shopping centres than is Woolco.

If the argument that department stores are a distinct market is valid, what is the current situation in Canada? Tables
3 and 4 shows that the combination of The Bay/Simpsons'/Sears/
Robinsons accounted for 64 percent of all department stores, 58
percent of total gross leasable space and 61 percent of dollar
sales in Canada in 1977. Even the elimination of Sears as a
non-controlled entity, still leaves The Bay group with 36 percent of dollar sales in 1977. This is well above the 20 percent threshold share. In addition, Table 4 suggests that the
degree of concentration will rise steadily during the next few
years. The Bay group accounts for 89 percent of all new construction completed, under construction or committed of through
1981. Eliminating Sears lowers that figure to 72 percent.

What about an "interchangeability in use" approach? Rather
than classify stores according to similarity of operation, which
is the basis for Statistics Canada DSM and DSTM data, we could
apply the concepts developed in the previous section. This
leads to definition of a retail market as the set of retail outlets (including stores and catalogue) judged by customers to be
competitive within purchase situations in which similar patterns
of benefits are sought. In this context the benefits sought
might include convenience, type and selection of goods, level
of services and so forth. Pertinent evidence would be the degree to which each retail outlet was utilized or judged to be
suitable as a source for each distinct purchase requirement.

The output from this approach is not a single share estimate, but rather a large number of shares, one for each of the
distinct purchase situations. While this analysis has not been
undertaken, the following data from two separate product categories illustrates the approach and the findings that would be
encountered.

During the period 1974-1977 large scale consumer surveys
in Toronto have included a series of questions to respondents
about "where they would be likely to shop" for each of a number
of product classes. The responses to the major appliance question generated the following response pattern:

TABLE 3

POTENTIAL CONTROLLING SHARE
OF TRADITIONAL DEPARTMENT STORE MARKET
BY THE BAY

Name of Store	% of Total Stores	% of Total Sq. Ft. Gla.	% of 1977 $ Sales
The Bay [1]	18.9%	20.2% *	21.3% [5]
Simpsons	10.5%	12.3%	13.3%
Simpsons-Sears [2]	31.3%	23.5%	25.2%
Robinson's	3.0%	1.8%	1.3%
Sub-Total Bay Share	63.7%	57.8%	61.1%
Eaton's [3]	25.4%	29.8%	29.2%
Woodwards [4]	10.9%	12.4%	9.7%
Total	100.0%	100.0%	100.0%
Alternative Bay Share [6]	32.4%	34.3%	35.9%

SOURCE: Larry Smith & Associates Ltd.
1) Excludes wholesale and fur sales.
2) Excludes catalogue operation.
3) Excludes 14 Horizon stores.
4) Excludes food stores in the Woodwards stores.
5) Total retail sales including stores of less than 75,000 Sq. Ft.Gla.
6) Excluding Sears
* A recent publication by The Bay shows 10 downtown stores with a total of 4,094,000 Sq. Ft., and 28 suburban units with 3,485,000 Sq. Ft. for a grand total of 38 stores and 7,579,000 Sq. Ft.

92

TABLE 4

NEW TRADITIONAL DEPARTMENT STORES
COMPLETIONS, UNDER CONSTRUCTION, COMMITMENT
1978-1981

STORE NAME	NUMBER OF UNITS	TOTAL SQUARE FOOTAGE (Sq. Ft.Gla.)
The Bay	27	2,413,000
Simpsons	4	470,000
Simpsons-Sears	8	883,000
Robinson's	2	206,000
Eaton's	4	530,000
Woodward's	1	150,000
TOTAL:	46	4,652,000
Potential Bay Share [1]	41	3,972,000
% of Total	89.1%	85.4
Alternative Bay Share [2]	33	3,089,000
% of Total	71.7%	66.4%

SOURCE: Larry Smith & Associates Ltd.
  1) Includes - The Bay, Simpsons, Simpsons-Sears, and Robinson's.
  2) Excluding Sears.

93

Chains Mentioned	"Where Would You Be Most Likely to Shop For Major Appliances?"			
	1974	1975	1976	1977
1. The Bay/Simpson/Sears[3]	36%	40%	41%	46%
2. Eaton's	33	28	26	26
3. Discount Department Stores	1	1	1	1
4. All other stores	30	31	32	27
Total	100%	100%	100%	100%

It is clear from the above that The Bay group would control almost half the total business and that the department stores would be the dominant retail outlets for this product class. The "all other" category would include the independent retail outlets for appliances such as Leon's, Tasco Distributor, Caplans, etc.

The Bay has not historically been a strong chain in appliances. It is therefore reasonable to assume that The Bay would attempt to join the Simpsons/Sears buying group for major appliances and initiate centralized buying in this product category in order to achieve maximum volume rebates from suppliers. Smaller producers who could not meet the volume requirements might be expected to be shut out from supplying the new Bay group. In addition, a significant reduction in competition could lead to higher prices as The Bay group forms the "umbrella" price level for the total market. It is also possible that under the new GATT agreement, The Bay group could begin shifting the buying of major commodity classes such as appliances to suppliers outside Canada, in a search for large volumes at the most attractive prices.

Other product classes do not show the same concentration of sales in the hands of The Bay group of stores. For example, the group captures only about 30 percent of a metro market in women's fashion items. In this product category, the independent boutiques are quite powerful, as are the national specialty women's fashion chains. In addition, the national specialty chains have grown much faster than the department stores in this

3 While Sears has announced its intention to go alone in major appliances, The Bay's 37% stock interest in Sears suggests that The Bay is not likely to jeopardize the overall appliance business.

FIGURE TWO

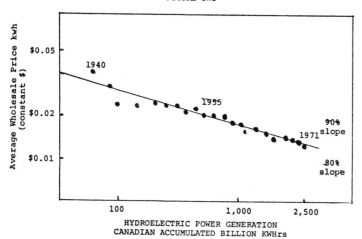

HYDROELECTRIC POWER GENERATION
CANADIAN ACCUMULATED BILLION KWHrs

Source: Research Program, Royal Commission on Corporate
         Concentration, Government of Canada.. Data
         compiled by Information Centre, Department
         of Energy, Mines and Resources, Government
         of Canada

FIGURE THREE

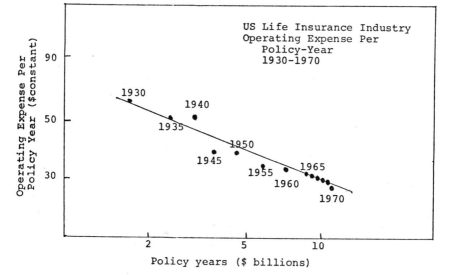

Policy years ($ billions)

Source: Institute of Life Insurance, reproduced
         in Review (1978), p.92

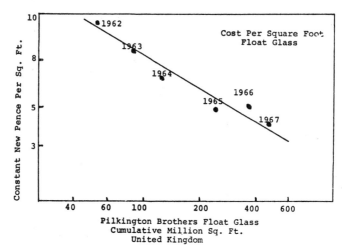

Source: United Kingdom Monopolies Commission,
reproduced in _Review_ (1978), p.92

FIGURE FIVE

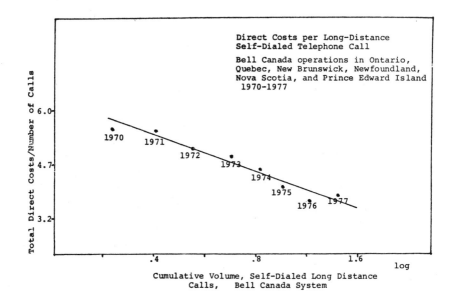

Source: Rate filings with Canadian Transport Commission
and Canadian Radio-television and Telecommunications
Commission (1976 and 1977)

Cost Elements

Each cost element, including overhead, sales expense, advertising, and research and development, has a different history of past experience. The cost of components obtained in the open market will decline as a function of the total usage of the relevant market, not the usage of the individual buyer. Some internal value-added elements will accumulate experience from multiple products or applications, while others accumulate experience from a single unique application. Thus a change in volume of one product can change the rate of cost decline of an otherwise completely independent product, if they share a common cost element. The cost of any product is the total of a set of experience curves for its component materials and assemblies. If one input dominates this total, or if the component curves reflect the same experience rate, the curve should be unbroken and characteristic.

Thus, the significant variables in relating cost reduction to experience are prior accumulated experience, shared experience, value added, component growth rate, and relative competitive volume. Growth rate in accumulated product experience is the most important of these; if the rate of production is not growing, then the rate of cost decline per year slows down and approaches zero.

It should be emphasized that inferred cost reductions with volume are not automatic. They depend upon a management that is under competitive pressure to force down costs as volume increases. It is competition that produces survivors who achieve the full potential reductions and who use the optimal combination of cost elements compared to competitor's combinations.

The two most important conditions of validity for the experience curve analysis seem to be that the product whose cost pattern is being observed be stable throughout the period of observation, and that value-added rather than total cost be measured (although the latter is less important if value-added is a large component of unit cost). Predictably, then, experience analyses are most clear-cut for heavy industrial goods, chemicals, synthetics and, more generally, in capital-intensive industries. Nevertheless, experience analyses appear to be helpful in understanding the competitive dynamics of an industry, and the strategic options for public policy, even in situations which do not satisfy these two conditions.[5]

[5]Another (and obvious) condition is that when performing experience curve analysis, one must correct for inflation by deflating the raw data and if necessary, reflating the forecast. Use of a gross national product deflator is necessary, because use of a sector deflator has the effect of minimizing evidence of the effect being measured.

Cross-Sectional Experience Curves

At any point in time, cost differentials between competitors may be far less than relative experience levels indicate. For example, a competitor with twice the experience typically has only a 5-10% cost advantage, rather than the 25-30% predicted by the experience curve. This differential is the "cross-sectional" experience curve at a point in time.

The explanation for relatively modest cross-sectional cost differentials is found in differing histories of competitors. For example, competitors who enter late should be able to start at lower costs than the pioneer did, through the purchase of state-of-the-art technology. (However a new entrant will always start at a higher cost point than that occupied by the leader at that point in time, if only for scale, capacity, utilization, and organizational reasons.) Competitors who enter late will almost always grow relatively faster than established companies, if only to approach competitive scale and utilize excess capacity. Also, some late entries from related fields bring with them cost advantages through prior experience in common components. They may also use materials and services common to competitors which decline in real cost on their own cost curves, without much regard for the relative growth of experience of specific users (See Cross Section Experience Curves, n.d., pp. 1-2).

Managerial Implications

There are a number of immediately obvious management and managerial strategy implications of experience curve analysis, and these have been extensively described in the literature (Hedley 1976; Delombre and Bruzelius 1977; BCG 1968). For example, if costs are inversely proportional to market share, then higher market share has a calculable value. If cost declines are predictable, they can be used as a basis for both cost control and management evaluation. Costs will decline proportionately faster when cost elements can be shared among more than one product, and a choice of design element alternatives can be made on the basis of whether initial experience is high or low compared to future expected volume.

Another important implication, particularly for Canadian companies operating under higher cost conditions than their U.S. competitors, is that the relative growth of companies in an industry is more important than absolute growth in a dynamic environment. A company with a structural cost disadvantage can compensate for it by a dynamic cost advantage, by accumulating experience faster than the competitor who enjoys a structural advantage. It can easily be calculated by how

much faster one must grow in order to overcome a given structural cost disadvantage.

An observation of particular importance in Canada is that
what appears to be a technological gap between competitors may
in fact turn out to be an experience gap.

Experience curve analysis can be used as a basis for industrial strategy, for both growth and mature stage products.
The most successful example historically is that of Japan.
Exploitation of product-specific economies, combined with a
willingness to sell initially at a very low margin while growth
in production experience is taking place, plus a home market
protected by non-tariff barriers, has enabled the Japanese to
achieve world-wide comparative advantage in shipbuilding,
steel, cameras, consumer electronics, and to bid for it in
areas like duplicating machines.

The balance of this paper will discuss some of the pricing
implications of the experience curve phenomenon. Using experience curve analysis, price reduction is predictable in some
situations. If prices are not paralleling costs, then price
instability is predictable.

Cost-Price Relationships

If costs decline at a predictable rate, then it is possible to examine related price curves for cost-price correla-
tion.[6] In stable markets, one might assume that as costs decrease due to experience, prices will decrease proportionately.
If profit margins remain at a constant percentage of price,
average industry costs and prices should follow identically
sloped experience curves. Figure Six shows such a stable
price pattern, where price follows costs and the margin between
them remains fairly constant over time as experience accum-
ulates.

This kind of stable price pattern is virtually never
found in North American marketing practice. Donald J. Daly of
York University has concluded that virtually the only stable

---

[6] The analysis usually used plots industry unit price or
weighted average unit price for different sizes or grades,
against total historical industry units. Average industry
costs are weighted by the unit production of each competitor.
If individual prices were plotted against appropriate costs for
individual competitor's experience, the slope of the price line
would vary based on whether the competitor were gaining or
losing substantial market share.

price patterns found are those in Japanese industry. This
observation contributes to the explanation of phenomenon such
as the great stability of market share in many Japanese industries over long periods of time and over various stages of
product life cycles.

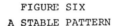

FIGURE SIX

A STABLE PATTERN

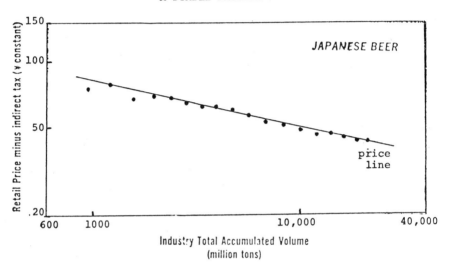

Source: Sallenave (1976), p.22

By far the most commonly observed North American pattern
is a stable-unstable-stable sequence, illustrated in Figure
Seven.[7] Prices at the introductory life-cycle stage are initially below average industry costs, being based on short-
term anticipated costs. Then the rate of cost reduction
exceeds price reduction over a period of time, creating a price
umbrella. The market-leader supported price umbrella typically
occurs in the rapid growth period of the product life-cycle,

_____

[7]It is important to remember that Figures One through Seven
are plots against accumulated units produced, not against
time. Although experience increases with time, the relation
may be quite irregular.

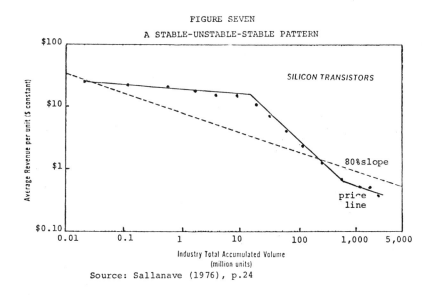

FIGURE SEVEN

A STABLE-UNSTABLE-STABLE PATTERN

SILICON TRANSISTORS

Average Revenue per unit ($ constant)

$100
$10
$1
$0.10

0.01   0.1   1   10   100   1,000   5,000

80%slope

price line

Industry Total Accumulated Volume
(million units)

Source: Sallanave (1976), p.24

where demand exceeds supply. However this phase is highly
unstable because, characteristic to the period, new competitors are attracted and/or production is expanded by existing
competitors, and the dominant firm loses market share.

At a point usually corresponding to the beginning of what
is called the "competitive turbulence" stage of the product
life-cycle, a shakeout period begins (See Wasson 1975, for
discussion of the stages). Either the leading producer, or a
secondary producer which has been gaining market share under
the price umbrella, decides to buy a larger market share by
reducing either actual or effective price. Such breaks in
price seem to occur earlier in the life-cycle the faster the
rate of growth of product output, the larger the number of
producers, the greater the difference between price and cost
for the lowest-cost producer, and the faster the rate of loss

111

of market share by the leading producer.

At some point, the price war ends - very often with price again below average industry cost, although not necessarily below cost for the leading producer. Marginal producers are either eliminated, or differentiate their product. Survivors recognize that they have more to gain from coexistence than from price competition, and evolve to a shared-oligopoly position (Rutenberg 1978; Robinson and Lackhani 1975). Decline in the unstable phase of the price curve will almost always have ended by the mature stage of the product life-cycle, when market growth has slowed down. At this point, when product characteristics have stabilized and technology is available by purchase, the leading producer is likely to have achieved a dominant market position which is virtually unassailable by domestic competitors.

In terms of strategic product portfolio analysis, a firm with products in the "star" position of high cash requirements because of high growth rate, but high cash generation potential because of high market share, might, in the absence of adequate policies, deteriorate to become "question marks" or "dogs," where cash generation ability is low because of low market share. It is very difficult to break out of a "question mark" or "dog" position with a mature product. The firm which fails to achieve dominant status either faces years of continuous cash investment with little return, or the need to divest.

In the mature stage, long-term competitive challenge for the leadership role is most likely to come from low-cost producers in other countries.

STRATEGIC IMPLICATIONS OF THE COST-PRICE RELATIONSHIP

In industries where a significant portion of total cost can be reduced due to experience or scale effects, cost advantages and ultimately profit position can be achieved by pursuing a strategy aimed at accumulating experience faster than competitors. The object of such a strategy would be to acquire the largest market share, relative to competition.

The leading competitor at the rapid growth stage of the product life-cycle has a choice. He can create a price umbrella, allow profit margins to widen, and achieve a rapid pay-back period of his initial investment. This alternative stabilizes price over the short run, but invites dramatic changes in price and market share in the long run.

The second alternative is to maintain constant margins

(which may be negative) and convert decreasing costs into lower prices. This option will both continue the cost decline, and also continue the high growth rate. The fastest growing competitor can,by maintaining a constant margin, lower prices faster than anyone else's costs can decline. Unless competitors have both abundant financial resources and excellent knowledge of industry cost curves, it is not likely that they will invest to maintain margins.

The advantages of leadership are greatest where both physical volume of the product is growing rapidly, and each year's volume is a high percentage of total previous experience. In a steady-state situation, an annual growth in physical production of 5% a year will double past experience in about 15 years; a growth of 10% in about 7 years, of 15% in about 5 years, and of 25% in just under 3 years.

Of course not every firm can or should aspire to leadership, because one implication of high growth rate is the rapid investment in human and financial resources necessary for leadership. The most important of these may be the great increase in capital investment in facilities to maintain or increase share in a growth market. To try to maintain or increase share is to be committed to a rapidly escalating series of investments during the rapid growth and competitive turbulence phases, with a long potential period of losses and negative cash flow ahead. An annual growth in physical production of 25% per year may require a doubling and redoubling of capital investment (and of paid-in equity) every thirty months. A good current example of inability to invest for leadership is found in the microprocessor industry, where rapid growth and evolving technology have left only four firms in the world able to sustain the capital investment and research and development expenditure necessary today, for market leadership tomorrow – and all of these firms are receiving generous direct or indirect assistance from their respective governments.

Failure to maintain investment at the necessary rate, either because of unwillingness to do so or inability to raise additional debt or equity capital, will cause a firm to drop off the experience curve and to fall into a market position which becomes less tenable as initial market share (or expected share) erodes. This sort of financial limitation has been cited as a disadvantage facing Rapid-Data in the Canadian hand-held calculator business, and facing the European aerospace industry in selling the Panavia Tornado fighter aircraft, and the various models of Airbus (Nuts and Bolts, 1978). The financial limitation is a particular problem in Canada, where planning horizons measured by payback periods tend to be shorter, and financial institutions more conservative in the provision of capital (RCCC 1978, chs. 10 and 11).

A strategy based on the experience curve phenomenon is much more difficult to undertake in low growth-rate stages of the product life-cycle. Abell and Hammond cite the example of a firm with a 6 percent of a market that is growing at an 8 percent real growth rate, in an industry where the leader has a 24 percent share. If the leader were to hold its share by growing at the 8 percent industry rate, the trailing firm would have to grow at a 26 percent annual growth rate for nine years to pull even. Sales and investment in productive capacity would have to expand by 640 percent. This analysis raises substantial questions as to whether the growth rate could be sustained, the necessary investment financed, and whether the market would be worth leading in nine years time. It is suggested that the implications of such calculations may have been involved in the withdrawal of RCA, Xerox and GE from the main-frame computer business. (Abell and Hammond 1979, pp. 118-9).

Given these caveats, experience curve analysis suggests that short or medium term pricing below cost may be rational behaviour for a competitor. In the turbulent growth period of a new product, it makes sense for the competitor with the necessary financial resources to lead in price cutting to insure a high continuing market share, and a low cost structure. Pricing below cost may also be rational behavior for a late-comer to a product area who has access to large financial resources compared to existing producers.

In both cases, and even when price is reduced below short-run cost to the point where competitors with limited financial resources cannot survive, this is not necessarily irrational. Under the right cost-reduction circumstances, the price cut need never be revoked. Moving down the experience curve should lower costs sufficiently to provide normal margins within a reasonable time span. Because of price elasticity, a very deep price cut may even increase the market enough to shorten the payback period to less than what it was prior to the cut.

A number of Canadian businessmen, while accepting this analysis and the premise that pricing below cost may be rational, have argued that such behavior would constitute predatory pricing under Canadian competition law, and thus be foreclosed to them. Indeed this argument was put forward by several large enterprises as a reason why Canadian firms could not benefit equally with U.S. firms from tariff cuts under the Tokyo Round. The final section of this paper will discuss the economics of predatory pricing, and will conclude that within limits, below-cost pricing under the experience curve phenomenon is not prohibited behavior in Canada.

PREDATORY PRICING AND THE EXPERIENCE CURVE PHENOMENON

It has long been recognized in law that a firm may reduce its prices with the intent to destroy its rivals or to deter new entry. However the statutes on such predatory pricing have been characterized by vagueness, the case law by a lack of cases, and case discussion and departmental opinions by a paucity of economic analysis. No case of which I am aware, in Canada or in the United States (at least under Section 2 of the Sherman Act), has specifically considered the experience curve phenonemon as a defense for a predatory pricing charge. This section will briefly analyse the predatory pricing offense in terms of defining a boundary between legitimately competitive prices, and those that are properly regarded as predatory.

One reason for the haziness of the predatory pricing concept is that rivals almost automatically assume predation when a competitor's price is below their costs for any extended period of time. As indicated in Figure Eight, it is quite possible for differential experience to give competitors quite different profit-margin positions at one point in time.

FIGURE EIGHT

EXPERIENCE - PROFIT MARGIN RELATIONSHIPS

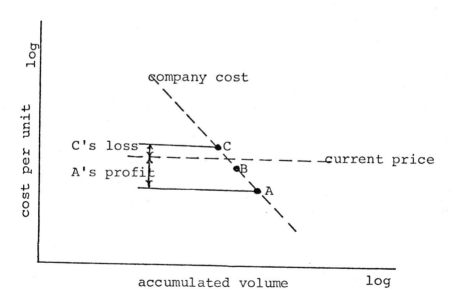

Court cases in predatory pricing cases have generally referred to highly general concepts such as "below cost pricing,"[8] "ruinous competition,"[9] and "predatory intent,"[10] in
assigning liability. Such undefined standards provide little
basis for analyzing the predatory pricing offense.

We would normally expect a rationally-managed firm to
attempt to maximize profits or minimize losses in the short-
run, by producing to the point where marginal cost equal price
(or in the case of the monopolist, equals marginal revenue).
A firm that sells at a short-run profit-maximizing (or loss
minimizing) price is clearly not predatory. A necessary condition for predation is the sacrifice of short-run profits
(which occurs in all the experience curve cases). It is not
a sufficient condition, because not all deliberate sacrificing
of short-run profits is predatory. A firm may assume short-
run losses in a situation where monopoly is not possible, for
example, to buy-in to a market where short-run average costs
are above existing market price. Thus a standard based on
short-run profit maximization cannot be used to define predatory or non-predatory price levels for firms in general.
(However long-run profit-maximization is not a sufficient
defense to alleged predatory behavior. A firm may calculate
that short-run losses can be recaptured by the higher monopoly
prices that can be charged after competitors have been driven
out).

Pricing At or Above Average Cost

When a leading firm sells at a price equal to or above
average cost (and thus above marginal cost), but could earn
higher short-run pofits selling at a higher price, the necessary element of predatory behavior is present. The classical
argument is that the firm is charging a lower price to deter
rivals. (These and subsequent arguments are set out in detail
in Areeda and Turner 1975, 1976; Posner 1967; Yamey 1972;
Scherer 1976, 1976-2; Williamson 1977). There are two cases
relavant to the experience curve. In one, the seller may

---

[8] Discussed in National Dairy Prod. Corp. v. US, 350 F.2d 321
(8th Cir., 1965), at 327.

[9] Discussed in Puerto Rican American Tobacco Co. v. American
Tobacco Co., 30 F.2d 234 (2d Cir.) at 236.

[10] Discussed in Moore v. Mead's Fine Bread Co., 348 US 115
(1954), at 118.

charge a profit-maximizing price, lower the price when rivals
appear, then raise the price when rivals have departed. In
the second, the firm may charge less than a profit-maximizing
price to deter entry, or to weaken existing competitors. In
both cases however, either temporary or permanent prices below
the profit-maximizing level but equal to or above average cost,
can be considered competition on the merits and not an abuse
of power or exclusionary behavior. Average cost pricing
includes a "normal" return on investment (which US courts recently have interpreted as industry average, rather than average for the economy).[11] The principle that earning an average
industry return over a 3-5 year term is "competitive" is an
important one in that it would permit most constant-but-posit-
ive margin cases of short-term, experience curve pricing.

Pricing At or Above Marginal Cost

In most normal situations, marginal cost is below average
cost.[12] The competition policy problem with marginal cost
pricing is the possibility that an equally efficient competitor
may be damaged, or its entry prevented, not because of normal
competitive factors but because it has less capital, or less
access to financial markets. Even in a situation where the
leading firm and its closest rival have similar cost curves,
pricing by the leading firm at marginal cost (which is below
average cost), may create a situation where the rival has in-
sufficient capital to cover losses and to service capital debt.
The rival either drops off the experience curve and seeks a
more sheltered market segment, or else withdraws from the
business.

Even with the possibility of marginal cost pricing driving
out equally efficient rivals, or deterring new entry, it is
hard to make a case for considering it predatory. If a leading
firm produces to the point where price equals marginal cost,
only less efficient firms will suffer larger losses per unit of
output. More efficient firms, if they exist, will be either

---

[11]The principle and appropriate length of time and rate of
return is discussed at length in the district court decision in
Telex Corp. v. IBM, 367 F. Supp. 258 (N.D. Okla. 1973).

[12]The exceptions are where the leading firm is producing beyond
the normal efficient plant capacity in the short-run, or where
the leading firm has a great deal of excess capacity in the
long-run. The first case does not eliminate equally efficient
rivals or potential entrants, and thus is not predatory. The
second case will not normally arise with experience curve
pricing.

making profits, or at least losing less. Also, to force a
firm in a rapidly expanding industry to maintain a price floor
above marginal price would reduce industry output and cause inefficient use of resources in the short-run. At least in the
rapid growth and competitive turbulence stages of the product
life cycle, it can be argued that pricing at marginal cost is
on balance a competitive and socially optimal objective (See
Areeda and Turner 1975; Scherer 1976; and Williamson 1977 for
differing views).

Pricing Below Marginal Cost

The practice of marginal cost pricing by a leading firm is
argued to be non-predatory even though losses could be minimized or profits increased at a lower output and higher price,
because marginal-cost pricing in an industry undergoing rapid
growth is consistent with proper resource allocation, and with
competition on the merits of the firms involved.

In normal circumstances, neither of these cases holds when
a leading firm prices below marginal cost. The monopolist not
only incurs private losses but wastes social resources when the
marginal cost of production exceeds the value of what is produced. From a competition policy standpoint, pricing below
marginal cost greatly increases the probability that competing
firms will be eliminated or deterred for reasons unrelated to
the efficiency of the leading firm. For all these reasons,
public policy and the courts have normally held that pricing
below marginal cost is a sufficient condition for a finding
of predatory or exclusionary behavior. The only common exceptions to this rule are justification of short-term price
reductions to new customers or new geographic markets, by non-
leading firms. The arguments supporting such reductions are
usually found inadequate when applied to leading firms, or for
general or long-term price reductions.

It has been recognized that the marginal costs that a
leading firm may not go below are "reasonably anticipated" marginal costs, but there is considerable doubt as to how "reasonably anticipated" costs may be established. In other words,
to establish predatory pricing, it is sufficient to show that
a leading firm has priced both below immediate marginal cost
and below the marginal cost at the output which he reasonably
anticipated he would attain in the near future, but the onus is
probably on the firm to provide a solid case for "reasonably
anticipated costs." It is here that the mathematics of the
experience curve may come to the rescue of a rapidly growing
firm. Pricing at a constant margin to anticipated costs, even
where price is below marginal cost at a point in time, would
seem acceptable if a proper analysis of cost levels and the

experience effect has been carried out before the fact. Such
an analysis would involve, at a minimum, a determination of
the unit of analysis, gathering of relevant historical cost
data for various cost components over a period of time, and
using a fitted line to project future costs of each cost component allowing for shared experience with other units of
analysis.

The same type of defense would be available to a non-
leading firm attempting to buy market share by pricing below
marginal cost. Normally, there are grounds for permitting a
non-leading firm to price below marginal cost to meet, but not
beat, a competitor's unlawful price. A non-leading rival might
be able to justify a below marginal-cost and below-competitors
price by cost-line projection, plus the assumption that a non-
leading firm would be permitted a longer time-frame for analysis than would a leading firm.

It should be emphasized however that the use of these
below-marginal cost arguments have far more validity in the
rapid-growth stages of the product life-cycle, where experience doubling and related cost reduction occurs over a short
time period. In the saturation and maturity stages of the
life-cycle, it would be more difficult for a leading firm to
justify below-marginal cost pricing, although a substantially
smaller rival might still justify it on the basis of rapid
relative experience increases.

Average Variable Cost as a Surrogate

The primary problem in defining predation based on the
economist's concept of marginal cost is an administrative problem of ascertaining what a firm's marginal cost is, at a point
in time. The incremental cost of making and selling the last
unit cannot easily be calculated from conventional accounting
conventions, which typically only show observed average variable cost. It is quite feasible to use this as a surrogate
for marginal cost, when pricing under an experience curve,
without unduly limiting flexibility. In particular, a firm
may still legitmately determine its price levels according to
expected future costs rather than historical accounting costs.

In this discussion we can dispense with distinctions
between fixed and variable costs. Virtually all costs are
variable when a firm plans on increasing its capacity substantially over a short time period. More costs become variable
over the time period involved in the growth-competitive turbulence stages of the product life-cycle. Thus for our
purposes, all costs can be considered as variable.

In a declining cost situation, average variable cost will always be above marginal cost, but in most cases only slightly above. By reference to the marginal cost standard, reliance on average variable cost will be less permissive, but probably only slightly so. Average variable cost can also be argued to be the correct test on principle, since a firm that sells below its average variable cost is clearly not loss-minimizing. At any price below anticipated average variable cost, a firm is earning no return and could cut uts losses by ceasing to operate.

REFERENCES

Abell, Derek F. and John S. Hammond (1979), Strategic Market Planning, Englewood Cliffs, New Jersey: Prentice-Hall, Inc.

Abernathy, William J. and Kenneth Wayne (1974), "Limits of the Learning Curve," Harvard Business Review, (September-October), 109-119.

Alchian, Armen (1963), "Reliability of Progress Curves in Airframe Production," Econometrica, 31 (October).

Areeda, Philip and Donald F. Turner (1975), "Predatory Pricing and Related Practices Under Section 2 of the Sherman Act," Harvard Law Review, 88 (1975), 697.

Arrow, Kenneth J. (1961), "The Economic Implications of Learning by Doing," Review of Economic Studies, 155-173.

Barkai, Hain and David Lebhari (1973), "Impact of Experience in Kibbutz Farming," Review of Economics and Statistics, (February), 56-63.

Boston Consulting Group (1968), Perspectives on Experience, Boston, Mass.: The Boston Consulting Group.

Buzzell, Robert D., Bradley T. Gale, and Ralph G.M. Sultan (1974), Market Share, Profitability, and Business Strategy, working paper, Cambridge, Mass.: Marketing Science Institute, (August).

Cross Sectional Experience Curves, Boston, Mass.: The Boston Consulting Group, n.d. (pamphlet).

Delombre, J. and B. Bruzelius (1977), "Importance of Relative Market Share in Stretegic Planning - A Case Study," Long Range Planning, 10 (August).

Fruhan, William E., Jr. (1972), "Pyrrhic Victories in Fights for Market Share," Harvard Business Review, (September - October), 100.

Goldschmid, H.J., H. Michael Mann and J. Fred Weston (1974), Industrial Concentration: The New Learning, Boston: Little, Brown and Company.

Gort, M. and T. Hogarty (1962), "New Evidence on Mergers," Journal of Law and Economics, 13 (April), 167-184.

Hamermesh, R.G., M.J. Anderson Jr. and J.E. Harris (1978) "Strategies for Low Market Share Businesses," Harvard Business Review, (May-June) 95-102.

Hedley, Barry (1976), "A Fundamental Approach to Strategy Development," Long Range Planning, (December), 2-11.

Hirsch, W.Z. (1956), "Firm Progress Ratios," Econometrica, Vol. 24.

Horvath, Dezso and Charles McMillan (1978), Industrial Planning In Japan, (Industrial Strategy Working Paper), Faculty of Administrative Studies, York University, Toronto, (December).

Lecraw, Donald J. and Donald N. Thompson (1978), Conglomerate Mergers in Canada: A Background Report, Ottawa: Supply and Services Canada, Government of Canada, (May).

Mason, R.H. and M.B. Goudzwaard (1976), "Performance of Con-glomerate Firms: A Portfolio Approach," Journal of Finance, 31 (March), 39-48.

McGee, John S. (1958), "Predatory Price Cutting: The Standard Oil of New Jersey Case, " Journal of Law and Economics, (October), 137.

McMillan, C.J. (1978), "The Changing Competitive Environment of Canadian Business," Journal of Canadian Studies, 13 (Spring), 38-47.

Nadler and Smith (1963), "Manufacturing Progress Functions for Types of Processes," International Journal of Production Research, Vol. 2.

Nuts and Bolts of the Economy: Background Papers (1978),
(Chapter Two: Productivity), London: Chief Secretary to
the Treasury, H.M. Government, (June 10).

Philips, Almarin (1979), "Predation and Antitrust Rules: The
Complications When Quality is Considered," Proceedings of
the Conference in Honor of E.T. Grether (working paper,
(March).

Posner, Richard (1967), "Exclusionary Practices and the Antitrust Laws," University of Chicago Law Review, 41 (1974),
506.

Rapp, William V. (1977), "Japan: Its Industrial Policies and
Corporate Behavior," Columbia Journal of World Business,
Vol. 12 (Spring), 38-48.

Report of the Royal Commission on Corporate Concentration (1978)
Ottawa, Canada: Government of Canada, Department of Supply
and Services, 449 pp.

Review of Monopolies and Mergers Policy: A Consultative Document (1978), London: Her Majesty's Stationery Office, (May).

Robinson, Bruce and Dhet Lackhani (1975), "Dynamic Price
Models for New Product Planning," Management Science, (June),
1113-22.

Rutenberg, David P. (1978), Umbrella Pricing, Kingston, Ontario: Queen's University School of Business, (working paper)
(January).

Sallenave, Jean-Paul (1976), Experience Analysis for Industrial
Planning, Boston, Mass.: Lexington Books.

Scherer, Frederick M. (1976), "Predatory Pricing and the
Sherman Act: A Comment, " Harvard Law Review, 89 (1976),
901.

_____ (1976-2), "Some Last Words on Predatory
Pricing," Harvard Law Review, 89 (1976), 901.

Schoeffler, Sidney, Robert D. Buzzell and Donald F. Heany
(1974), "Impact of Strategic Planning in Profit Performance,"
Harvard Business Review, (March-April), 137-145.

Skeoch, L.A. and B.C. McDonald, Dynamic Change and Accountability in a Canadian Market Economy, Ottawa, Queen's Printer.

Thompson, Donald N. (1979), "Mergers, Effects, and Competition
  Policy: Some Empirical Evidence," Canadian Competition
  Policy, (Robert Pritchard, ed.), Toronto: University of
  Toronto Press.

Wasson, Chester R. (1978), Dynamic Competitive Strategy and
  Product Life Cycles, (3rd ed.), Austin Texas: Austin Press.

Williamson, Oliver E. (1977), "Predatory Pricing: A Strategic
  and Welfare Analysis," Yale Law Journal, 87 (1977), 284.

Wright, T.P. (1936), "Factors Affecting the Cost of Airplanes,"
  Journal of the Aeronautical Sciences, Vol. 3.

Yamey, Basil S. (1972), "Predatory Price Cutting: Notes and
  Comments," Journal of Law and Economics, (1972), 129.

THE DECLINE OF THE INDEPENDENT STORE IN CANADA:
SOME PUBLIC POLICY QUESTIONS[1]

Mel S. Moyer, York University
Hart E. Sernick, York University

ABSTRACT

During the first half of this century the independent
store occupied a prominant place within retailing in Canada.
This strong position was maintained despite the appearance of
large scale retailing institutions (e.g. chain stores) which
could have been expected to significantly erode the independent's share of market.

However, since the 1950's, the share of the market held by
the independent store has declined rapidly. This decline appears to be linked to the rise of the shopping center. Consequently, this paper examines the relationship between the independent retailer and the rise of the shopping center and
questions whether the position of the independent retailer is
the result of tolerably fair competition or is the result of
undue power exercised by developers and large retailers.

In examining the relationship between developers and small
retailers, the paper notes that the small retailer is disadvantaged by many requirements of the shopping center developers.
On the other hand, it is apparent that small retailers may
avoid shopping center locations to maintain their independence.
In view of this conflicting evidence it is unclear whether the
independent store warrants intervention to stem the decline.

Finally, in order to answer the public policy questions
raised by this paper, it is noted that further research is

---

[1] The following research assistants made valuable contributions
to this paper: Ms. June Francis, Mr. Ken Goode, Mr. Tom Mc-
Cullough, and Ms. Anne Moyer. The authors are also indebted to
the following executives for critiquing drafts of the paper:
Mr. S.H. Witkin & Mr. H. Haber of the Cadillac Fairview Corporation Ltd.; Mr. J.G.W. McIntyre & Mr. D. Rogers of the
Hudson's Bay Company; Mr. E. Bodner & Mr. G. Becker of S.B.
McLaughlin Associates Ltd.; Mr. T. Davies of W.H. Smith Ltd.;
Mr. S. Sell of Lehrdorff Management Ltd.; and Mr. J.F. Bull-
ock, Mr. W.R. Worth & Ms. P. Johnson of the Can. Fed. of In-
dependent Business.

needed in two areas. The first concerns the need for empirical
evidence showing that small retailers are in fact important to
the retailing landscape. The second relates to the needs and
requirements of independent retailers in shopping centers which
could make the latter environment more appealing to the small
retailer.

Au cours de la première moitié du siècle actuel, le magasin indépendant a occupé une place importante dans la vente au
détail au Canada. Cette position marquée fut maintenue malgré
l'apparation d'établissements faisant la vente au détail sur
une grande échelle (exemple: les magasins à succursales multiples) qui auraient dû miner considérablement la section de
marché du détaillant indépendant.

Toutefois, depuis les années cinquante, la section du
marché détenue par le magasin indépendant a déclinée de facon
dramatique. Ce déclin semble être lié à l'essor des centres
d'achats. De plus, il est à croire que ce déclin est irréver-
sible. Conséquemment, une certaine inquiétude se fait sentir
en ce qui concerne la situation du magasin indépendant en tant
qu'institution commerciale.

Au début, cet article trace la position du magasin indépendant sur le marché durant les cinquante dernières années.
Ensuite, il examine les rapports existants entre le déclin ré-
cent du magasin indépendant et l'essor pris par le centre d'-
achat. Ensuite, il questionne si la position actuelle du détaillant indépendant est le résultat d'une compétition passable-
ment loyale, ou si elle est le résultat de pressions indues
faites par les promoteurs des centres d'achats et les gros détaillants.

En examinant les rapports qui existent entre les promoteurs et les petits détaillants, l'article note le fait que le
petit détaillant est défavorisé par les exigences multiples im-
posées par les promoteurs des centres d'achats. D'un autre
côté, il est évident que les petits détaillants évitent les em-
placements des centres d'achats afin de conserver leur indépen-
dance. Etant donné cette évidence contradictoire, il est difficile de décider si une intervention est nécessaire pour ar-
rêter le déclin du magasin indépendant.

Finalement, afin de pouvoir répondre aux questions d'ordre
publique soulevées apr cet article, il est à noter qu'une recherche plus approfondie est nécessaire dans ces deux domaines.
Le premier concerne le besoin d'évidence empirique démontrant
que les petits détaillants sont en fait très importants dans le
royaume de la vante au détail. Le deuxième touche aux besoins
et aux exigences des détaillants indépendants dans les centres

d'achats, ce qui pourraient rendre l'environnement de ces
centres plus attirants pour le petit détaillant.

INTRODUCTION

After many decades of maintaining his dominant position in
Canada's marketing channel, the independent merchant has been
giving ground rapidly since the mid-1950's. The timing of this
decline appears to be linked to the rise of the shopping center
in Canada.

Since the independent merchant has traditionally been considered central to the health of the distribution trades, this
decline is seen as a threat to the marketing system. This
paper examines the relationship between the rise of the shopping center and the decline of the independent store and high-
lights the public policy question that evolve from this analysis.

THE CHANGING COMPETITIVE POSITION
OF THE INDEPENDENT STORE

Since the late 1800's, Canada has seen a succession of institutional innovations in retailing, including the department
store, the mail order house, the corporate chain, the supermarket, and the discount house. Each has posed a threat to
smaller rivals. Thus, each has sparked questions about the ability of the independent merchant to hold his historically
prominant place in retailing. For some, these questions go beyond a narrow curiosity about the share of the "small man" to a
broad concern for the vigour of the distributive system.

Exhibit I shows how the small man has fared. It traces
the changing competitive position of the independent store as a

---

2 The Statistics Canada defintion of an independent store on
  which all these data are based is in effect any store not defined as a unit of a corporate chain or a department store.
  A corporate chain is defined as "an organization operating
  four or more retail outlets in the same kind of business under
  the same legal ownership" (Snyder 1976, Appendix B).
  A department store is defined as a retail outlet which sells
  "at least three different commodity lines are: a) Family
  Clothing and Apparel; b) Furniture, appliances and home fur-
  nishings; and c) All other (miscellaneous). No one line can
  represent more than 50% of total sales and at least 10% of
  the outlet's sales must be derived from the "All other" group
  (Snyder 1976, p. 64-65). Consequently, independent stores include those affiliated with voluntary chains and co-op groups.

EXHIBIT I

SALES OF INDEPENDENT STORES AND SALES OF SHOPPING CENTRES AS A

PERCENTAGE OF TOTAL RETAIL TRADE - CANADA, 1935-1973

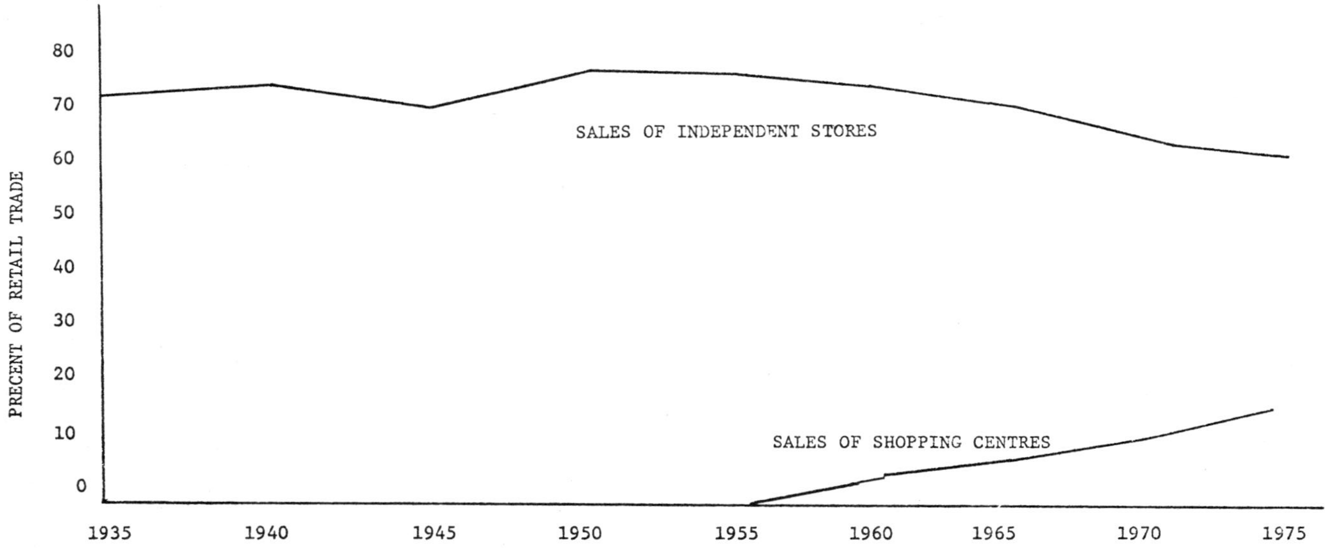

SALES OF INDEPENDENT STORES

SALES OF SHOPPING CENTRES

PERCENT OF RETAIL TRADE

80 70 60 50 40 30 20 10 0

1935 1940 1945 1950 1955 1960 1965 1970 1975

Sources: Moyer and Snyder 1967, p. 159
Statistics Canada - Retail Trade, Cat. #63005, 1965-1973
Snyder 1976, p. 37

retailing institution in Canada.[2] During the 1920's, independent stores lost at least a fifth of their business to corporate chains and department stores. During the Depression they regained a small amount of ground. Then, during the second World War they slipped back again. In the postwar period, the independents' fortunes improved again. The reasons for these ebbs and flows are discussed elsewhere (Moyer and Snyder 1967, pp. 147-163). What is important is that, as of the early 1950's, the position of the independent store was as strong as it had been for three decades.

However, in the quarter century since that time, Canada's independent merchants have been losing ground. Moreover, their decline has been steady and substantial. In 1952, the proportion of retail trade going to independents was over 75%. Every year since then, it has decreased. Today, the independent retailer's share of the Canadian market is about 58%. This is the longest and steepest slide experienced by the independent store-keeper over the period for which records exist. In fact, it is among the most dramatic declines recorded by a major retailing institution in the history of a country.

The Link With the Shopping Center

This significant decline of the independent merchant appears to be linked, in several ways, to the rise of the shopping center. The shopping center appeared in Canada in the middle 1950's. The plunge in the market share of independents also began at that time. By the late 1960's, it was clear that, "measured by the speed and success with which it occupies a large place in its environment, the shopping center is probably the most significant innovation in retailing to appear in Canada in half a century" (Moyer 1973, p. 30).[3] The retreat of the independent outlet has coincided with the advance of the shopping center.

There is another link. It is clear that the shopping center has been a relatively inhospitable setting for the independent merchant. Exhibit II contrasts the market share of independent merchants inside and outside of the shopping center setting. Clearly, the independent gets smaller shares of the shopper's dollar inside shopping centers than it does outside of them.

Although the independent's relative lack of success in

---

3 For other statistical analyses of shopping centers in Canada plus descriptions of their historical development, see Moyer and Snyder (1967), pp. 181-199 and Snyder (1976), pp. 3-29.

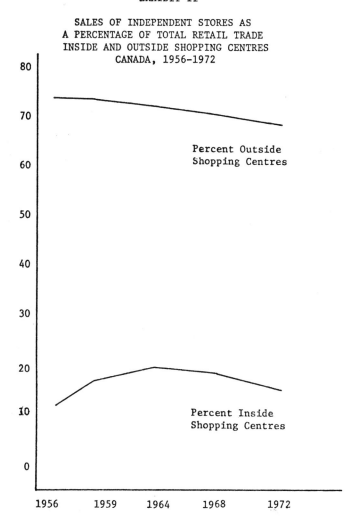

EXHIBIT II

SALES OF INDEPENDENT STORES AS
A PERCENTAGE OF TOTAL RETAIL TRADE
INSIDE AND OUTSIDE SHOPPING CENTRES
CANADA, 1956-1972

Percent Outside
Shopping Centres

Percent Inside
Shopping Centres

1956   1959   1964   1968   1972

Sources: Moyer and Snyder 1967, p. 192
           Statistics Canada - Retail Trade, Cat. #
                                             63005

129

shopping centers varies from trade to trade, the small man is less well represented in every line of trade (Exhibit III). For example, in variety stores, service stations, drug stores, furniture outlets and jewellery stores, the independent has a fairly strong presence inside shopping centers compared to elsewhere. At the other extreme, among grocery and combination stores, the independent gives up much of the shopping center market to chain stores. In the middle range are hardware stores and the four kinds of stores that deal primarily in apparel, namely men's clothing, women's clothing, family clothing and shoes.

Behind these differences, there is a tendency worth noting. In general, as one goes from the market outside to the market inside the shopping center, the weakening in the independent's market position is least severe among specialty goods outlets and most severe among convenience goods outlets.

To this generalization there are three exceptions. In service stations and variety stores, which sell convenience goods, and in drug stores, which sell some convenience goods, independent stores do quite well in shopping centers compared to elsewhere. For service stations, the explanation of their success lies in the fact that the dealer is nearly always franchised and closely supervised by a single supplier. In functional terms, service station dealers can be linked to chain store managers, thus fitting them into the pattern described for grocery and variety stores. Among drug stores, part of the explanation is the immense success of one plaza-oriented voluntary chain.

These data cannot demonstrate causality. However, they strongly suggest that the rise of shopping center has been a contributor to the decline of the independent store. This apparent causal connection will be strengthened in subsequent sections, which show why smaller merchants encounter unusual difficulties in shopping centers.

It should be noted that the available data used in the preceding analysis are not all that one might wish. First, the Statistics Canada definition of a chain noted previously is not equivalent to the U.S. definition, thereby limiting Canadian-American comparisons.

Second, in a lengthy longitudinal study such as this there are changes in definition and measurement which threaten comparability over time. To the extent possible, such changes have been identified and compensated for, leaving what the authors and research assistants believe to be reasonably reliable portrayals of the overall trends.

Third, the data treat independent stores as that significant body of outlets which are, in terms of behaviour, interde-
pendent parts of a larger families of enterprises. This includes closely franchised outlets, as in the automobile, gasoline and fast-food fields, members of co-operative chains and
voluntary groups as in the grocery, hardware automotive and
drug fields, and other stores which are in some measure, "chain
stores."[4] The inclusion of these "grey areas" overstates the
market share of independent stores, particularly in those commodities previously mentioned. These neo-chains have increased
their market shares since the 1930's. Consequently, the long-
term decline of the fully independent merchant is understated
and his present market standing is overstated.

A fourth data problem is that some enclosed downtown malls,
(for example the Eaton Center in Toronto or the Pacific Center
in Vancouver) do not meet the Statistics Canada definition of a
shopping center, and are excluded from those data. The effect
is to understate the inroads of the shopping center and to overstate the strength of the independent store.

A fifth problem, in concept rather than in measurement, is
that shopping centers do not challenge independent merchants
equally in all fields. For example, in the sale of motor vehicles, lumber and building materials and farm implements, shopping centers are a relatively unimportant setting. Were fields
such as these eliminated from the calculations, the impact of
the shopping center on the independent store would appear more
dramatic than has been shown here (Moyer and Snyder 1967, p.
181).

All of the above represent difficulties in the analysis.
However, what is equally important is that where the limitations
of the data obscure the true situation, the effect in each case
cited here is to understate rather than to overstate the trends
shown, the relationships discussed and the conclusions drawn.

MEASURING THE IMPACT OF THE SHOPPING CENTER
ON THE INDEPENDENT STORE

While the shopping center appears to be a contributing
cause to the significant decline of the independent merchant,
it may well not be the only one. One might ask to what extent
the erosion of the independent store can be attributed to the
relative inability of the independent store-keeper to compete
in shopping centers.

---

4 For a fuller treatment of this analytic problem see Moyer and
    Snyder 1969, pp. 163-177.

Any answer to this question must be speculative. Nevertheless, it can be estimated by determining what the total sales of smaller merchants would be if independent stores had done as well in shopping centers as in the outside world, and by noting the difference between that aggregate and the total revenues which smaller merchants do in fact have. This difference can be taken as a measure of the business which independents have forfeited in the arena of the shopping center.

In the latest year for which we have data, the independent's share of the market outside of shopping centers was about 68%; inside of shopping centers, it would be about 16% (Exhibit III). This is a shortfall of 52%. If independents were able to get the same market share inside the shopping center as outside of it, then their total annual sales would be larger by about almost $3 billion. This can be taken as a rough measure of the annual business which independent outlets lost because of their inability to compete as effectively in shopping centers as in the wider world. Put another way, this forfeited $3 billion due to their relative unsuccess in shopping centers diminished their overall position in Canadian retailing by about one seventh.

Taking this approach, one can estimate, annually for the last two decades, the share of total retail trade than independents could have been expected to have in the absence of the shopping center. Exhibit IV graphs these imputed annual market shares and compares them with the shares that independent stores actually had in each year.

Exhibit IV puts the impact of the shopping center in some perspective. First, it underlines that not all of the decline of the independent retailer can be attributed to shopping centers. As the graph shows, small merchants would have lost some ground even without the shopping center.[5] However, with the imputed effects of shopping centers removed, the loss of market share takes on a different character: it is reduced to about the amplitude of the swings in market position which the independent store experienced in the decades before the 1950's. This suggests that, without the shopping center, independent stores would still have suffered a setback since the 1950's, but of the kind that, over earlier decades of this century, they had always managed to reverse.

---

[5] These "non-shopping center" causes, while important to understand, are outside of the scope of this paper. For a discussion of these causes, leading to the conclusion that the small retailer will play a much less substantial role in retail distribution in the future, see Cady 1976.

EXHIBIT III

SALES OF INDEPENDENT STORES
AS A PERCENTAGE OF SALES
INSIDE AND OUTSIDE OF SHOPPING CENTERS
BY KIND OF BUSINESS
CANADA 1972

Kind of Business	(1) Market Share Outside Shopping Centers	(2) Market Share Inside Shopping Centers	(2) As a Percentage of (1)
Variety	19	16	84%
Garage & Service Stations	91	76	84
Drug	84	66	79
Furniture	84	51	61
Jewellery	69	40	58
Men's Clothing	95	54	57
Women's Clothing	77	36	47
Hardware	87	40	46
Shoe Stores	60	21	35
Family Clothing	82	25	30
Grocery	56	8	48
Department Stores	10	0	0
TOTAL ALL STORES	68	16	22%

Source: Statistics Canada – Shopping Centers in Canada – Cat. # 63-214

133

EXHIBIT IV

ACTUAL AND IMPUTED SALES OF INDEPENDENT STORES
AS A PERCENTAGE OF TOTAL RETAIL TRADE
CANADA, 1956-1972

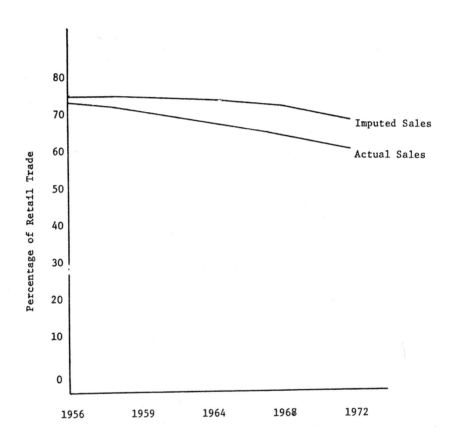

Source: Statistics Canada, Retail Trade, Cat. 362-209
         Annual

Conversely, the graph allows an estimate of what proportion of the smaller merchants' loss of position is attributable to shopping centers. Over the period covered by the graph, the independent's share of Canada's retail trade declined by about 12.8%. This compares to an estimated loss of 5.2% had the shopping center not come on the scene. Put another way, about half of the ground given up by the independent storekeepers in the last two decades has been taken up by non-independent merchants in shopping centers.

WILL THE TREND CONTINUE?

Finally, one might ask whether the independents' problems occasioned by shopping centers will become more acute or less.

One determinant will be the rate of growth in shopping center sales. The available data indicate that, for at least the next decade, shopping centers will continue to account for a growing share of the country's retail trade. However, there is some evidence that this advance is slowing, and there are persuasive reasons to believe that the slowdown will continue (Moyer 1973, p. 28; Snyder 1976, pp. 26-29; Chain Store Age 1975). Thus, if these projections hold, the three quarters of all independent storekeepers who are outside of shopping centers will continue to lose further access to Canadian shoppers, but at a slackened pace.

Another governing factor will be the pattern of growth among shopping centers. Independent merchants have a lesser place and a lower market share in large shopping centers than in small ones (Moyer 1973, p. 28).[6] Most observers expect that, as "the years of explosive growth of shopping centers are probably over" (Snyder 1976, p. 29), further development will tend to be in neighbourhood and community centers (McNair and May 1976). This would shift shopping center sales toward independent tenants. A related change with the same effect would be a trend toward "specialty shopping centers" or "mini-malls" (Brown 1976; Chain Store Age 1973; Globe and Mail 1977). These consortia cater to those specialized, personalized, shopper needs not met by regional centers by building on the strengths of local sole proprietors. However, it is not clear that a shift to "the independent's kind of shopping center" will be either strong or sustained.

One other change may improve the independents' access to shopping center business. It is the developer's desire to

6 This also holds for the U.S.; See Dollars and Cents of Shopping Centers, Part II: Tenant Characteristics (1962) p. 19.

differentiate his center from others. "How long can we continue to have centers with similar merchants, similar merchandise and similar styles before our uniqueness wear thin?" (Baxter 1975, p.9). As retail markets become "overstored" (a condition few define but many foresee), developers "can no longer maintain their share of market by blindly opening stores with a cookie-cutter sameness, and expect customers to wander in and spend $150 a square foot" (Marketing 1978, p. 12). In Canada, where the number of different retailing organizations is much fewer than in the U.S., the problem is more acute. Developers consulted in this study often observed that "the consumers biggest complaint is that all centers look the same" (Monday Report on Retailers 1979, p. 6), and that this blandness can only be overcome by "bringing in more independent retailers to add variety and interest" (Monday Report on Retailers 1979, p. 6).

To get perspective on these ameliorating changes, one can project their potential impact on the independent's overall position. First, one can determine how strong these changes would have to be in order to significantly help the independent store as an institution. Calculation shows that there is no foreseeable combination of a slowdown in the growth of shopping centers, together with a shift to smaller ones, that would halt the loss of market share by independent stores (Appendix I).

If that is the case, then one can ask what effect these favourable trends could be expected to have. Projection shows, that even under the most favourable conditions that can be forecast, these changes will do very little towards equating the independent's market share inside and outside of shopping centers, and will do almost nothing to slow the independent's loss of market share in retailing as a whole (Appendix II). It seems reasonable to conclude that the continued play of existing market forces will not materially alter the threat to the independent as represented by the shopping center.

QUESTIONS OF PUBLIC POLICY

If independent merchants are losing position as never before in Canada, if shopping centers are an apparent key cause, and if the situation is unlikely to change under prevailing conditions, then Canadians confront some substantial questions of public policy.

Central Questions

A central question is whether shopping centers are offering Canadians the retailing system they want, and if not what actions should be taken. That will depend to an important extent on whether, in shopping centers, the position of the independent store is the outcome of tolerably fair competition and is therefore a reasonable reflection of the public will.

Those who think not might see the shopping center as an enclave not subject to the free play of market forces, its tenants being selected - and rejected - by a small number of large developers and dominant retailers. Additionally, it could be alleged that these gatekeepers tend to direct their discrimination in favour of corporate outlets and against independent stores.

Conversely, it could be argued that ultimately developers must compete for the shopper's dollar, that they are therefore forced to reflect the consumer's wishes, that they do so by choosing what the market identifies as the most acceptable set of tenants and that, as businessmen, they have no motive or duty to act in any other way.

Subordinate Questions

To resolve these central questions, one must settle several subordinate issues. One is whether deveopers and major tenants have undue power in shopping centers. The view that they do gain support from developments in the U.S. In recent years, the Federal Trade Commission has charged several developer landlords and major retail tenants with restraint of trade through the use of restrictive leases (Chain Store Age 1971; American Druggist 1972). Further, the FTC has been able to obtain consent judgements in almost all these cases. Limiting or excluding certain other merchants, according to an FTC representative, "seems to be very common practice in the industry" (Chain Store Age 1971, p. E6). This generalization is supported by other authors, and appears not to have been challenged by either industry spokesmen or the business press (Business Week, 1975). Other lease covenants, called "inducement clauses," guarantee the flagship retailer that no more than a stated number of square feet will be occuped by other tenants carrying competing lines. Restrictive lease covenants are common enough to have caused some debate within the industry as to their use as a management tool (Farber 1962; Rubloff 1962; Weiss 1963).

A related question is whether developers and dominant retailers have used power to exclude or limit independent merchants. While restrictive leases may have been "virtually the rule ... in the shopping center industry" (Chain Store Age 1971, p. E6), not all have been aimed at indepedent stores. Often, the trade reports indicate, the targets have been discount stores. "In some cases they even named the discount stores they objected to" (Chain Store Age 1971, p. E6).

Nevertheless, it does seem evident that, at least in the U.S., gatekeeper power has been used to disadvantage small retailers. One FTC charge claims that in 24 cases Gimbel Brothers made shopping center leases which gave them "the right to disapprove leases of smaller tenants and limit the floor space available to them and the power to exercise continuing control over their business operations" (American Druggist 1972, p. 30).

To what extent this practice exists in Canada is difficult to establish. Canada's recent Royal Commission on Corporate Concentration considered the issue and decided that the matter did not deserve their further attention. In addition, no arm of the federal or provincial governments has initiated a restraint of trade action comparable to that of the FTC. Thus the question of exclusion and control of independent merchants in shopping centers is a matter that has attracted little attention and discussion in Canada.

But this may not settle the question. An absence of evidence does not in itself preclude the existence of unreasonable limitations on independents in shopping centers. Therefore it may be appropriate for Canadians to question whether these restrictive trade practices are unseen because they are common or undetected because they are effective.

Independent merchants may also be disadvantaged by having to pay higher rental rates than larger tenants. This seems to be a common requirement in North America. Many published sources, including a good proportion of trade literature, support the conclusion that "Lessors ... have traditionally assessed the independent merchants a higher rental per square foot than for the triple-A chain and department store" (Snyder 1976, p. 25; Dollars and Cents of Shopping Centers 1962; Harris 1968; Carr 1965; Gorman 1968; Foster 1967). The result is that, if they do participate in shopping centers, "small independents may have to operate on a higher gross profit margin than the average for their line of business" (Foster 1967, p. 27).

It does not necessarily follow, though, that heavier rents mainfest unfair competition. While critics of unequal rents could claim that this is discriminatory pricing which reflects the unbalanced power of the large and small competitors, defenders of the practice could argue that it is flexible pricing which responds to the unequal contributions for the major and minor tenants. "The key store in the shopping center is the drawing card which makes the people come to the center; as such it pays a relatively low rate. The smaller stores which hope to attract some of the customers which come to the key stores are willing ... to pay a higher rate of rent ... in order to .. . be neighbours ..." (Community Planning Review 1975, p. 1).

It should be noted, too, that the keystone store does not acquire its pulling power at no cost. In part, dominant retailers buy it by incurring advertising expense rates which are higher than the small tenant would probably accept.

In addition, large retailing organizations use their financial strength to enter into unusually long-term leases. Thus, it can be claimed, their advantageous rents are not unlike quantity discounts given for buying large amounts of space for long periods of time. "Even if the general merchandise stores and supermarkets in a center were independently owned, a similar pattern of quantity discounts for large space usage would hold true. Independents ... typically operate less space on a much shorter lease term" (Foster 1967, p. 34).

Lower rents can also be an acknowledgement of the scarcity of key tenants. "Particularly in the case of department stores, developers rarely find more than one ... in a given city interested in expansion into a proposed shopping center at that particular moment. The developer is commonly faced with the alternative of either signing that one department store or not building a center at all. The developer normally has to grant concessions ... The usual areas for concessions are on rent and co-tenants" (Foster 1967, pp. 32-33). The chapter by Day and Tigert demonstrates how constrained the Canadian developer has become in seeking keystone retail tenants.

The superior bargaining power of key retailers has several sources. Developers take the position that, faced with that power, they must offer lower rents to large tenants - and higher rents to small ones. Thus a smaller retailer reports that "many developers have told me that after they have completed negotiations with their major tenants, their rent schedule for the balance of the schedule - to make a project economical for the developer - is so high that it is no longer economically feasible for small independents to become tenants" (Harris 1968, pp. 3-11).

Beyond the higher rents charged to the independent retailer, there may be other, more important financial constraints. The rigorous design criteria imposed upon retailers entering a shopping center may push the smaller merchants' store construction costs well beyond what they would otherwise be. It may take two to three years for a shopping center to become viable. These factors can greatly extend payback periods. In such situations, chains and department stores are more likely to have the resources necessary to absorb initial losses and thus gain the ultimate profits.

Taking all of these factors into account, one must then

make a judgement as to whether, in the hands of dominant retailing organizations, lower rents are the unjustifiable profits of a monopolist or the legitimate rewards of a competitor who has earned command of a rare resource.

A further issue is whether, ultimately, the difficulties of the independent should be laid at the door of the developer and the large retailer, or whether they lie elsewhere. It could be argued that, given his substantial power and strategic position, the developer has a responsibility to help preserve retailing's entrepreneurs. Some think so: "Although many independent specialty stores ... have found a 'niche' in the regional center ... the future of the independent store is clouded. ... Lessors will have to take steps to insure the survival of the independent entrepreneur through a change in the traditional method of allocating cost" (Snyder 1976, p. 25). Others would disagree taking the position that, so long as they operate within the law, developers have no responsibility but to seek their own self interest. They might add that, in development companies which are publicly owned, managers have no right but to maximize company profits. If that is accepted, then strict limits for the independent seem to follow: it can be asserted that the developer, aiming to minimize his equity investment, facing the demands of mortgage lenders for a high proportion of triple-A tenants, and needing flagship retailers, has no economically viable alternative but to accept only a few independent merchants, to constrain them through disadvantageous lease covenants, and to charge them high rents (Foster 1967, pp. 25-37).

When developers argue that they are caught in this ineluctable arithmetic, they often claim that the real enemies of the independent are the lenders. "Why haven't the lending institutions ... come around to figuring what the independent merchant is really worth to the developer from the standpoint of credits on mortgages? ... While shopping center developers ... are becoming much more sophisticated with experience, the lending institutions are archaic" (The Independent Retailer and the Shopping Center 1968, p. 45).

Developers also implicate urban planners. Municipal regulations, it is claimed, place ceilings on the number of stores permitted in individual shopping centers and put limits on the proximity of one center to another. This fosters larger stores in larger centers. If centers were located nearer one another, it is argued, developers would have more need to differentiate their centers using their major instrument of differentiation - the independent retailer.

Developers also argue that, rather than disadvantaging the

140

independent merchant, they encourage him to expand by opening
new stores in other shopping centers. When this happens, the
independent store becomes a local chain, and thus the share of
the market held by independents is reduced. Those who have examined this issue suggest that it would not significantly alter
the share of market held by independents in shopping centers
(Snyder 1976, pp. 14-16).

The factors considered so far have been economic. To
these economic considerations some non-economic ones could be
added. Those who would go beyond an economic calculus might
claim that small-scale retailing is not only a way of doing
business but a way of life - one that promotes industry, responsibility, innovativeness, enterprise, and self-reliance -
these being not only economic assets but civic virtues (Wismer
1977). They might state that this point of view is one that has
shaped public policy in agriculture, and that it should in distribution.

Those who would focus on economic considerations could argue that valuable societal qualities are fostered to no less degree in corporate organizations, and might add that such claims
and counter claims defy resolution because of insoluble problems of definition and measurement.

Those who would minimize the case for intervention on behalf of the independent could add that it is a self-imposed
non-economic consideration that keeps some entrepreneurs out of
shopping centers. To a merchant who gives high value to business independence, operating in a shopping center can be an un-
attractive undertaking. The labour he can use in finishing his
store interior, his insurance coverage, the date he can open,
his opening hours, his store signs, his advertising, his mem-
bership in a merchant's association, the kinds of cash registers
he can use, the records he must keep for purposes of calculat-
ing his rent, and his powers to sublet - all of these may be
subject to covenants in the shopping center lease (Carr 1965).
It follows that some independent merchants are outside shopping
centers, not because of the developer's discrimination, but because of the merchants' decision. Developers consulted in this
study argued that this is in fact the main reason for the reduced number of independent stores in shopping centers.

TOWARD A MORE INFORMED DEBATE

It seems clear that, in a debate on what actions to take
on behalf of the independent merchant in Canada, several positions could be taken. On one hand, a case could be made for
nonintervention on the grounds that the shift away from

independent outlets is an unarguable rendering of the public will as expressed through a workably competitive market mechanism. On the other hand, a case could be made for intervention on the grounds that the decline of the independent merchant is the unacceptable outcome of unfair competition sited in shopping centers, and that social costs are also involved. However, if the examination is to move beyond the arguments noted in this paper, then much research remains. Two areas of ignorance deserve mention.

The first concerns the value of the independent merchant to the Canadian economy and society. Those who are inclined toward intervention can cite an abundance of writings which state that the independent makes an immense contribution. What they cannot bring to bear is reasonable evidence that the statements are true. The literature on the subject suffers from several defects: it tends to deal with small manufacturers rather than small retailers, it is European and American rather than Canadian, and it relies on empty abstractions rather than relevant evidence. Thus, those who would fight for special assistance to the independent merchant in Canada have armed themselves with remarkably little empirical ammunition.[7]

Another subject deserving research is the survival needs of independents in shopping centers. Those who would oppose intervention on behalf of the small man need to show that shopping centers are no more inhospitable to independents than they need to be. Developers and major retailers insist that this is so, stating that they very much want independents as tenants. Indeed, the suggestion that they might be, however unintentionally, the instruments whereby independents are disadvantaged was met with apparent shock and dismay. Nevertheless, it must be observed that neither the trade literature on shopping centers, or discussions with leaders in the field reveal thoughtful attention to the problem of encouraging a healthy mix of outlets. Thus, those in the shopping center business do leave themselves open to claim that they have not understood the motives and needs of the traditional independent merchant and have not recognized the impact of their shopping center regulations in discouraging the independent tenant. To bolster their position, the International Council of Shopping Centers, the Retail Council of Canada, and the Canadian Federation of Independent Business might promote investigation of how to minimize those factors which make the shopping center inhospitable to the independent store.

---

7 For a general discussion on the value of small business in Canada, see Peterson (1977). For a brief discussion concerning the lack of scholarly attention focussed on small business, see McGuire (1976).

CONCLUSION

Is there now a sufficient case for intervention on behalf of independents in shopping centers? The authors think not. However, the question does deserve further research, reflection, and debate. During the past quarter century there has been a significant change in the place of the independent merchant in Canada and in the character of Canadian retailing. That change has gone largely unremarked. Now it warrants further examination to determine whether Canadians are, in fact, getting the retailing system they want.

APPENDIX I

OPTIMISTIC ESTIMATE OF
SALES OF INDEPENDENT STORES IN SHOPPING CENTERS

CANADA 1980

Optimistic projections of currently available data to 1980 would be as follows:

Annual increases in rates of sales of small shopping centers: 25%; of medium shopping centers; 20%; of large shopping centers: 10%.

Independent stores' share of retail sales in small shopping centers: 25%; in medium shopping centers: 17%; in large shopping centers: 12%.

Independent stores' share of retail sales outside of shopping centers: 68%.

Under these assumptions, the independent stores' share of total retail trade would be 55%.

APPENDIX II

MOST LIKELY ESTIMATE OF
SALES OF INDEPENDENT STORES IN SHOPPING CENTERS

CANADA 1980

Most likely projections of currently available data to 1980 would be as follows:

Annual increases in rates of sales of small shopping centers: 17%; of medium shopping centers: 14%; of large shopping centers: 28%.

Independent stores; share of retail sales in small shopping centers: 18%; in medium shopping centers: 14%; in large shopping centers: 10%.

Independent stores' share of retail sales outside of shopping centers: 60%.

Under these assumptions, the independent stores' share of total retail trade would be 52%.

REFERENCES

American Druggist (1972), "FTC Is Probing Shopping Center 'Exclusives'; Class Action Filed," (April 17), 30.

Baxter, Richard C. (1975), "Pause in Growth Offers Opportunity for Industry to Hone Its Operations," Real Estate Forum, 9.

Brown, Lawrence E. (1976), "Specialty Shopping Centers: A New Trend in Retailing," The Appraisal Journal (April), 226-235.

Business Week (1975), "Antitrust Action in Shopping Malls," (December 8), 51.

Cady, John F. (1976), "Structural Trends in Retailing: The Decline of the Small Business," Journal of Contemporary Business, (Spring), 67-89.

Carr, Donald (1965), "Shopping Center Leases," a special lecture to the Law Society of Upper Canada, in The Lease in Modern Business, Toronto: Richard De Boo, 245.

Chain Store Age (1973), "Developers Vote Top Tenants in Tight Market," (September), E35.

_____ (1975), "Shopping Centers: What's Ahead?," (May), 23-24.

_____, Executive Edition (1971), "FTC Restraint of Trade Probe May Hit Many More Centers Before Ending," (December 1), E6.

Community Planning Review (1975), "Malls -- Who Really Pays," (August), 1.

Dollars and Cents of Shopping Centers Part II (1972), Washington: Urban Land Institute, 19.

Farber, Leonard J. (1963), "Some Disturbing Trends in Shopping
  Center Development," in Profitable Shopping Center Development and Management, proceedings of the 1962 convention of
  the International Council of Shopping Centers, New York:
  ICSC, 9-16.

Foster, John R. (1967), "The Effect of Shopping Center Financing on the Opportunity for Occupancy by Independent Retailers," Southern Journal of Business, (April), 25-37.

Globe and Mail (1977), "Mixed Use Development Bans Chain Stores," (March 18), B3.

Gorman, Aubrey (1968), "What Does the Landlord Like About Independent Retailers? Everything!" in Proceedings of the Independent Retailers' Shopping Center Conference, New York: Retail Merchants Association, 29-34.

Harris, Earl (1968), "What the Operator of Small Stores Wants
  from Shopping Center Owners," in Proceedings of the Independent Retailers' Shopping Center Conference, New York: Retail Merchants Association, 4-11.

Marketing (1978), "Warning to Big Stores and Malls: Please
  Fickle Public or Go Broke," (May 8), 12.

McGuire, J.W. (1976), "The Small Enterprise in Economics and
  Organization Theory," Journal of Contemporary Business, (Spring), 115-138.

McNair, Malcolm P. and Eleanor G. May (1976), The Evolution of
  Retailing Institutions in the United States, Boston: Marketing Science Institute.

Monday Report on Retailers (1979), "ICSC Idea Exchange, Toronto,"
  (April 9), 6.

Moyer, Mel S. (1973), "Shopping Centers in Canada: Their Impact, Anatomy and Evolution," The Business Quarterly, (Summer),
  23-31.

_____, and Gerry Snyder (1967), Trends in Canadian Mar-
  keting, Ottawa: Queen's Printer.

Peterson, Rein (1977), Small Business: Building a Balanced Economy, Erin, Ontario: Procepic Press.

Rubloff, Arthur (1962), "Shopping Center Development and Operation," The Appraisal Journal, (January), 83-84.

Snyder, Gerry (1976), Shopping Centers in Canada, 1951-1973,
Ottawa: Queen's Printer.

The Independent Retailer and the Shopping Center (1968), Proceedings of the Independent Retailers' Shopping Center Conference, New York: Retail Merchants Association.

Weiss, E.B. (1963), "Retailing by Treaty," Advertising Age,
(March 11), 94.

Wismer, Cathy (1977), "A Nation of Shopkeepers," Canadian Business, (December) 75-79.

PUBLIC POLICY ASPECTS OF ELECTRONIC FUNDS TRANSFER IN QUEBEC[1]

Roger C. Bennett, McGill University
Roger J. Calantone, McGill University

ABSTRACT

Canadian government policy has worked against the setting up of consumer oriented electronic funds transfer systems in Canada. In 1975, the federal government proposed a single system for all Canada organized by the Bank of Canada. This met with immediate opposition from Québec, which has a large and influential network of credit unions - les Caisses Populaires Desjardins - that do not want to keep reserves with the Bank of Canada.

This paper describes this political background and a study, funded by the government of Québec, which attempted to study the likely reaction of Québec consumers to EFTS.

The study was in two parts. The first was a series of focus group interviews which produced a number of hypotheses that were tested in the second stage. This consisted of a modified form of thematic aperception testing conducted among 776 area respondents.

The main conclusions were that Québec consumers are unlikely to give a favorable initial response to EFTS. They are concerned about the possibilities of fraud, personal assault and overspending. They believe that the consumer should be provided with legislative protection. But they are not particularly concerned about loss of privacy, an issue that has been frequently mentioned by American consumerists. Anglophones, who, because they are more likely to have seen border television EFTS commercials, are, perhaps, better informed than francophones, are more likely to be opposed to the idea.

As a general conclusion it is clear that banks will have to proceed very cautiously. A strong marketing effort and

---

1 This research was funded by le Ministère des Communications, Gouvernement du Québec.

clear consumer protection mechanisms will be vital for the success of EFTS in Québec.

Les politiques du gouvernement canadien n'ont pas favorisé l'établissement au Canada des systèmes de transfert de fonds orientés vers les consommateurs. En 1975, le gouvernement fédéral a proposé qu'un seul système soit établi au pays et qu'il soit organisé par la Banque du Canada. Le Québec s'est immédiatement opposé à cette proposition, en raison de l'important et influent réseau des Caisses Populaires Desjardins qui n'ont pas et ne veulent pas déposez de reserves auprès de la Banque du Canada.

Cet article dresse cette toile de fond politique et rapporte les résultats d'une étude financée par le Gouvernement du Québec qui avait pour but de rechercher la réaction probable du consommateur québecois au système de télépaiement. L'étude comprend deux parties. La première consiste en une série d'entrevues de groupe qui ont donné lieu à une série d'hypothèses testées dans la deuxième phase. Celle-ci consistait en l'administration d'une version modifée du test TAT à 776 personnes.

Les conclusions pricipales de l'étude sont que les consommateurs québecois ne sont pas de prime abord favorablement disposés envers le système de télé-paiement. Ils sont concernés par les dangers de fraude, d'aggression, et de dépenses excessives. Ils pensent que le consommateur devrait être protégé par un législation adéquate. Par contre, ils ne voient point de risquer d'intrusion dans leur vie privée, crainte qui a été souvent mentionée par les mouvements de consommateurs américains.

Les anglophones, qui sont davantage susceptibles d'avoir été exposés aux annonces publicitaires sur les systèmes de télépaiement des chaines de télévision périphiques américaines, sont peut-être mieux informés que les francophones et sont généralement davantage opposés à l'idée.

En conclusion générale, il semble que les banques doivent procéder très prudemment en ce domaine. Un effort de marketing important et des mécanismes évidents de protection des consommateurs semblent être la clé du succès de l'introduction du système de télépaiement au Québec.

INTRODUCTION

Users of bank services in Québec were questioned about their reactions to the possible introduction of various forms of EFTS. A modified form of thematic aperception testing was used in order to obtain responses from consumers about services about which they knew little or nothing. Differences between the known reactions of American consumers, the likely reactions of Québec bank users and between anglophone and francophone were discovered.

This introduction is followed by a brief study of Canadian policy on EFTS and shows why this has led to federal-provincial disagreements. It places the study in its context, gives a brief description of the research and presents the major con-clusions.

EFTS and Canadian Policy

Two major Canadian policy initiatives have affected the development of consumer-oriented EFTS in this country. In addition, events associated with its arrival in the United States have led to a far slower approach being taken here. The area is complex, but what in 1976 might have been viewed as healthy caution, in 1979 might be seen as a lack of important progress.

Before proceeding further it is necessary to define EFTS and some of the acronyms associated with it. Electronics funds transfer systems are of many sorts. Here, we are concerned with consumer-oriented EFTS, consisting of those systems with which the consumer interacts. The major types are shown in Exhibit 1. A variety of systems are in use in various parts of the U.S. and many of them have been part of standard banking practice in the U.K. for ten years. In Canada, the Bank of Montreal has installed a limited number of ATM's but other banks and financial institutions have been slow to adopt con-sumer-oriented EFTS.

The first major policy statement by a Canadian body was the 1972 report of the Privacy and Computers Task Force that dealt with electronic banking. The maintenance of confiden-tiality was viewed as important.
> "An individual has an interest beyond that original
> access of another person to any particular fact
> about him, in whether and how, it is further dis-
> seminated to third and fourth parties and the public
> at large." (Gillman 1972, p. 14)
But having reached this conclusion the author of the report prefers to concentrate on problems of ensuring accuracy of data rather than on their confidentiality. The remainder of the re-port presents a cogent argument for the necessity of electronic banking citing the colossal growth in the number of cheques

being cleared, the likelihood of the banking system grinding to a halt and presenting the interesting argument that credit cards have tended to increase cheque usage. The final comment concerning privacy almost seems to argue that there is nothing to fear from potential abuses of privacy:

"The banks in Canada have established good reputations for preserving confidentiality and protecting privacy." (Gellman 1972, p. 51)

Thus Canadian government authorities, unlike their U.S. counterparts,[2] have shown little concern about record keeping problems and the effects that errors might cause. This is in contrast to the position in the United States, where privacy is one of the six major areas of concern voiced by consumerists. One of the areas to be researched, therefore, was whether Québec consumers would mention privacy as a problem associated with the introduction of EFTS.

The second government document that influenced the research was a report by Information Canada, "Towards an Electronic Payments System," which defined the federal government's policy with respect to EFTS. In a remarkably brief paper it was announced that the government favored a single nationwide EFT communications system to which all financial institutions would have access. The aim was to create "a common user communications network" which would include the following characteristics:

-It would be a nationwide system
-It would be publicly accessible
-It would be a shared facility with the only cost being user fees
-It would be a secure system
-It would allow access from a wide variety of computer and terminal equipment

The paper did not provide much insight into the reasoning behind such a policy, a policy, indeed, that was totally different from those that other western countries were pursuing. But some observers, such as the Economic Council of Canada, suggested that the main motivation behind the proposal was the desire to prevent EFT systems being dominated by or even being operated from the U.S. (Economic Council of Canada 1976). The new single system would, presumably, be Canadian-operated and Canadian-owned.

---

2 For a discussion of privacy in banking transactions in the U.S. see The Economist pp. 48-49, May 19, 1979.

3 For a discussion of these concerns see Bennett and Strang 1978.

EXHIBIT 1

Glossary of Frequently Used EFTS Terms and Acronyms

ACH	Automated Clearing House. Allows the automatic transfer of funds among account holders of member banks.
ATM	Automated Teller Machine. These can be found away from financial institutions but are presently most often found inside or outside banks. They permit deposits, withdrawals, and transfers between accounts.
CBCT	Customer Bank Communication Terminal. Full ATM at a distance from a clearing bank.
Pay-by-Phone	Customers may make direct transfers to the accounts of merchants, utilities, and others who have joined the scheme. In some cases, customers with push-button phones may gain direct access to the computer without going through an operator.
POS	Point-of-sale Terminal. A machine most often found in supermarkets that performs a variety of services. In the most simple cases it verifies checks. More complex machines provide full banking services, as well as direct transfers between customers' accounts and those of retail stores.
RSU	Remote Service Unit. This is the equivalent of a CBCT when operated by a thrift insitution.
Switch	The switching center operated by a bank or group of banks that receives instructions from remote terminals. In ten states the sharing of the facilities provided by a switch is mandatory.

Whatever the reasoning behind such a policy it has had one deadening effect. There have been few advances in the implementation of any electronic funds transfer system in Canada since the paper's publication.

Québec's Position

The two documents outlined above appear, on the surface, to have little to do with federal-provincial relations. In 1975 the Bourassa government was nationalist and would surely have been in favour of safeguards for consumers and would prefer a Canadian to an American owned network. But the reaction of the provincial government to the policy statement was speedy. In a lengthy correspondence between Bourassa and Trudeau[4] it became clear that Québec would have great

---

4 Not quoted here but read by the researchers.

difficulties in accepting the newly announced "one system" policy.

There were two reasons for this conflict. Québec has a unique banking (or, more correctly, near bank) system and any single nationwide system would require a clearing agent, a body with whom all members would maintain accounts and through whom all debits and credits would be balanced. Naturally it was thought that the Bank of Canada would assume such a role. And these two factors made a single system unacceptable to Québec.

Québec has a unique network of credit unions. The "caisses," short for the independent members of a group of credit unions known as Les Caisses Populaires Desjardins, are a powerful financial and popular force. Four million Quebecers have accounts at a caisse. Total deposits exceed $7 billion. The provincial government guarantees these deposits, and, in rural Quebec, the caisses are an integral part of the community, run by local people for the benefit of the town or village.

One of the distinctive features of this network has been its consistent refusal to retain reserves with the Bank of Canada. Indeed, the system retains practically no non-cash reserves at all. A small sum was (in 1975) kept with the Banque Provinciale for cheque clearing services and the caisses paid 1.5¢ a cheque for each transaction. Otherwise, assets were invested in the communities. The problem for the caisses was that a proposed single system would require them to keep reserves for clearing purposes with the Bank of Canada.[5] This they would not do and the provincial government strongly supported them.

Due to the existence of the caises and the need for a federal clearning agent, the Québec government had a particular

[5]This problem, which seemed to be insoluble under the provincial liberal government, has recently been neatly circumvented. Under an agreement between the Bank of Canada and The Caisses each keeps notional but non-existant off-setting balances with each other. The Bank of Canada's balance with the Caisses is maintained to allow the instant cashing of federal cheques at a Caisse (as happens at a chartered bank). The offsetting balances of the caisses are used for clearing purposes. Thus, cheques drawn on a caisse are now cleared directly by the Bank of Canada without the use of an intervening agent. It can be assemed that this removes technical difficulties in setting up a single system. There now remains the nationalistic problem for Quebec of who should control the system? This problem has, to date, remained dormant.

interest in EFTS. However, there were other reasons for continued research in this field. In any part of Canada the likely reactions of consumers to EFTS are important concerns and are of vital interest to governments. Experience in the U.S. suggests that consumers tend not to use expensive systems to the degree expected and consumerists will even attack such systems for various reasons. In 1969 it was generally agreed that the cashless, chequeless society would have arrived in the U.S. by 1980. In 1979 it is clear that the cheque is being used more frequently than ever before and people still carry dollars around with them. Although the technical ability for many types of EFTS has been available for years, for many reasons, the consumer has rejected them (Bennett, Strang 1978).

In many ways, however, the Quebec consumer differs from his U.S. counterpart and this study attempts to study whether the same or even different concerns will pose similar problems for banks and regulatory agencies in this province. It does not, however, make recommendations about possible actions the government might take. It provides some data upon which policy decision might be based.

It must be stated here that research among consumers about a product they do not know and have never seen presents problems. When that product is a service the difficulties are multiplied. While these results present good indications as to likely reactions to certain forms of EFTS nobody could guarantee that, in years to come, the picture might not be very different.

Methodology

The research took part in three stages. The first stage consisted of a visit to a U.S. mutual savings bank (The Dollar Savings Bank of Pittsburgh). This bank had introduced a pay-by-phone system that was the largest in the United States. More important, however, was the fact that there had been no objections from consumerists at any stage. The scheme was accepted by the public without any adverse comments. This visit suggested how some of the typical fears of consumers could be assuaged. It also produced some indication of the type of marketing effort necessary for success in this field.

The second stage involved a series of five focus group interviews with people with bank accounts. Two of the groups consisted of anglophones, three of francophones. Between five and eight people were invited to talk together about banks and their opinions of them. They were then asked to comment about various proposed EFTS schemes.

Each group discussion lasted about one and a half hours. In order to ensure comparability there were:

-one group of francophone middle age males
-one group of anglophone middle age males
-one group of francophone middle age females
-one group of anglophone middle age females
-one group of francophone young males

The purpose of this stage was to check that each element of consumers' likely reaction had been considered. It was hoped that hypotheses they had not considered might arise that could be checked.

The third stage of the project consisted of interviews with 776 respondents chosen at random in the Greater Montreal area.[6] The interviews were conducted by students who were completing a market research course. They were trained and instructed by one of the researchers, who also checked randomly that they interviewed where they were directed and in a satisfactory manner.

The questionnaire consisted of five parts. The first three questions were a modified form of thematic aperception tests (TAT). Respondents were shown pictures and statements and asked to comment on them. This method was chosen to avoid the difficulties involved in asking questions about services, of which most respondents were unaware. The nature of the comments made suggest that useful results were obtained. But it should be noted that these opinions were based upon individuals' own immediate impressions. No opportunities for opinion leaders to mold public attitudes could be provided. Despite this fact, clear results to some questions did emerge.

The fourth series of questions, based on the researchers' preliminary hypotheses and on results obtained from the focus group interviews attempted to gain more specific attitudes about consumers' attitudes to banks and proposed EFT services. A six point scale was used and respondents were asked to agree or disagree with ten statements. It was hoped to obtain clear indications of problem areas from this series of questions.

The fifth series of questions consisted of general demographic data and questions about banking habits. It should be noted that this research concentrated on likely consumer reactions. It was conducted within the background of the political situation which is described above and which motivated

---

6 The sampling procedure is explained in the text.

154

the project. But it was in no way designed to solve those political problems. Nor, once it had started, was the research influenced by any political consideration.

Hypotheses

Before starting the project we had developed certain hypotheses. These were based on experience in the U.S., previous research on general matters among Quebec consumers and factors unique to the Quebec environment. The first hypothesis was general:

> Consumers will be generally antagonistic to EFT
> systems. They will not trust them and will say
> they will not use them.

This hypothesis was based on the U.S. situation where, as stated above, there has been significant opposition to many forms of EFTS.

The second hypothesis arose from the same background and was reinforced in the focus group interviews:

> Consumers will expect governments to provide
> legislative protection from arbitrary bank
> decisions with respect to EFTS.

In the U.S. there are approximately 30,000 commercial banks and saving institutions. In Canada there is a far smaller number and the commercial banks tend to compete only on a marginal basis. This led to the third hypothesis:

> There will be a large amount of general
> dissatisfaction with commercial banks. The
> Caisses Populaires Desjardins will be better
> regarded.

The final major hypothesis considered arose from the fact that previous research suggested that francophones and anglophones often have different attitudes to products and services. In this case the reasons for any differences were believed to be obvious. In 1976 and 1977 American banks in Maine and Vermont had been advertising pay-by-phone services extensively on U.S. television channels that are viewed in Montreal. For this reason it was believed that anglophone respondents might be more receptive to EFTS than francophones:

> Anglophones will be more positive to EFTS than
> francophones and will have significantly different
> attitudes to proposed services.

These hypotheses and others that arose during the preliminary
stages were tested in the survey and the analysis concentrated
on time.

THE RESEARCH

The Pittsburgh Experience

Most of the efforts to introduce EFTS in the United States
have been unsuccessful. They have been far more costly and
far less utilized than had been forecast before implementation
One important exception to this trend has been the pay-by-
phone system introduced by the Dollar Savings Bank of Pittsburgh. A description of this system would be too long for this
paper but is available in English or French from the authors.

There are four major features that distinguished the Dollar Savings Bank scheme:

- A careful planning process
- Clear safeguards against fraud
- A four pronged marketing effort
- A strong advertising campaign.

The planning process was thorough. First there was a
clear need established for the system. Second, there was a
careful examination of pay-by-phone systems that had already
been implemented. Third, there was intensive research among
potential participating businesses and consumers.

The safeguard against fraud has been so successful that
no funds have been lost in four years of operation.

The system was aggressively marketed to four groups:

- bank employees
- potential customers
- bank customers in the branches
- potential business customers.

The bank's recognition that it had to market the idea to its
own employees was of particular interest. There has been evidence that some EFT systems have been badly affected by an
unconvinced bank staff.

The advertising of the system was intense. At the beginning it concentrated on attracting prospective customers into
the branches. Later it dealt with the number of businesses
whose bills it was possible to pay by phone.

The reason for this stage of the study was to demonstrate that a carefully planned system, with safeguards against fraud, well marketed and aggressively advertised can be successful and attract new customers and funds.

THE FOCUS GROUP INTERVIEWS

The five groups met at McGill and discussed the questions relating to banks and EFTS. All groups came from the Montreal area with the exception of one francophone male group which was recruited from the suburbs.

Banks

Most group members were dissatisfied with certain aspects of their bank or caisse. All groups mentioned waiting times as a major problem. While two of the francophone groups expressed annoyance at the 'one line' policy, both the anglophone groups expressed approval of it. Other complaints mentioned by at least two groups were the high turnover of tellers (FF, Fm, AF, Am)[7] leading to inefficient service, computer problems (FF, AM), difficulties in banking at other branch of your bank (FMS, AM) and language problems (FF who objected to customers who cannot speak either French or English and AF who objected to French speaking managers who, it is said, have been impolite to anglophone customers).

EFTS

The next question dealt with automated teller machines (ATM's). The anglophone groups were familiar with them while most francophone group members were not. However, reactions to them were similar. For example, both francophone males and anglophone females were concerned about the possibility of having deposits incorrectly credited. Three groups (FMS, AM, AF) mentioned personal safety as a problem.

The pay-by-phone system itself was then discussed. As expected, most of the anglophone group members had seen television ads for such a system but only one francophone (female) had heard of it. There was a good degree of opposition to the system, although many respondents tended to preface their remarks with such statements as:

"I like the idea but..."

---

[7] FF refers to the francophone female group, FM to francophone male, FMS to francophone male suburban, AM to anglophone male, AF to anglophone female.

Problems typically mentioned were:

- the costs of setting a system up or the charge per transaction (FMS, AM, AF);

- the problems of mistakes. "How can we argue with a computer?" (FF, AM, AF);

- the problems of fraud (AF);

- encouraging overspending (FM);

- no need as credit cards could be used (FMS);

- fear of having it imposed (FM).

When specifically asked what problems they foresaw most groups repeated the ideas mentioned above. All groups expressed concern about the role of the computer. In some cases, however, opposite concerns were expressed. For example, the francophone male suburban and the francophone female groups thought a pay-by-phone system would lead to difficulties in record keeping while the anglophone males thought it would force accurate record keeping.

Other interesting observations about the system that arose were:

- people like money in their pockets (FM);

- people like to pay by cheque (AM, AF);

- a lot of education will be necessary (FM, AM);

- the system will encourage kidnapping and extortion (FM);

- "it's part of the dehumanizing process. We'll have one number from birth and it will be stamped on our coffin." (AM)

The next group of questions involved specific matters of concern that have been voiced publicly by consumerists with respect to EFTS. The first was the loss of float[8]. The francophone male suburban group had previously suggested that

---

8 Float can be obtained by writing a cheque against an account that does not have enough funds in it. The account is credited before the cheque arrives at the bank. The use of credit cards is a common method of obtaining lengthy personal float.

- Consumers do not worry about loss of privacy.

- Consumers are not clear what, if any, protective legislation is necessary.

THE QUESTIONNAIRE

The questionnaire was designed in light of the hypotheses mentioned in the introduction. The first three questions consisted of photographs and/or statements about which respondents were asked to give opinions. This method was chosen as being the only way to obtain large scale response about services that either did not exist at present or were not widely known.

The fourth section consisted of a series of ten questions concerning banks and EFTS. Respondents had to rate, on a six point scale, the degree to which they agreed or disagreed with each statement. Finally, nine demographic questions were asked.

The questionnaires were administered in either French or English, according to the preferred language of the respondent, randomly over the geographic area of Montreal, including the South Shore (e.g., Longueuil, Laval, Boucherville, etc.). The method chosen was randomized geographic block with systematic vertical and horizontal choice according to the spatial density of the population in that block. Areas were spot checked to insure the non-introduction of bias or other systematic drawing errors. Uniform representation of language groups resulted in both completed interviews and usable questionnaires.

After the questionnaires had been returned, answers to the open ended questions were grouped and coded. The replies to all questions were broken down by whether the responses came from francophones or anglophones.[9] Owing to problems of vocabulary, differences between anglophone and francophone difference of opinions in the first three questions should not be regarded with more than passing interest. Differences in the other questions were tested for statistical significance.

Results

The results were summarized in the tables appearing in the Appendix. Just under two thirds of respondents suggested

---

9 Four percent of respondents categorized themselves as "other". These were included in the anglophone category for the analysis.

159

the use of float was unfair in some ways to people who did not use it. The other groups claimed it would make no difference to them.

Another major problem often mentioned is that of maintaining privacy. In every group, respondents said that there is so much information available now that a little more would not make any difference. There was no evidence that loss of privacy was a matter of concern to any group member.

When asked about what protective legislation might be necessary, few concrete proposals were forthcoming. The anglophone males said there should be somebody in banks to whom one can complain. The francophone females were very anxious about legislation to protect their money if Quebec separates. The francophone male suburban group believed there are too many laws already and that new ones are useless.

Conclusions

Certain hypotheses arose from the group discussions that had not necessarily been expected. Others confirmed earlier ideas. These will be put in the form of statements but it should be noted that there was little evidence to support them at this stage:

- Banks are easily and frequently criticized by customers on a wide range of subjects.

- The main problem with banks and caisses is the waiting period to make a transaction.

- Anglophones are more familiar with ATM's than francophones. Both groups show concern about dealings with them.

- Consumers' ideas about improving bank service are limited to adjustments to present services rather than radical new ideas.

- Pay-by-phone systems will be met with a certain degree of opposition. Individuals are afraid of the possibilities of fraud, mistakes, encouraging overspending and having the system imposed on them.

- Consumers recognize the need for education about bank services.

- Consumers are not afraid of losing the use of float.

that the user of the pay-by-phone system shown in the first
question was either happy or satisfied. Other positive comments were limited but there were very few negative remarks.
At first sight, then, it can be suggested that consumers <u>do</u>
<u>not object</u> to pay-by-phone systems. However, the respondents
were not actually involved with the system at this stage.
While they may have perceived that the woman in the picture
was satisfied, they might not enjoy the experience themselves.

The second question revealed the group of respondents
who were opposed to the concept. Over one third of the sample
stated they were against or not interested in a pay-by-phone
system. Those who suggested possible problems, mentioned the
areas that the focus groups had identified:

- Computers
- Fraud
- Loss of control.

At this stage, however, a new objection was mentioned by over
one tenth of those questioned. They said they preferred
"personal contact" when banking.

Those who were in favour of the scheme suggested four
main advantages:

- Convenience
- Good for those who have problems leaving home
- Saves time
- Cheap.

Francophones were significantly more likely to mention the
help such a system would be for people who cannot get out.

Respondents were then questioned as to why consumers do
not use ATM's. A wide variety of suggestions were made, many
of them repeating earlier stated objections. Responses given
by at least one tenth of the sample were:

- Fear of fraud
- Fear of mugging
- Not needed
- Fear of overspending

Despite the fact that the groups mentioned the liklihood of
errors as being an important factor, only a small proportion
(5%) of respondents mentioned concern in this area as a reason
for ATM's lack of use.

The most important reason for their failure, mentioned by

one third of all those questioned, was consumers' lack of
familiarity with the machines. It is interesting, in view
of the preliminary hypotheses, that francophones were much
more likely than anglophones to suggest lack of familiarity
or the need for advertising.

The fourth group of questions produced interesting
results. Respondents tended to disagree (2.482 out of 6) with
the statement "I find that most bankers are not pleasant."
On the other hand, they were more likely to agree (3.18 out of
6) with the idea that ATM's are a sign that banks are cold and
efficient.

There was a marked tendency, particularly among francophones, for people to agree (4.782) that their bank or caisse
is important to them. Francophones also tended to be more
likely to agree that "the caisse is more personal than a bank."
On the other hand, anglophones were much more likely (4.537
compared to 3.961 for francophones) to agree that Saturday
banking hours would be helpful.

Both groups agreed very strongly that "there should be
tough laws to protect individuals who use telepayment." The
score of 5.038 was the result skewed most clearly in either of
the directions "definitely agree" or "definitely disagree."
This conclusion also slightly contradicts some of the views
expressed in the focus group discussions where one group said
there are already too many laws.

A little surprisingly, perhaps, was the marginal tendency
to agree (3.580) that "telepayment is the most convenient way
to bank" but there was also a slight belief in fallibility of
ATM's with a score of 3.560 on the statement "automatic teller
machines won't work when you need them."

Francophone respondents tended to trust telepayment to
a significantly greater extent than anglophones, scoring 2.640
compared with 3.292 on the statement "telepayment could
result in the bank losing some of my money accidently."

In the final section the most important information
came from the statement "I would apply for a telepayment
account if they were available at my bank." One third of
respondents definitely would not. But while a third of
francophones said they would apply for such accounts only
one quarter of the anglophones would do the same. The remainder wanted more information.

Conclusions

Certain major conclusions arise from these results obtained from the survey. It should again be noted that these opinions came from people with little knowledge about EFTS. Views might change markedly after prolonged exposure to systems.

- Initial response to EFTS is likely to be poor. Under one third of respondents expressed positive interest.

- Typical concerns with EFTS are fear of fraud, fear of mugging, fear of over-spending and the belief that such systems are not needed.

- There is some criticism of banks. EFTS might accentuate that criticism.

- Anglophones, who might be better informed about EFTS, are more doubtful about telepayment schemes. They want more information. An important preliminary hypothesis, that those who know more about the services will have different attitudes, has been confirmed. But it has been confirmed in an unexpected way. Those who know more about EFTS are likely to have greater doubts.

- There is massive support for legislation to protect the consumer.

- There is no evidence that the Quebec consumer is concerned about privacy.

Implications of the Study

Certain implications arise from the three parts of the study. It has been found that there is a favourable response to carefully planned and designed EFT systems which incorporate safeguards and which are well marketed. But, on the other hand, consumers find it extremely easy to criticize banks and they will have to proceed slowly, probably obtaining a very poor initial response.

Consumers believe that they require legislative protection in this area. But, despite massive support for this concept, there are few clear proposals as to what exactly is required. It is an interesting situation. Further research might produce more concrete proposals but the chances are not good that anything useful would arise. Blindly following American precedence would not necessarily help. The American is very concerned about confidentiality. It is clear that the Quebec consumer does not believe that privacy exists; nor is it worth fighting for. One might hazard a guess that the consumer is primarily concerned with the "facelessness" or impersonality of the banks. It is difficult to imagine that governments would legislate in such areas. On the other hand, perhaps this is an indication for firms and governments alike, that one of their next major problems is to handle the alienation of the individual to the large, anonymous corporate or political entity.

APPENDIX

TABLE 1

Positive Comments about Pay-by-Phone Picture

	All (776)	Francophone (445)	Anglophone (321)
Happy, etc.	48%	41%	57%
Likes it	8	9	5
Satisfied	14	20	5
Useful	9	9	10
O.K.	4	6	1
Efficient	1	1	1
Saves time	5	6	3
Can do it from home	9	11	7
Businesslike	1	2	0
Good idea	4	4	3
Interested	2	2	2
Other	6	5	7

TABLE 2

Negative Comments about Pay-by-Phone Picture

	All (776)	Francophone (445)	Anglophone (321)
Lonely	1%	1%	0%
Does not like it	1	1	1
Confused	2	0	4
Fraud	1	1	1
Other	5	6	4
Personal Comment	4	4	5

TABLE 3

Positive Comments about Pay-by-Phone Press Release

	All (776)	Francophone (445)	Anglophone (321)
Great	33%	37%	29%
O.K.	11	11	10
Convenient	26	26	25
Home related	16	19	11
Saves time	16	18	13
Cheap	13	11	15
Other	9	9	8
Perhaps	7	7	7

TABLE 4

Negative or Doubtful Statements about Pay-by-Phone Press Release

	All (776)	Francophone (445)	Anglophone (321)
More information	3%	2%	4%
Against/not interested	37	36	38
Record keeping problems	6	6	+
Computers go wrong	5	4	6
Fraud possibilities	6	6	6
Prefer personal contact	11	11	12
Have to go to the bank	3	3	2
Use cheques	5	5	5
Loss of control	2	2	3
Other negative	7	7	8

TABLE 5

Comments about why Consumers do not use ATM's

	All (776)	Francophone (445)	Anglophone (321)
Fear of fraud	11%	9%	13%
Fear of mugging	11	10	13
Errors	5	5	5
Not interested	1	2	0
Not needed	12	12	11
Spend too much	12	8	16
Breakdowns	5	5	4
Consumers not familiar with it (Not advertised)	34	39	27
New, habit	5	5	5
Use credit cards	4	4	5
I do use it	4	3	5
Don't know	6	6	6

TABLE 6

Opinions of Banks and Telepayments
(6 definitely agree, 1 definitely disagree)

	All (Mean response)	Francophone (Cell Size) (Mean response)	Anglophone (Cell Size) (Mean response)
Bankers are not pleasant	2.482	2.382 (447)	2.635 (288)
ATM's are a sign that banks are cold, efficient institutions	3.180	3.259 (436)	3.055 (275)
My bank of Caisse is very important to me*	4.782	4.943 (445)	4.521 (288)
The Caisse is more personal than a bank*	3.482	3.555 (411)	3.165 (199)
Saturday banking hours would be very helpful to me*	4.188	3.961 (439)	4.537 (285)
There should be tough laws to protect individuals who use telepayment	5.038	5.034 (435)	5.043 (279)
Telepayment is the most convenient way to bank	3.580	3.550 (429)	3.627 (276)
Like a lot of machines today, automatic teller machines won't work when you need them+	3.560	3.658 (386)	3.414 (261)
I am worried that telepayment could result in the bank losing some of my money accidentally*	2.894	2.640 (437)	3.292 (277)
Telepayments would be better for large depositors	3.660	3.735 (441)	3.540 (276)

* Differences between francophone and anglophone responses significant at the 99% confidence level.
+ Differences between francophone and anglophone responses significant at the 95% confidence level.

166

TABLE 7

Banking and General Factors

	All	Francophone	Anglophone
Person who _generally_ goes to the bank			
Man	30%	30%	31%
Woman	30	27	35
Both	40	44	34
Person who _generally_ writes the cheques etc.			
Man	36	35	38
Woman	36	34	39
Both	27	30	23
Person who decided on bank of caisse*			
Man	36	32	42
Woman	20	18	23
Both	44	50	35
Most of business done at*			
Caisse	27	39	8
Bank	65	49	89
Credit Union	1	1	1
Caisse and Bank	7	10	3
I would apply for a telepayment account if they were available at my bank*			
Yes	31	35	24
No	35	35	34
Need to know more	35	30	43

* Difference between francophone and anglophone responses significant at the 99% confidence level.

167

REFERENCES

Bennett, Roger C. and Roger A. Strang (1978), <u>Banks and the Cashless Society: Time for Reappraisal</u>, Business Horizons, Volume 21, Number 3, Bloomington, Indiana.

Economic Council of Canada (1976), <u>Efficiency and Regulation of Deposit Institutions</u>, Supply and Services Canada, Ottawa.

Gellman, H.S. (1972), <u>Electronic Banking Systems and their Effects on Privacy</u>. Part of series of the Privacy and Computers Task Force. Department of Communications, Department of Justice, Ottawa.

Government of Canada (1975), <u>Towards and Electronic Payments System</u>, Information Canada, Ottawa.

CONSUMER ISSUES:
APPLICATION OF THE CONCEPT OF MARKET MATURITY[1]

James G. Barnes, Memorial University of Newfoundland
Karen R. Kelloway, Memorial University of Newfoundland

ABSTRACT

This paper examines the possibility that consumer markets might be segmented on the basis of the relative need for consumer protection and education programs demonstrated by consumers who form identifiable market segments. The concept of 'market maturity' is introduced as an explanation for differences among various markets or market segments. This concept suggests that all markets are not alike in terms of the abilities of their members or in terms of the opportunities which they provide for consumers to learn about new or different products or consumption experiences. A mature market is one which is comprised of mature consumers who are likely to be exposed to a diversity of consumption experiences. The result is hypothesized to be that consumers in more mature markets are better prepared to anticipate problems in the marketplace and to avoid them and better able to deal with problems when they do arise.

Data collected from two Canadian provinces, which have been described as more mature and less mature markets, are examined and the conclusion is drawn that important differences do exist between consumers in these markets in terms of their concerns and problems; their attitudes toward business, government, and the consumer movement; the problems which they encounter and the manner in which they deal with these problems; and their awareness and use of consumer information and legislation.

---

[1]The authors wish to thank Professor Mel Moyer of York University and the Ministry of Consumer and Commercial Relations, Ontario, for permission to quote the results of the study entitled Ontario Consumer Issues, August 1978, and Professors Elizabeth C. Hirschman of New York University, Jacques C. Bourgeois of Carleton University and Donald W. Barclay of Memorial University of Newfoundland for their comments on a draft of this paper. The authors also acknowledge the contribution of The Consumers' Association of Canada, Newfoundland.

The conclusions drawn are that differences do exist across markets with regard to the ability of consumers to handle problems which they encounter in the marketplace. There appears to be a link between the level of market maturity present and the preparedness of consumers to cope with the marketplace. If such is the case, then a global approach to the development and implementation of consumer protection and education programs is clearly inappropriate.

Cet article examine la possibilité que les marchés de consommation peuvent être segmentés, en se basant sur le besoin relatif de protection du consommateur et sur les programmes éducatifs démontrés par des consommateurs qui forment les segments identifiables du marché. Le concept de "maturité du marché" est introduit comme explication des différences existant parmi les divers marchés ou segments de marché. Ce concept suggère que tous les marchés ne sont pas semblables en terme de la compétence de ses membres ou en terme des opportunités qu'ils fournissent aux consommateurs de connaître des produits nouveaux ou différents, ainsi que des expériences en consommation. Le résultat hypothétique est que les des marchés ayant une plus grande maturité sont mieux préparés à anticipier les problèmes que surviennent sur la place du marché et savent mieux les éviter. Ils sont aussi plus en mesure de venir à bout de ces problèmes.

Les données recueillies dans deux provinces canadiennes, lesquelles ont été décrites comme étant les marchés ayant le plus et le moins de maturité sont examinées et la conclusion qui en est tirée démontre que de sérieuses différences existent entre les consommateurs de ces marchés én terme de leurs soucis et problèmes, de leur attitude envers les affairs, le gouvernement et le mouvement des consommateurs; les problèmes à laquell ils se heurtent et leur manière de les résoudre; leur connaissance et usage de l'information et de la législation du consommateur.

Les conclusions tirées sont que des différences existent dans ces marchés, tenant compte de l'habileté des consommateurs à résoudre les problèmes rencontrés sur la place du marché. Il parait y avoir un rapport entre le degré de maturité du marché et l'état de préparation des consommateurs à pouvoir affronter la place du marché. Si tel est le cas, alors une approche globale sur le développement et la réalisation de programmes de protection et d'éducation du consommateur est nettement peu appropriée.

Branch, in the collection of data from the Province of Newfoundland.

INTRODUCTION

The concept of market segmentation has been widely accepted by practising marketers and leads to the development of appropriate strategies to capitalize on the differences across market segments. While market segmentation has demonstrated its usefulness as a management tool, it might also find increasingly appropriate applications in a macromarketing context where emphasis would be not on increasing sales, but on optimizing the social benefits which accrue to consumers as a result of marketing processes (Bartels and Jenkins 1977). It is the thesis of this paper that consumer markets might be segmented on the basis of the relative need for consumer protection and education demonstrated by the consumers who form each segment. The concept of market maturity is introduced as a basis for segmenting markets.

The first part of this paper will examine the concept of market maturity and will relate that concept to associated concepts of modernity and consumer creativity. Factors which are **hypothesized** to contribute to the level of maturity present in a market are discussed. Two markets are then examined with regard to these factors andthe conclusion drawn that one might be labelled more mature and the other less mature for the purposes of testing the hypothesis that differences exist between consumers in more mature and less mature markets in terms of their abilities to cope with the complexity of the modern marketplace.

The second part of the paper will test for an effect of the level of maturity present in a market on the general well being of consumers, their attitudes toward business, government and the consumer movement, their awareness of and use of sources of consumer information and assistance, and the manner in which they seek to resolve consumer problems.

Finally, conclusions are reached concerning differences which exist across markets at different levels of market maturity. The differences in terms of problems encountered and the ability of consumers to cope with such problems testify to the appropriateness of a differential approach to the development and implementation of consumer protection and education programs based on the relative degree of maturity present in different markets.

THE CONCEPT OF MARKET MATURITY

It is a basic thesis of this paper that markets may be described in terms of their level of maturity. **The term 'maturity'** relates to the ability of an individual to function within a particular environment. Thus, some individuals who lack certain skills to function as consumers and to cope with the modern marketplace may be termed less mature. Conversely, consumers who possess such skills may be considered more mature. Clearly, some individuals are more mature in their abilities to function as consumers than are others. Some are more receptive to innovation, more knowledgeable of product characteristics, better able to solve market-related problems, better able to obtain good value for their shopping dollar. What factors contribute to the level of consumer maturity which an individual possesses?

This concept of maturity as consumers is closely related to that of "consumer creativity." Hirschman (1979) has viewed creativity in consumers as "the problem-solving capacity which is possessed by the individual and enhanced by environmental inputs". Thus, creative consumers are those who are best able to solve consumer problems and are considered mature consumers in the context of this paper. A market may also be described in terms of its level of maturity as it relates to the maturity of its consumer members. Therefore, a mature consumer market is the collectivity of mature, less naive, better equipped consumers.

The degree of maturity present in a market may be expressed on a continuum as some societies are more mature than others in terms of the abilities of individuals to solve consumer problems. The concept of a continuum of market maturity is analagous to that of modernity. As societies or markets develop from traditional to modern, the individuals who reside therein become better equipped to solve problems: that is, more creative, more mature.

The maturing of a consumer is a process which is influenced by forces both internal to and external to the individual. The equipping of the individual with skills which better prepare him to cope with the problems of the marketplace is a function of certain characteristics of the individual and of elements of his environment. The ability of the individual to solve consumer problems, to exhibit consumer maturity or creativity, has been related to six sociocultural factors: (1) parental socioeconomic status; (2) early childhood stimulation; (3) formal educational attainment; (4) occupational stimulation; (5) social structure; and (6) consumption processes (Hirschman 1979). While the first four factors are clearly characteristics of the individual, the latter two are characteristics of his environment.

The mature consumer is more likely to be better equipped economically and educationally to cope with the modern marketplace. He will tend to be more receptive to new products and new shopping experiences and will possess the skills and resources to solve problems which are related to the purchase and consumption of products and services.

The environmental factors which are related to consumer maturity may be divided into two categories: those relating to the structure of the society and those relating to consumption processes to which the individual is exposed. The extent to which a society encourages creative behaviour has been shown to be related to an individual's ability to solve problems. The characteristics of such a society include greater urbanization and complexity. Finally, the greater the diversity of products and consumption situations to which an individual is exposed, the greater will be his ability to learn from such experiences and to benefit from that learning (Hirschman 1979).

Therefore, a problem-solving or creative or mature consumer is the product of a background characterized by higher socioeconomic status and of an environment which encourages creative behavior and which is more urbanized and more likely to expose the individual to a diversity of consumption situations. A more mature market is one comprised of mature consumers and is, therefore, likely to be characterized by higher levels of education and income, by greater urbanization and complexity and by the availability of a broad range of different types of shopping experiences.

The consumer in a more mature market is in a position to take advantage of the attractions which that market offers and is sufficiently equipped to benefit from the experience of participating in the market. Therefore, consumers in a mature market are likely to be better off economically and able to purchase the types of products which would be found in such a market. Also, these consumers are likely to be better educated and, therefore, better able to cope with the variety of shopping experiences and to benefit from these experiences. The educational and economic characteristics of consumers also contribute to the mix of products and services which is created to serve them.

The extent to which a market might be termed a mature market relates in part to the actual size of the market.

Trading areas which are supported by a large population base are able to sustain a larger number and greater variety of retail stores. Such a mix of retail stores in large urban centers provides residents of these markets with an opportunity to gain relatively more experience dealing with a broader variety of shopping experiences. Clearly, small markets cannot provide as rich a shopping experience.

The major factors which contribute to the labelling of a market as mature or not relate to the variety of consumption experiences which it provides. Clearly, as a market matures by growing to serve a larger population base and as it assumes a greater degree of importance as a shopping area, a number of changes are likely to take place. First, it will attract an increasing number of retail stores and types of stores. Second, its size will permit the establishment of a variety of specialty businesses which could not be supported by a smaller market. Third, the market would be more likely to be receptive to innovations and to new forms of retailing. Finally, the market is likely to become significantly more competitive.

The level of competition present among the retail stores in a mature market is likely to produce a number of effects which influence the extent to which consumers in that market experience problems or are satisfied with the level of service they are receiving. The competitiveness of a mature market should lead to a diversity of prices, or even to lower prices (Burt and Boyett 1979) and to the development of more efficient distribution systems which will facilitate the movement of products from producer to consumer. Similarly, a more competitive market is likely to necessitate that businesses offer customers a higher level of personal service, better value, and a higher order of personal selling skills than are available in less developed or less mature markets.

Mature markets are also more complex markets in that they expose the consumer to a broad range of social institutions, including the mass media. While the shopper in a mature market may have access to a variety of media, including one or more daily newspapers, cable television and a large number of radio stations, the consumer in a less developed market is served possibly by a weekly newspaper and by a small number of radio and television stations. The result is that a consumer in a less mature market has greater difficulty in acquiring information about the market and about specific products and services.

The concept of market maturity is one which might be applied in a variety of different contexts. Certainly, it is possible to compare countries on the basis of the relative sophistication or maturity of their markets, much as economies are now compared in terms of their level of development (Moyer and Hutt 1979). The concept might also be applied in comparing, as is done in this paper, two or more regions or provinces within a country, or even groups of consumers within a country or city. Just as we would find certain countries with more mature markets, so too are certain retail markets or consumer groups more mature than others. The importance of the concept lies in the theory that less mature consumers are less prepared to face the sophisticated market of today, less knowledgeable concerning their rights as consumers and concerning programs and legislation which exist to protect them, and less aware of procedures which they might **follow** to seek advice, assistance or redress.

The second part of this paper examines the results of consumer surveys conducted in two provinces of Canada. The Provinces of Ontario and Newfoundland were selected for study because they conform to the descriptions of more mature and less mature markets respectively. The determination of the relative levels of market maturity present in each province was based on an examination of secondary data which revealed marked differences between the two provinces. This review determined that, in comparison with Newfoundland, the Province of Ontario is characterized by higher levels of per capita income and higher education levels, and by lower rates of unemployment and lower consumer price indices. In addition, Ontario has a large population base and is more urbanized. This greater density of population supports a broad diversity of retailing institutions and mass media. The Ontario consumer is much more likely to be exposed to a larger number of retail stores and to a broad range of types of retail operations, including shopping centers, national and regional chains, department, discount, and specialty stores. Finally, consumers in that province are more often exposed to innovations in that Ontario is often used as a test market and as the base for introducing new forms of retailing into Canada.

In terms of the factors which have been put forward as influencing the level of market maturity present in a market, Newfoundland is clearly less mature. The secondary data show that Newfoundland has lower per capita levels of education and income and higher prices and unemployment rates. The population of the province is dispersed over a wide geographic area and the absence of large population centres means that consumers are much less exposed to a variety of media and do not encounter a broad mix of consumption experiences. The rate of new product introduction and of retailing innovation is much slower than in Ontario.

The Provinces of Newfoundland and Ontario have been selected for comparison in part because the socioeconomic differences between these provinces are often large. Similar comparisons might be made between cities or regions within provinces.
The conclusions, however, would be comparable. There clearly
exists important differences across markets in terms of the
economic and educational ability of consumers in less mature
areas to deal in the market as do consumers in areas where
income and education levels are higher. A final conclusion
which might be drawn from this discussion is that differences
also exist across regions in terms of the nature of the markets.
More mature markets tend to offer their consumers a broader
variety of shopping experiences, greater opportunity to gain
experience in a number of different settings and with new
products and new forms of retailing, better access to retail
information andto information on stores, products, and brands
through the media.

RELATIONSHIP BETWEEN MARKET MATURITY AND CONSUMER ISSUES

This review of market differences leads naturally to the
conclusion that consumers are different across regions and
that such differences are related to characteristics of both
the consumer and the market in which he resides. These differences essentially represent the existence of market segments
which are of obvious interest to marketers as they represent
differential levels of demand for their products. They should
also be of interest to policy makers, consumer protection
agencies, and to marketers, because they represent differential
levels of consumer expertise and of need for consumer programs
and services. The consumer in the more mature market is hypothesized to be better educated and to have a higher level of
income. He benefits from the broader mix of shopping experiences to which he is potentially exposed. Through shopping
in a variety of situations, he learns to better cope with
situations and problems which might arise. Conversely, the
consumer in a less mature market who has less education and a
lower income and whose opportunity to gain consumption expertise is limited, is more likely to be confused or misled by
new shopping experiences. The consumer in a mature market also
is hypothesized to benefit from the competitiveness of the
market in which he shops in that he is more likely to encounter
more variety, more retail 'sales,' lower prices, and a higher
level of service. The consumer in the less mature market often
faces a situation where he has little choice but to deal with
a small number of retailers, or even a single retailer, in
the purchase of most items which he buys.

Hypotheses

The overall hypothesis of the research which is described in the following pages is that consumers in a mature market, such as Ontario, are likely to be better equipped to face the marketplace and to avoid and solve consumer problems, than are their counterparts in less mature markets, such as Newfoundland. Specifically, the following hypotheses will be addressed:

1.   that consumers in a more mature market (Ontario) will assign different priorities to social issues and consumer issues than will consumers in a less mature market (Newfoundland);

2.   that consumers in a less mature market will demonstrate a more negative attitude toward business and will hold a less positive opinion concerning the accomplishments of the consumer movement and the progress being made to improve the lot of the consumer;

3.   that consumers in a less mature market are less likely to complain when problems are encountered in the marketplace;

4.   that consumers in a mature market will advocate different actions to solve consumer problems than those advocated by consumers in a less mature market;

5.   that consumers in a mature market will be more likely to seek information on consumer rights and on major purchases and that they will seek such information from different sources than will consumers in a less mature market;

6.   that consumers in a mature market are more knowledgeable and experienced concerning retail shopping and more knowledgeable concerning consumer rights and consumer legislation which is designed to benefit them.

Research Methodology

The differences, discussed above, between the Provinces of Ontario and Newfoundland are sufficient to permit the conclusion that Ontario represents a more mature retail market than does Newfoundland. This being the case, a research project was undertaken to test the hypotheses which have been stated. The remainder of this paper contains a comparison of the results of a study undertaken on behalf of the Ministry of Consumer and Commercial Relations of the Province of Ontario in 1978 (Moyer et al. 1978) and those of a similar study conducted in Newfoundland in early 1979 with the support of the Consumers' Association of Canada (CAC), Newfoundland Branch. As is obvious from the description of the two projects, the results in many areas are not directly comparable since they were designed, not for comparative purposes, but to meet the information needs of their sponsors. Nevertheless, the basis for comparison is sufficient to permit the drawing of conclusions concerning differences between Ontario and Newfoundland.

The Ontario sample was made up of 956 consumers aged 18 years and older. The province was divided into six regions and data were collected through a personal interview. The Newfoundland sample of 499 consumers was selected at random from the most recent voters' list. Data from the Newfoundland sample were obtained through a mailed questionnaire to which the effective response rate was 27.3%.

The questionnaires used in both studies were designed to measure the attitudes of consumers on a variety of consumer related issues. While both used similar questions, the method of data collection used in the Newfoundland survey necessitated more detailed instructions. Also, to satisfy the objectives of the survey for the Consumers' Association, additional questions were asked of participants. Questions dealt with attitudes toward various consumer matters, use of information sources, awareness of consumer legislation, shopping behaviour, and demographic and socioeconomic characterists of the respondent and his or her family.

The analysis presented in this paper consists of a cross-tabulation analysis of responses of the Newfoundland sample as compared with the similar analysis presented in the Ontario report. As the actual data from the Ontario survey were not available to the authors, no statistical tests were performed. Discussion of results will, therefore, consist of what the authors perceive to be noteworthy similarities and differences.

Results

Personal and government priorities - social issues. Consumers in both samples were asked to indicate, from a list of fifteen social issues, the three which they considered to be of greatest concern to them personally and also the three which should be of greatest concern to government. Table 1 presents the results of this question both in terms of the percentage who mentioned the issue and how each issue ranked in

TABLE 1

PRIORITY OF SOCIAL ISSUES

Percentage of respondents who mention that issue*

Issues	Issues Which Concern People Personally				Issues Which Should Have Government Priority			
	Ontario		Newfoundland		Ontario		Newfoundland	
	%	Rank	%	Rank	%	Rank	%	Rank
Unemployment	44	1	34	2	55	1	58	1
Inflation	41	2	33	3	46	3	41	2
Government Spending	33	3	11	10	47	2	33	3
Education	30	4	24	6	16	7	18	6
Cost of Health Care	26	5	16	8	25	4	15	7
Energy	22	6	27	4	22	5	28	4
Lower Taxes	22	7	26	5	20	6	22	5
Fair Deal for Consumers	19	8	38	1	14	8	14	8
Law and Order	17	9	13	9	14	9	10	9
Pensions	11	10	10	11	13	10	6	12
Environment	11	11	9	12	11	11	8	10
Abortion	10	12	20	7	3	15	8	11
Immigration	8	13	2	14	11	12	2	15
Public Safety	6	14	7	13	6	14	3	14
National Security	3	15	1	15	8	13	4	13
Other	0	-	1	-	0	-	1	-

*The answers total more than 100 percent because respondents were asked to name the three issues that concerned them personally the most and the three issues which should have the highest priority for government.

179

terms of importance. While both groups tended to rate unemployment and inflation as being very important and immigration, public safety, and national security as not very important, striking differences were shown on the level of importance attached to certain other issues. For instance, government spending was ranked much higher by Ontario respondents (33% of the Ontario sample indicated that this is an important issue to them personally as compared with only 11% of the Newfoundland sample). Also, a fair deal for consumers was most often mentioned as an issue of personal concern for Newfoundland respondents, although this result may have been influenced by the fact that the project was sponsored by the CAC. Noticeable differences were also observed on such issues as abortion and cost of health care.

On the issues which respondents thought should be of highest priority for government, similar results were obtained for both groups. Unemployment, inflation, and government spending were the three most often cited issues, whereas immigration, public safety, and national security were again the least often cited. The only noticeable differences concerned the issues of the cost of health care (Ontario respondents ranked higher) and abortion (Newfoundland respondents ranked higher).

Degree of concern - consumer issues. Respondents were asked to indicate their level of concern regarding various consumer issues. As may be seen from Table 2, a large percentage of both groups expressed at least moderate concern over most issues. The prices of food and other products were most frequently mentioned, with a larger percentage of the Newfoundland sample expressing concern about the quality of products and after-sales service and repairs, guarantees and warranties, the amount of information available on products and services, and knowing what to do if a product fails. Ontario respondents, on the other hand, expressed greater concern over the cost of renting or owning a house or apartment, the availability of too much credit, and such marketing aspects as the amount of packaging and advertising.

The results of this series of questions tend to corroborate several of the hypotheses put forward earlier concerning mature markets. These results indicate that subject in Newfoundland, the less mature market, are more concerned about economic issues and prices in particular, the quality of products and of the service and repair facilities available to them, the amount of available information, the perceived adequacy of guarantees and warranties, and particularly knowing where to turn for assistance in the event of a problem. On the other hand, subjects from the more mature market are rela-

TABLE 2
PRIORITY OF CONSUMER ISSUES

Issues	Percentage of respondents who are extremely or moderately concerned about each issue	
	Ontario	Newfoundland
Food prices (The price of food)*	88	99
Prices of many other products (The prices of products other than food)	86	97
Cost of renting or owning a house or apartment	80	76
Poor quality of many products (The quality of products in general)	74	83
Poor quality of after-sales service and repairs (The quality of after-sales services and repairs)	66	74
Too much packaging (Packaging and labelling)	65	43
Too much advertising (The amount of advertising)	64	50
Too much credit available (The amount of credit available)	63	43
Failure of many companies to live up to claims made in their advertising (The extent to which companies live up to claims made in their advertising)	60	64
Inadequate guarantees or warranties (Product guarantees or warrangies)	56	68
Misleading and confusing labelling	54	–
Not enough information about different products and services (The amount of reliable information available about different products and services)	46	63
Knowing what to do if something is wrong with a product	39	68

*Statement within parentheses indicates the slightly modified wording used in the Newfoundland survey.

181

tively less concerned with such matters and are in a position to turn more of their attention toward such "higher order" consumer issues, such as the amount of credit available and the volume of packaging and advertising.

Consumer attitudes toward business and marketing activities. Tables 3 and 4 present some atttitudes of respondents toward business, marketing activities, and the consumer movement. A large majority of the Ontario sample saw business as being at least fairly interested in the needs of consumers but a much smaller majority of both groups felt the same way about government's interest (Table 3).

Consumers were asked their level of agreement with various Likert-type statements and the results are presented in Table 4. The percentages expressed in this table represent the percentage of respondents who responded "strongly agree" or "agree" to each statement. While a large percentage of both groups agreed that "most people don't know how to use credit wisely," a larger percentage of the Ontario sample agreed on the success of the consumer movement in **improving** product quality and that the consumer's carelessness is the cause of most of the problems he experiences. Ontario respondents also were likely to see competition as the best way to keep prices down and to think that there is too much government regulation of business.

Respondents from the **mature** market expressed more strongly the opinion that both business and government are interested in consumer needs. Those from the less mature market were more likely to feel that business and government are somewhat less interested. Similarly, possibly as a result of their more advantageous economic position, Ontario respondents generally feel that the consumer movement has been of some help and are more willing to attribute at least some of the consumer's problems to his own carelessness. They see a competitve marketplace, rather than government regulation, as an important ingredient in assisting consumers. Conversely, the Newfoundland respondents did not feel so strongly that much progress has been made in consumer matters and were more likely to advocate greater government involvement rather than trust in the free marketplace to solve their problems.

Problems and complaints. Subjects were asked various questions concerning the problems and complaints they experienced in the marketplace. Aspects included frequency of complaining, types of complaints, whether a complaint was actually made and if not, why not, to whom the complaint was taken, the result of the complaint action, and the level of satisfaction with the outcome. The two surveys differed in

TABLE 3
INTEREST OF BUSINESS AND GOVERNMENT IN CONSUMER NEEDS

| | Percentage of respondents who report that degree of interest | | | |
| | By Business | | By Government | |
Degree of Interest	Ontario	Newfoundland	Ontario	Nfld.
Very interested	31	15	12	7
Fairly interested	51	46	47	48
Not too interested	13	32	28	36
Not at all interested	4	7	11	9
Don't know	1	—*	2	–

*In this and subsequent tables, a dash (-) indicates that the alternative was not listed for that sample.

TABLE 4
ATTITUDES TOWARD BUSINESS AND CONSUMERS

| | Percentage of respondents Agreeing or Strongly Agreeing with the statement | |
	Ontario	Newfoundland
Most people don't know how to use credit wisely	89	88
The consumer movement has helped improve the quality and standards of products and services	89	74
Competition among companies is the best way to keep prices down	85	74
There is too much government regulation of business	54	27
Most consumers' problem result from their own carelessness	46	30

183

their approach in that while questions were asked generally (across all product and service categories) of the Ontario sample, the Newfoundland survey covered these dimensions of complaints for three specific products categories - grocery, appliance, and clothing.

In Ontario, 35 percent claimed they had good reason to complain about a product or service during the past year and of these 31 percent said they had lodged a complaint. Of the three product categories, the Newfoundland sample experienced more problems with groceries (32 percent had good reason to complain and 48 percent actually did). Though less problems were experienced with clothing (25 percent) and appliances (15 percent), at least **half** of those who felt they had legitimate complaints actually voiced their complaint.

In the Ontario survey, of all complaints, most had to do with the product not being as durable as claimed (39 percent), the quality not being as advertised (23 percent), and the product being misrepresented (14 percent). The complaints with groceries by Newfoundland consumers dealt mainly with product spoilage or damage or the inferior quality of ingredients. The few problems experienced with appliances were mainly concerned with poor performance, while clothing complaints were due to the poor quality of material and the garment not wearing satisfactorily.

Consumers were asked their reasons for not complaining when they experienced a problem. For both samples, the majority gave reasons which reflected indifference (not worth the time and effort) and defeatism (would not make any difference), while only a small percentage cited ignorance of how and where to complain.

As can be seen from Table 5, consumers in both provinces, but particularly in Newfoundland, brought the vast majority of their complaints to the dealer or retailer. The Ontario respondents were more likely to complain to manufacturers, the Better Business Bureau, or their legal adviser. Little or no use was made of government representatives or agencies.

The various outcomes of complaints are presented in Table 6. A substantial percentage of complaints were resolved through repair, replacement, exchange or refund. This was particularly so with the Newfoundland complainants. However, on a large minority of complaints, the consumer gave up or received no satisfaction. As can be seen in Table 7, about two-thirds of the Ontario complainants reported that they were reasonably satisfied with the outcomes. Similar results were obtained with the Newfoundland sample, except with appliances,

TABLE 5
WHERE COMPLAINTS ARE TAKEN

| | Percentage of respondents* | | | |
| | Ontario | Newfoundland | | |
		Grocery	Appliance	Clothing
Dealer, retailer or store	72	89	92	97
Manufacturer	22	8	8	3
Better Business Bureau	9	0	0	0
Lawyer	4	0	0	0
Utility Company	4	–	–	–
Local elected official	3	0	0	0
TV or radio station	2	0	0	0
Trade Association	2	0	0	0
Newspaper action line/Newspaper	1	1	0	0
Consumers' Association of Canada	1	0	0	0
Letter to Editor	1	–	–	–
Ombudsman	0	0	0	0
Government agency/ department	–	0	0	0
Other	5	1	0	0
No response	2	–	–	–

*Percentages for the Ontario sample add to more than 100%
because some respondents mentioned more than one answer.

TABLE 6
OUTCOMES OF COMPLAINTS

Percentage of respondents who gave
that result*

Result of Complaint	Ontario	Newfoundland		
		Grocery	Appliance	Clothing
Item repaired	21	–	37	12
Item replaced or exchanged	20	58	24	45
Money back or credit note	13	17	10	23
Explanation of reason for problem	9	7	3	5
Apology	9	0	0	0
Item delivered	3	0	0	0
Accounting/Clerical error fixed	2	0	0	0
Person responsible was reprimanded	–	0	0	0
Took court action	–	0	0	0
Other	4	3	5	0
No settlement yet	15	8	3	2
Gave up – no satisfaction	19	7	18	13

*Percentages add to more than 100 percent because some respondents in the Ontario sample mentioned more than one outcome.

TABLE 7
DEGREES OF SATISFACTION WITH OUTCOMES OF COMPLAINTS

Percentage of respondents who were
that satisfied

Degree of Satisfaction	Ontario	Newfoundland		
		Grocery	Appliance	Clothing
Very satisfied	35	39	27	51
Fairly satisfied	32	39	19	16
Not too satisfied	13	11	15	12
Not at all satisfied	20	11	39	21

where the majority indicated some dissatisfaction.

The results of this section of the study are difficult to
interpret owing to the differences in the manner in which the
questions were asked in the two studies. It is practically
impossible to compare the two samples on the basis of complaining behaviour and to address the hypothesis that consumers in
less mature markets are less likely to complain.

Perceived effectiveness of various consumer actions. Respondents were asked to rate the effectiveness of various
actions which might be employed as a means of solving consumer
problems. Different approaches were taken with each sample.
In the Ontario survey, respondents were asked to rate each
action on a 5-point scale (5 = excellent, 3 = average, 1 =
poor) while the Newfoundland respondents rated each item on a
5-point Likert-type scale from "very effective" to "very inef-
fective." Table 8 presents the effectiveness rating for each
action by the Ontario sample and the percentage of Newfoundland respondents who saw the action as very or somewhat
effective. In order to compare both samples, the ratings and
percentages were rank ordered. Teaching consumer education in
the schools was rated the highest, followed closely by media
publicity in the Ontario sample, while the media and consumer
representation on supervisory boards were ranked as most effective in the Newfoundland sample. Actions which were not
considered very effective included contact with elected representatives, taking manufacturers to court, and public
demonstrations.

While these results do not indicate a marked difference
between the two samples, they do suggest that consumers generally are interested in long-run solutions to problems through
consumer education, consultation, and consumer representation.
Newfoundland respondents were slightly more likely to advocate
media publicity, but both groups expressed relatively little
support for more radical actions such as taking marketers to
court or organizing public demonstrations.

Perceived improvement concerning various aspects of
consumerism. Respondents were asked whether changes have
taken place in recent years concerning various aspects of
consumerism. More specifically, they were asked to indicate
whether, over the last three years, certain situations have
improved or worsened or whether there has been no change.
Table 9 presents the results of this question. Areas in which
respondents from both provinces perceived improvements included
product safety, product content information, and information
on product care and operation. Although 30 to 40 percent felt
that improvement had been made, larger percentages of respon-

187

TABLE 8
EFFECTIVENESS OF CONSUMER ACTIONS

Kind of Remedy	Ontario		Newfoundland	
	Effectiveness Rating (5 = Excellent, 3 = Average, 1= Poor)	Rank	Percentage of Respondents who see action as very or somewhat effective	Rank
Teaching consumer education in schools	4.1	1	81	3
Getting the media to publicize issue	3.9	2	83	1.5
More consultation between consumer groups and government	3.6	3.5	80	4
Getting consumer representatives on supervisory agencies such as marketing boards	3.6	3.5	83	1.5
Refusing to deal with specific companies or not buy their product	3.5	5	74	5
Getting consumer representatives on company boards of directors	3.4	6	73	6
Writing or phoning elected representatives	3.2	7	55	8
Taking manufacturers, dealers, etc. to court	2.8	8	65	7
Sit-ins or other kinds of public demonstrations	2.1	9	51	9

TABLE 9

EVALUATION OF THE PRESENT SITUATION CONCERNING VARIOUS ASPECTS OF CONSUMERISM

Percentage of respondents who see the situation as better or worse*

Aspect	Ontario			Newfoundland		
	Better	Worse	No Change	Better	Worse	No Change
Safety testing of products (The safety of most products)	77	6	17	60	9	20
Information about content of products	69	9	22	64	6	21
Information about how to take care of/operate/assemble products	52	10	38	50	5	32
Handling of consumer complaints by business	40	14	46	35	10	37
Relationship between consumer and business	37	19	44	29	20	33
Treatment of consumer by business	33	18	49	27	17	38
Misleading claims about products	31	25	44	16	31	33
Getting things repaired properly	19	39	42	22	30	40
Fair cost of having things repaired	7	70	23	5	73	13

*Figures for the Newfoundland sample add to less than 100 percent because of the additional alternative "Not Sure" which was included.

189

dents, particularly in Ontario, saw no change with respect to the handling of complaints by **business,** the relationship between the consumer and business, the treatment of the consumer by **business,** and the extent of misleading product claims. A large percentage of both groups felt that the cost of repairs had worsened and more saw no change in getting **things repaired** properly.

Apart from the question relating to "getting things repaired properly," members of the Newfoundland sample were generally less likely to express the opinion that the situation has improved over the past three years. This result supports the hypothesis stated above that consumers in a less mature market are likely to be less satisfied with the accomplishments being made in the area of consumer affairs and with the situation they face in the marketplace. Respondents from the more mature market are likely to express more positive opinions regarding the progress being made, in part because the nature of the mature market leads to a competitive retail situation which benefits the consumer, and because the consumer in this market is more likely to be made aware of such progress through the media and to experience it first hand when he shops.

Sources used for information about consumer rights and major purchases. Two questions dealt with the sources consumers use for information concerning their rights and those consulted prior to making a major purchase decision. As may be seen from Table 10, respondents in both provinces state that they would be most likely to contact the Better Business Bureau concerning consumer rights. A much larger percentage of Ontario respondents mentioned government sources, particularly provincial. A large percentage (32 percent) of the Newfoundland sample cited the Consumers' Association of Canada. This figure is felt to be inflated because of the indicated sponsorship of the survey by the CAC.

Table 11 shows the percentages of respondents who indicated they would go to, or have gone to, various sources for information in making purchase decisions. Here we find some striking differences. Thirty four percent of the Ontario sample as compared wth 11 percent of the Newfoundland sample would go to, or have gone to, retail stores for their information. While a fairly large percentage of consumers in both provinces would consult friends or relatives and the media, this percentage is slightly larger for the Ontario sample. It is also interesting to note that, although more than 40 percent of consumers in both provinces would go to the Better Business Bureau for information on consumer rights, only 16 percent of Ontario respondents and 11 percent of Newfoundland respondents have used or would use that source for purchase

TABLE 10
SOURCES OF INFORMATION ON CONSUMER RIGHTS

Source	Percentage of respondents who would go to that source*	
	Ontario	Newfoundland
Better Business Bureau	43	41
Government - Provincial	20	5
Government of Canada	12	1
Lawyer	12	4
Newspaper, TV or Radio	9	1
Friend or Relative	6	4
Chamber of Commerce	6	–
Banks	1	0
Consumers' Association of Canada	–	32
Other	21	0
Don't Know	16	12

*Figures for Ontario add to more than 100 percent because some respondents mentioned more than one source; the Newfoundland sample was asked for the first source they would go to.

decisions. A relatively large percentage of the Newfoundland sample claimed they have used Consumer Reports magazine and product literature from the manufacturer (two alternatives not listed for the Ontario survey).

These results indicated that consumers in the more mature market are more aware of the role of government in the area of consumer rights but they would not necessarily contact government for information on major purchases, feeling somewhat more confident of their own ability to rely on information from

TABLE 11
SOURCES OF INFORMATION AND ASSISTANCE
ON A MAJOR PURCHASE DECISION

Source	Percentage of respondents who have gone or would go to that source*	
	Ontario	Newfoundland
Stores	34	11
Friends or Relatives	32	26
Paper, TV, Radio, Magazines	20	15
Better Business Bureau	16	11
Lawyer	13	8
Banks	5	15
Library	4	4
Chamber of Commerce	2	–
Community Information Centres	2	–
Provincial Government	1	6
Federal Government	1	3
Consumers' Association of Canada	–	5
Consumer Reports Magazine	–	12
Canadian Consumer Magazine	–	7
Product literature put out by companies	–	17
Other	–	2
Don't Know/ Can't Recall	9	19

*Figures add to more than 100 percent because respondents were asked to indicate all of the sources they would use or had ever used.

retailers, from friends, and the media. On the other hand, consumers in the less mature market are less aware of the role of governments in the consumer rights field and are less trusting of information from retailers. They are also more likely to know where to go for information (19 percent) and would be more reliant on information from banks and non-commercial sources such as Consumer Reports magazine.

Shopping behaviour. Consumers were questioned on their buying habits and were asked whether they performed certain actions always, sometimes, or never. As may be seen from Table 12, a large percentage of both groups indicated that they comparison shop, but a much larger percentage of the Newfoundland sample than of the Ontario sample say they use a shopping list at least sometimes. A somewhat contradictory result shows a large percentage of the Newfoundland sample claiming to both make a budget and stick to it and also to overspend. These results do, however, reflect somewhat the economic problems of the less mature Newfoundland market. These respondents indicate that they are at least as likely to comparison shop and are more likely to use a shopping list and to operate on a budget. They also, possibly because of more limited resources, feel that they overspend at least sometimes.

Awareness of consumer laws. Respondents were asked to list any federal and provincial consumer laws of which they were aware. Both groups were largely ignorant concerning legislation: 62 percent of the Ontario sample and 89 percent of the Newfoundland sample claimed no knowledge of any laws. Among respondents who could name at least one law, the most often cited included the cooling-off period for direct sales, packaging and labelling laws, and truth in advertising legis-

TABLE 12
SHOPPERS' BUYING HABITS

| Buying Behavior* | Percentage of respondents who do | | | |
| | Always | | Sometimes | |
	Ontario	Nfld.	Ontario	Nfld.
Comparison shop	54	57	35	35
Use a grocery shopping list	53	50	22	41
Make a budget and keep to it	25	38	30	34
Overspend	10	22	54	70

*The wording of statements was slightly different for the Newfoundland sample.

lation. These results support the contention that consumers in a less mature market are less likely to be aware of legislation which exists to protect them.

CONCLUSIONS AND IMPLICATIONS

This paper has explored the concept of market maturity and related concepts of modernity and creativity and the relationships between maturity and the degree to which consumers are likely to experience problems and to be able to cope with the complexities of the marketplace.

The concept of market maturity is one which has not yet been examined in depth by these authors or others. The discussion of the concept has been preliminary and the variables which have been proposed as descriptors of market maturity are rough and unproven. It would appear, however, to be a concept which merits further discussion and exploration. Clearly, additional work is needed in order to refine the concept.

Similarly, the differences between a more mature and a less mature market which have been examined in this paper are also lacking in some respects. Additional work is needed in order to permit not only a clearer definition of a mature market, but also to facilitate an improved examination of the differences across markets which result from differences in the level of market maturity. However, despite the inadequacy of the basis for comparison used in this paper, there is evidence to suggest that differences in Consumer sophistication, preparedness and attitudes, and in consumer problems and their approaches to solution, do indeed exist between markets at different levels of maturity. This link between market characteristics and consumer abilities and problems needs to be more firmly established.

If such a link does exist, as it appears from this paper, it calls into question a global approach to dealing with consumer problems. It would appear that a program designed to protect consumers in mature markets would be inadequate to protect consumers in less mature markets. Similarly, the approach taken to the drafting of legislation, to its enforcement, and to consumer education should vary according to the needs of consumers in each market (Wallendorf and Zaltman 1976).

These results suggest a genuine need for a segmentation approach to the resolution of consumer problems and to the development of strategies **and programs which would be most** appropriate to deal with the issues and problems experienced by various segments of consumers. Just as a marketer would be

194

interested in the level of market maturity as a basis for market segmentation, since consumers in more mature markets are likely to be more demanding and more receptive to new products and innovation in·general, so too should consumer groups, educators, and public policy makers adopt a differential approach to serving consumers in different market maturity segments.

As has been indicated earlier, the concept of market maturity may be applied in a variety of contexts. Consumers who are part of a less mature market - a remote area, a rural community, a central city neighbourhood - are more likely to be less educated, have lower incomes, have less exposure to complex markets and to a diversity of shopping or consumption experiences. They have had fewer opportunities to learn how to be efficient consumers and less experience at solving problems. Their information handling and problem solving abilities are not as well developed as are those of consumers in a more mature market. Such differences demand the development of consumer protection and education programs which are appropriate to the level of consumer maturity present in a market.

REFERENCES

Bartels, Robert and Roger L. Jenkins (1977), "Macromarketing," Journal of Marketing, 41 (October), 17-20.

Burt, David N. and Joseph E. Boyett, Jr. (1979), "Reduction in Selling Price After the Introduction of Competition," Journal of Marketing Research, 16 (May), 275-79.

Hirschman, Elizabeth C. (1979), "Creativity: Consumer, Societal, Marketing," Working paper, Institute of Retail Management, Faculty of Business Administration, New York University.

Moyer, Mel. S., Margaret MacIver, Dagmar Stafl, and Marika Prymych (1978), Ontario Consumer Issues, Report for the Ministry of Consumer and Commercial Relations, Province of Ontario.

Moyer, Reed and Michael D. Hutt (1978), Macro Marketing, (2nd Edition), Toronto: John Wiley and Sons Canada Limited.

Wallendorf, Melanie and Gerald Zaltman (1976), "Perspectives for Studying and Implementing Consumer Education," Advances in Consumer Research, Volume IV, Edited by William D. Perreault, Jr., Proceedings of the Seventh Annual Conference of the Association for Consumer Research, Atlanta, 376-379.

MARKETING BOARDS: THE IRRELEVANCE AND
IRREVERENCE OF ECONOMIC ANALYSIS[1]

R.M.A. Loyns, University of Manitoba

ABSTRACT

The increase in importance and the geographic extension of
the powers of agricultural marketing boards has been one of the
most significant changes in the macroeconomics of Canadian food
marketing in the last decade. This development has sparked a
corresponding increase in interest in marketing boards on the
part of the economics profession, who criticize boards because
they are monopolistic, distort resource allocation, have unde-
sireable distribution effects and contribute to inflation of
food prices.

However, the wares of the economist are not nearly as valuable in the real world as they appear from within the discipline. Economic analysis of marketing boards is so at variance
with other over-riding considerations that it approaches irreverance and economists become iconoclasts when evaluating marketing boards.

This paper examines the definition, evolution and status
of marketing boards, reviews selected findings of recent economic studies and looks at the boards in their political and organizational settings. The basic hypothesis developed therein
is that marketing boards are political instruments for the
transfer of income and the shifting of market power. As such,
critical economic analysis is irrelevant in developing an understanding of the existence and operation of marketing boards.

L'importance accrue et l'extension des pouvoirs des commissions en marketing de produits agricoles a été l'un des
changements les plus considérables dans la macro-économie de
commercialisation des aliments au Canada, durant la dernière
décade. Ce développement a éveillé un intérêt correspondant

1 A.W. Wood has been a major source of assistance in presenting
and publishing this paper. The views and opinions remain my
own responsibility, however, and are not necessarily reflec-
tive of his or of the University of Manitoba.

dans les commissions en marketing de la part de la profession
économique, qui critique ces commissions parce qu'elles sont
monopolisatrices, parce qu'elles altèrent la répartition des resources, parce qu'elles apportent des conséquences indésir-
ables à la distribution et contribuent à l'inflation du prix
des aliments.

Cependant, les connaissances de l'économiste ne sont pas
aussi précieuses dans la vie réelle qu'elles n'apparaissent
l'être à l'intérieur même de la discipline. Les analyses des
économistes sur les commissions en marketing sont tellement en
désaccord avec d'autres études prépondérentes que cela frise
l'irrévérence et les économistes deviennent de véritables icon-
oclastes dans leur évaluation des commission en marketing.

Cet article examine la définition, l'évolution et la situation des commissions en marketing, donne un compte rendu de
résultats sélectionnés parmi les études faites dans le domaine
de l'économie et jette un regard sur les cadres de leurs politiques et organisation. L'hypothèse de base développée à cet
égard expose le fait que ces commissions en marketing sont des
instruments politiques pour la transmission des revenus et le
changement des pouvoirs du marché. Telle qu'elle est, l'analyse économique critique est hors de propos dans le développement
d'une compréhension de l'existence et du fonctionnement des
commissions en marketing.

INTRODUCTION

A Supply Management quota scheme can never increase producer net income because the benefits are capitalized into
the limiting resource.
British Columbia Select Standing
Committee on Agriculture

The past decade has produced a number of important changes
in the macroeconomics of Canadian food marketing. One of the
most important of these changes has been the increase in importance and geographic extension of powers of agricultural marketing boards. There has been a corresponding increase in interest in marketing boards by several sections of the economics
profession, a development which is somewhat out of character
for economists because they have ignored other much more important segments of the food industry. As a consequence of the
attractiveness of marketing boards to analysts, a considerable
body of economic literature, both theoretical and empirical,
has been built up. In general, it appears that economists are
critical of marketing boards because boards are viewed as in-
competitive in nature, as producing undesirable resource

allocation and redistributive effects, and as contributors to
inflationary pressures in food. Economic research generally
supports these prior expectations, and to the credit of the ob-
jectivity of the inexact science of economics, the expectations
and research results are the same whether presented by government or non-government economists. In short, most economists
see agricultural marketing boards as a structural form within
the Canadian economy which requires modification or abandonment.

If any significance can be attached to the public debate on
marketing boards which has occurred during the past five or six
years, there appears to be widespread sympathy for this economic prescription. Despite this, governments have continued to
defend boards, even those which have the most rigid control and
operate at the greatest public and consumer expense, and the
support is independent of political philosophy. Moreover, governments provide strong indication of willingness to consolidate
and extend marketing board powers.

The purpose of this paper is to develop several hypotheses
that seek to place the economics, and economic analysis, of
marketing boards in a perspective which is believed to correspond to today's marketing environment. Basically, my proposition is that agricultural marketing boards, although potentially powerful economic organizations, are much more political
entities than they are economic organizations. As a consequence,
political and organizational theory are more relevant to understanding them than is economic analysis. In this important
sense then, economic analysis is <u>irrelevant</u> to the existence and
operation of marketing boards. In addition, the results of economic analysis are often so much at odds with the entire value
system underlying boards and with the basic rationale for them,
that economic analysis approaches, or achieves, <u>irreverence</u>.

AGRICULTURAL MARKETING BOARDS:
DEFINITION, EVOLUTION AND STATUS

A great deal has been written about the history and evolution of boards in Canada (Hiscocks 1972; Federal Task Force on
Agriculture; Loyns 1971; Veeman, Loyns 1979). In order to provide a background for the substance of this paper, the following
brief review of definition, legal basis, and powers is provided.
The interpretation of evolution since the early 1970's will differ from previous versions since an important aspect of that
evolutionary period plus the present status is part of what this
paper is about.

The most common definition of boards is "a compulsory,
horizontal marketing organization for primary or processed

natural products operating under authority delegated by the government," (Hiscocks 1972, p. 2). These organizations have a number of characteristics which distinguish them from other forms of intervention in agriculture. First, they exist by virtue of broadly defined enablying legislation. Second, the motivation for implementing a plan under the legislation usually but not always, comes from the producers themselves. Third, the regulation once implemented is compulsory for producers in the defined area, and on the commodity or specific set of commodities defined to be regulated. Finally, the programs are administered from funds generated by levies on the regulated product. The enabling legislation may be provincial or a combination of federal and provincial with a corresponding federal-provincial agreement required to operationalize a plan under federal legislation. The kinds of economic powers which are permitted is extensive ranging from fee collection through promotion and market development, to price and volume control (Loyns 1971; Veeman, Loyns 1979).

Despite the scope of powers permitted under legislation, not all boards use them. In fact, few boards use the entire scope of powers that are available. A further important characteristic of boards, which is overlooked and clouds the ability to have useful economic dialogue about them, is their diversity. There are many different kinds of marketing boards, different in their economic characteristics, and therefore different in their effects and distribution of impact. To illustrate these points, consider what may be the polar extremes in boards, the Canadian Dairy Commission (CDC) and the Alberta Cattle Commission (ACC). The CDC has rigid price, volume, and surplus disposal controls and is supported by non-tariff trade barriers and large subsidy payments; the CDC costs the Canadian treasury and Canadian consumers hundreds of millions of dollars per year. The Alberta Cattle Commission collects a fee for conducting promotion, education and research activities, but the fee is reimbursable on request; consistent with their free enterprise, anti-government value system, Alberta cattlemen even refuse to call the ACC a marketing board. Between these extremes are about 100 boards with a wide range of powers. (Appendices I and II).

A useful method of classifying boards and their operation is the summary given in Table I. "Locus of Control" refers to those who make the major decisions. Since boards are monopolistic organizations within the limits of their plans and legislations, the more decisions made by producers themselves, the closer the process is to a self-regulated monopoly. Alternatively the more decisions made by government, the more public policy orientation the board would be expected to have. The identification of boards by the economic powers they exercise

199

Table 1

Strength and Locus of Control
of Marketing Boards

TYPE OF BOARD	LOCUS OF CONTROL — Increasing Self Regulation →		
Increasing Power →	Cabinet	Public Appointees	Producers
Promotional Boards	None	None	Alberta Cattle Commission Quebec Maple Products Boards
Negotiating Boards	None	Ontario Apple Commission	Many Fruit and Vegetable Boards
Central Selling Agencies	None	Freshwater Fish Marketing Corporation	Some Fruit and Vegetable Boards
		Saltwater Fish Marketing Corporation	Hog Boards
Price/Output Regulation	CWB (Some)	Canadian Wheat Board	Poultry Boards before Supply Management
Supply Management	CDC	Canadian Dairy Commission	Poultry Boards

are ranked from the least to greatest control. Supply management boards are those with close to (or the full) range of powers, complemented by tariff and/or quantitative border restrictions which eliminate import competition. These are very powerful boards in an economic sense and represnt very tight industry regulation. When associated with complete producer management of the board, as the original National Egg Agency was, a very powerful self-regulated monopoly is the result. In response to public criticism of this structure, changes have been made in composition of the National Agencies and to its overseer the Farm Products Marketing Council but producers are legislatively guaranteed a majority representation at both levels of administration.

This particular classification is also used because it provides a useful benchmark against which to discuss economic effects of boards. Briefly, it is primarily the supply management boards, and secondarily the Price/Output regulating boards, which bears the brunt of economic criticism and generate the greatest amount of public controversy. There is only periodic irritation expressed with Central Selling Agencies, and then much of that originates with producers themselves. Rarely are the negotiation boards challenged, and the promotional boards are much more like trade associations; indeed, most people do not even know these organizations exist.

My estimate is that marketing boards as defined above account for at least two-thirds of the value of farm output in Canada; supply management boards would represent upwards of one-quarter of the value of farm output. For purposes of economic analysis, if resource allocation and redistributive effects are the concern, analysis can concentrate on the last three types in Table 1. For purposes of this paper, however, there is no basis for distinguishing among the five categories; they are all important.

A BRIEF HISTORY OF THE DEVELOPMENT
OF MARKETING BOARDS

Although a board existed at the end of the First World War for selling wheat under war conditions, the origins of boards as we know them today began in the late 1920's. Any generalization on the causes for their existence can be challenged but boards in their early period seem to have been motivated by three basic considerations:

1. an effort to offset the disadvanted bargaining position of farmers;

201

2. an effort to reduct instability in returns to farmers;

3. the need to reduce the perceived high margins earned by marketing firms and suppliers.

The 1920's produced a concerted effort by governments, farmer organizations, and farmers to accomplish these objectives through co-operatives but this voluntary approach met with only limited success. Hence the motivation for legislated, compulsory, marketing organizations.

Prior to 1935, the first efforts were at the provincial level. British Columbia passed its Produce Marketing Act in 1927, and although it was later declared ultra vires provincial jurisdiction, it was the forerunner of much of the provincial marketing legislation that was to follow. Manitoba placed milk under its Public Utilities Act in 1929 and established the precedent for fluid milk regulation. In 1935, the Canadian Wheat Board Act was passed and the first federal-provincial agreement for this form of regulated marketing was established. The Canadian Wheat Board (CWB) has never been a producer agency as such. The original purpose of the Board was to bail the Western Pools and provincial governments out of high inventories and debt acquired in the depression wheat economy. However, during the war effort, the role of the CWB began to change. Quotas were implemented and the Board became much more a vehicle of national policy; but coincidentally, and perhaps paradoxically, it became a respected and essential institution of the farmers that the war era spawned. Today the CWB is by far the most important institution in Canadian grain marketing; indeed the CWB is one of Canada's largest corporations in terms of sales volume. The private grain trade has been a very docile, regulated service sector and apparently the majority of farmers are satisfied to have conditions stay this way.

During the 1950's and early 1960's marketing board growth was in the form of product coverage under provincial legislation. This growth appeared to be motivated by the same objectives as the original boards. Also, producers sought, and governments gave, powers directed towards altering the fundamental structure related to a selected set of marketing activities. For example, fruit and vegetable boards developed collective negotiation and selling procedures, and returns pooling mechanisms. Honey producers concentrated on collective processing and promotion. Hog boards sought to sharpen the competitiveness of bidding for their product by packers as well as returns pooling. Poultry boards expanded across Canada but under provincial legislation. They began to apply some of the quota procedures which fluid milk boards had been using, but they were limited in what they could achieve because the product moved relatively freely among provinces.

In 1967 the Canadian Dairy Commission (CDC) came into existence to regulate industrial milk on a national scale. At this
time the Canadian dairy industry, located heavily (but not concentrated) in Eastern Ontario and Quebec, was in trouble. Canada has never been able to show itself as low cost producer of
milk products by international standards; butter and cheese
prices in the 1960's did not provide Canadian industrial milk
producers with an acceptable return. The number of milk producers was declining rapidly, but milk was still produced by a
relatively large number of small producers. It is said that the
CDC was intended to rationalize the dairy industry and place it
on a more economic basis. This, however, soon came to mean concentrating production in Eastern Canada and more rapidly reducing the number of farmers. This process continued on into
1972 or 1973, while conditions remained depressed in the dairy
industry. Coincident with the rapid farm and food price increases in 1973, the policy approach in dairy changed. Prices
were increased rapidly, tighter cheese quotas were applied, subsidies were increased dramatically, and, "cost-of-production
pricing" was accepted as the industry norm in pricing. The so-
called "Long-Term Dairy Policy" announced in April 1975 marked
the climax of a process of tightening regulation in the Canadian dairy industry.

The last development of significance (in the context of a
brief historical review) was the passage in 1972 of the National Farm Products Marketing Agencies Act, and the subsequent increased regulation of the poultry industry by "supply management" poultry boards. The NFPMA Act established the National
Farm Products Marketing Council, and provided the federal powers
by which marketing agencies (boards) can be established on a
wide range of farm products. Production and price control can,
however, only be used in poultry products under the existing
Act. The egg agency (CEMA) was established in 1972, the turkey
agency (CTMA) in 1975, and the chicken agency (CBMA) in 1978.
"Cost-of-production pricing" has been the objective of each of
these boards but became completely operational only after July
1975 when the federal government established guidlines for use
of permits under the Import-Export Permits Act. This move by
the federal government closed the "supply management" circle of
eggs and turkeys at a time corresponding very closely to the
same policy in dairy.

The purpose of this review has been to show the specific
steps in the evolution of boards. Clearly there has been a
gradual expansion in board coverage (under provincial legislation) across commodities and across regions. However, without
federal-provincial agreements, this growth is of limited

203

economic consequence in most commodities (tobacco and fluid milk are the exceptions). Also, in the early 1970's the federal government presence became much stronger in boards; the CDC was strengthened and received much greater public funding, national poultry boards were created. Third, (although the point has not been developed) boards take many different forms irrespective of the economic conditions surrounding the industry. Boards seem to acquire the characteristics sought by the commodity group seeking them and range from tight control on dairy, to relaxed control on feed grains, to no control (except promotion) on beef cattle. In addition, there has been a very definite progression in development away from the "marketing" side of boards to production control. Supply management boards cannot be considered "marketing" boards in any conventional sense of that word, and certainly not in any historical sense of board development. Finally, the set of objectives for which boards exist is now expanded. It includes the very clear objective of raising farm prices, specifically in many cases to raise producer prices to the level of "average production costs" and provide assurances that prices will remain there. But the objectives now also seem increasingly to include "maintenance of the family farm."

These developments, particularly those occurring in the 1970's are remarkable. Farm population has been declining, the conventional wisdom is that that would imply less influence by farmers; these changes represent a significant increase in control of the farm sector both for and by farmers. Moreover, some of this change has involved substantial price raising, and it has come during a period when food prices have risen at unprecedented rates of increase. It has also come at a time when farm incomes have risen at average rates at least equal to that of "average" Canadians; when capital assets are considered, farm wealth has risen dramatically. Moreover, it has occurred during a period when "consumerism" has been the catchword. Finally, it has been a process of structural rigidification and market regulation when we claimed to have had an anti-inflation policy directed at reducing structural rigidities in the Canadian economy. Finally it has occurred in the face of much criticism from economists, and very little economic support. And the economic criticism has been reflected in a continuing public debate. The process should defy any logic of timing and it definitely defies economic logic.

SOME ECONOMIC EVIDENCE ON MARKETING BOARDS

The past few years have produced an array of empirical analyses of the operation and effects of marketing boards. The Food Prices Review Board, beginning in early 1974, contributed a number of commodity reports on regulated commodities during its existence. Also in 1974, the Consumer Research Council published the first comprehensive analysis of contemporary boards, and although that report was consumer-issue oriented, it covered a wide range of economic considerations. Since then analysis and analysts have proliferated, and now includes such prestigious organizations as the Competition Bureau, the Fraser Institute and the Center for Studies on Inflation and Productivity.

This section will selectively review the findings of a few of the very recent studies, and proceed to posit one or two personal observations regarding the status of economic analysis. Referring back to Table 1, the studies that will be referenced here fall primarily into the last two categories, i.e., Price/Output Control and Supply Management. The evidence has not been intentionally complied that way; I simply could not find any analysis of the other three categories of boards - which was definitive in indicating any of the following:

1. significant resource allocation implications either positive or negative;

2. significant changes in production and/or marketing efficiency, either positive or negative; or

3. significantly changed pricing performance, either positive or negative.

This is not to say that many economists, including myself, believe that these changes do not occur, or that these boards (increasingly as powers are increased) do not have some of these effects. On balance, it probably is believed that the effects are favorable. But we have not produced, nor have the boards themselves produced, the evidence to substantiate these beliefs.

I think this observation is important in at least one sense. It was stated earlier that an important characteristic of boards is their diversity. In terms of numbers of boards, numbers of producers, and perhaps, value of product, these first three categories are extremely important. Although these boards are not part of the criticisms leveled at marketing boards, neither have they really been studied, probably because no problems were perceived. Now we find that they are not part of the economic analysis. But they do represent a very important form of marketing organization in agriculture. I expect that most of the audience touched by the Workshop would agree that boards which improve information flows, reduce aspects of price or sales uncertainty, conduct market research which

205

otherwise would not be done, and generally introduce modern marketing technology to agriculture, could have some very positive benefits, especially when this is accomplished by leaving production decisions in the hands of the entrepreneur. To the extent that this expectation is valid, the exclusion of these boards from serious inquiry raises some doubts about the direction and relevance of our economic inquiries.

The Food Prices Review Board

Of the fifty-odd reports produced by the Board from late 1973 to February 1976, at least ten dealt with the price and quantity regulating boards, including supply management. The Boards produced evidence of mismanagement in eggs, product wastage in eggs and dairy, excessive prices in eggs, milk products and chickens, and sources of economic inefficiencies in most commodities they investigated. The Boards findings are perhaps best expressed in its own words from the Final Report:

> It is now clear that throughout 1973-75 producer marketing boards in Canada contributed substantially to increased food prices. Portions of those increases were often unwarranted in the food price circumstances pertaining to that period.

> As a consequence of all these factors, including the availability of reasonable alternatives, the Board has concluded that the Marketing Board approach to monopolistic supply management has become an inappropriate instrument for dealing with legitimate producer concerns. Its costs exceed its benefits, and it is possible to achieve those true benefits through other means. (Food Prices Review Board 1976, p. 45).

A few paragraphs earlier, the Board also noted "Despite strong arguments against the marketing board concept, federal and provincial government policies continued to promote and protect their continued and expanded operations throughout the 1973-75 period." (Food Prices Review Board 1976, p. 44)

Several efforts were made to challenge these findings of the Board. Farm organizations and Ministers of Agriculture chastised the Board and its staff for their prejudice, incomplete and biased research, unwarranted conclusions, and unrelenting attack on marketing boards; i.e., the Board was displaying unmitigated irreverence. The National Farm Products Marketing Council produced a rebuttal of the first Egg Report but, to this day, that rebuttal has not been made public nor have any other documents refuting the Board's findings. It is not inaccurate to say that events which unfolded during the life of the Board, and since, substantiate most of the findings of the FPRB's analysis. Significantly, there has not been any economic evidence produced to refute the Board's major findings despite the serious accusations that are still circulating. The Board research, from an economic standpoint, has stood the test of time.

Martin and Warley

In a 1978 paper, in the American Journal of Agricultural Economics, the results of a statistical analysis of board effects is reported. The researchers tested the hypothesis that Canadian marketing boards had successfully reduced market instability on four market variables -- industry output, producer price, industry gross revenue, and consumer price -- on five commodities -- pork, tobacco, chicken broilers, turkeys and eggs. Means and variances of the variables were compared before and after control. Although their results were not definitive in terms of each of the particular tests, the results certainly could not lead one to the conclusion that boards had unequivocally stabilized conditions for the commodities. One of their observations was "... because we would argue that if marketing boards do not deliver stabilization benefits that are unequivocal, large, and widely distributed, then, at a minimum, society should avoid over-valuing this aspect of the case for boards and their practices."[2] Their closing statement is even more revealing:

> The tradeoff between stabilization benefits that seem 'spotty' and uncertain at best, and the demonstrable worsening of competitive efficiency and impairment of equity that are attributable to the supply management boards does not strike one as being immediately favorable to Canadian society at large, or ultimately, to Canadian farmers themselves. (Martin, Warley 1978, p. 883).

The Center for Studies on Inflation and Productivity

In an address to the National Dairy Council in September 1978, Mr. R.C. Douglas, Executive Director of the short-lived CSIP outlined some concerns on milk policy in Canada. A supplemental note issued in Decmeber, 1978 detailed the Centres concerns. This analysis is particularly significant because the research was done by an economist who had had extensive, high-level experience with federal dairy policy, including

---

2 A similar analysis undertaken by this author on poultry products in 1974 produced similar results. However, the Martin and Warley analysis is more credible because it encompasses the period of tightened poultry regulation after 1973.

several years of directing research on policy matters in Agriculture Canada. The results could hardly be rejected as academic, hasty, superficial, or as is common in bureaucratic vernacular, "missing the nuances." These results represent one of the most thorough economic analyses of a very complex and significant public program currently available in economic literature.

The study commented and produced evidence on three general areas:

1. Basic performance norms.

The level of technology and scale of the average dairy farm in Canada lags far behind that existing in neighbouring states in the U.S. This lag results in lower real productivity, lower incomes to labour and capital, and greater amounts of capital tied up in the industry than is necessary. (p. 9)

2. Basic resource misallocation.

It is shown how, at the margin, reduction in milk production in Canada equivalent to 1.0 million cwt. of milk could:

- increase returns to all dairy farmers by $5.1 million
- reduce federal subsidies by $79.8 million
- create losses in revenue to processors and transporters of $58.2 million
- credit Canadian tax payers a net amount of $20 million, implying "... all of those groups could be paid not to produce and the country would be better off." (pp. 20,21)

3. Pricing inefficiency.

The pricing policy of the CDC established support prices on butter and skim powder and removes these products from the market at fixed prices. This "biases the utilization of milk towards the production of the products with the lowest market value and poorest market prospects," thereby aggravating an already excess supply situation.

Also, the pricing policy encourages milk shipment instead of cream shipment, which further aggravates the skim power surplus problem.

All milk producers could benefit—or remain as well off—if a premium of up to $3.00 per cwt. were to be offered

208

to producers who switched from milk shipping to on-farm cream separation and farm feeding of skim powder. (p. 27)

In October of 1978, the Dairy Farmers of Canada countered Mr. Douglas' arguments with one economic observation, that elimination of the skim powder exports would cost the economy the loss of "industrial activity at farm, processing and farm supply levels in the amount of $452 million." The rebuttal also argued that dairy production is part of social fabric of the areas where milk is produced, and that reductions in milk production would both reduce farmer numbers and alter rural communities.

In April of 1978, the following observations were picked up in an editorial (Cattlement 1978): the federal subsidized cost of the Canadian Dairy Commission in 1977-78 was about $9,500 per dairy farmer. The total amount of transfer to industrial milk farmers if a very conservative estimate of consumer costs were included would be about $15,000 per dairy farmer or $33 per Canadian. These estimates were checked with the Canadian Dairy Commission and were not rejected as inaccurate. There are significant and growing economic problems and high costs associated with market regulation in the industrial milk sector but the regulation continues.

British Columbia Select Standing Committee on Agriculture

The most recent literature on boards is a six volume set of reports completed for the Standing Committee appointed in 1977 to study the British Columbia food industry (British Columbia Select Standing Committee on Agriculture 1978, 1979). The reports are staff studies and working papers more than reports from the Committee. Although they are of varied quality and tend not to reach conclusions on sensitive areas, they do provide some useful up-to-date information. For example, the Reports point out that 1977 British Columbia quota values were as follows:

Milk - $75 per pound (per day; a 50 cow herd would require 3,000 pounds of quota in British Columbia).

Eggs - $800 per case (per week; average quota size would be about 144 cases).

Broilers - $5-6 per bird (per 11 week cycle; average size would be about 25,000 birds).

The reports show that, in British Colubia, prices of many farm products have been stabilized, farm incomes have risen dramatically, and the size and ownership of production units

209

have remained in the small, family classification. But the reports also show prices higher than in Washington, and many sources of production, pricing and market inefficiencies in the tightly regulated commodities. Finally, the reports brought us the quote at the beginning of this paper. The quote was used not only because it represents an irrelevance and irreverance, but because, except under very stringent assumptions, it is wrong. The statement is irrelevant because quotas are required to make a supply management system work; it is irreverant because it is believed that supply management will improve producer returns; it is wrong unless it is assumed that the production function is of a very peculiar nature and that the purest of purely competitive conditions exist; and it is wrong because whatever captialization does occur may take years, thus generating "short-term" excess returns. There is, however, a great deal of useful economic evidence contained in these reports.

To conclude this section, I will posit my own summary of the economic information and make two addition brief points.

1. Price Stability and Price Performance over time. In the tightly regulated commodities the evidence in the future should increasingly show that reductions in short-run price instability have occurred. However, the evidence available now shows that during the past several years, the supply managed commodities have performed no better, and sometimes worse, than unregulated commodities. The differences lie in how the changes are distributed over time.

2. Farmer Security. There is evolving from boards an increased level of security in pricing and decision making by farmers in relation to market uncertainties, but this is being accomplished at present in many cases at a considerable cost to consumers in terms of price, a cost to trade in the loss of sales, and a cost to the treasury in the case of dairy products.

3. Market Insecurity vs. Bureaucratic Uncertainty. Some, and in certain cases a significant amount, of the reduction in market uncertainty is replaced by bureaucratically or politically induced uncertainty. This very real form of producer uncertainty is extremely difficult to deal with.
Examples: quota changes in eggs 1974, 1975
          quota changes in milk 1975, 1976
          levy changes in milk 1975, 1976, 1977
          CWB quota changes in rapeseed August 1978
          CWB quota changes in feed grains April 1979

210

4. There are large numbers of farmers, earning very much
larger returns to their resources than would be the case
in the absence of regulation; the incidence of abnormal
profits almost certainly increases with size of operation.

5. The existing structure of supply management boards removes important sources of resource adjustment within
firms, and between firms and between regions. This absence
of adjustment mechanisms is a fundamental economic weakness of regulatory programs and has significant long-run
consequences.

These conclusions, unsupported and undeveloped here because of space limitations, lead to two very important economic
consequences of tight regulation as we now know it. These are
the "second generation effects" and the "indirect" or vertical
effects.

Second Generation Effects

This term refers to the impacts of regulation which show
up only after significant resource adjustment has occurred in
response to regulatory activity. They may be "second-best"
solutions or they may be second-worst solutions. In economic
terminology they may be considered "long-run resource misallocation problems" but that description is not very enlightening.
The term also relates to the bureaucratization effects which
necessarily accompany regulation. I am coming to believe (hy-
pothesize) that these effects may be more important to overall
economic performance of boards than the short-run, price raising
impacts that are the subject of most economic analysis.

Because the Canadian Wheat Board has been regulating the
grain trade for over a human generation, examples are most
easily found there:

- the CWB emphasis on wheat during the 1940's, 1950's and
  1960's meant that feed grains, especially barley, was
  relatively ignored. Its production was partly discour-
  aged, it was not "marketed," and the absence of an active
  grain trade meant that when wheat surpluses hit in 1968,
  a longer (and more expensive) adjustment into alternative
  crops was required. It does not require much missed opportunity in western Canadian grains to total $100 mil-
  lion in lost revenue.

- quotas on grain movements, admittedly partly a consequence of an inadequate transportation system which itself is a regulatory problem, tend to encourage summer-
  fallow, discourage chemical and fertilizer use, and alter

cropping patterns. To illustrate the scope of implications of second generation effects, it is pointed out that there is a growing problem in Saskatchewan related to summerfallowing. Some Saskatchewan land may have been irreversibly damaged. It would not be correct to attribut the problem solely to quota policy. But if it is even a contributor the consequences are significant.

- highly productive areas of the prairies are forced to produce special crops, sometimes livestock, and make other adjustments in order to move all their production.

Important as these iluustrative "second generation effects" may be, it should be noted that the western grains economy, because of its huge net export position, has had to remain internationally competitive. This pressure does not exist at present in the supply managed commodities. The obvious source of these effects in dairy and poultry is the freezing of production patterns across the country, the limitations on production by producer quotas, and the cost-of-production pricing procedures -- i.e., the lack of economic adjustment mechanisms. These changes cannot be measured directly because they are a form of opportunity cost and they will accrue over a considerable time period. They imply, however, greater upward pressure on prices, reducing international competitiveness, and increasing costs of exiting from supply management if and when that happens.

This raises the last point on second generation effects: the longer a program is in effect, the more likely that it will be difficult to adjust out of the program. This is so because institutions and procedures necessarily adjust around the program. A very real example of this is the effort to alter negotiable quotas now that they are in place and represent real costs to some farmers. Quota values can be reduced and eliminated, but at a capital loss to some farmers. The Manitoba government attempted to eliminate quota values on its regulated commodities over the period 1972-76. The efforts to accomplish this objective were extremely unpopular among farmers and that particular government is no longer in office.

Indirect Effects

The indirect or vertical effects of boards relate to the impact that regulation has at points in the marketing system before or after the actual point of control. They may be intended or unintended; my hypothesis is that in many instances the unintended (and unknown) benefits accruing to suppliers, processors and retailers may be as great or greater than those realized by the producers for whom control was designed.

This hypothesis is based upon the argument that the reduction in competition which occurs when price and quantity controls are established, and particularly when border controls are imposed, also reduces competition for other participants. Import and interregional competition have been effective regulators of many food industry participants, board and border controls alter the nature of this competition. In addition, they may remove some of the motivation to compete within the region. With the cost-pass-through procedures employed by the supply management boards, producers have less motivation to put downward pressure on input prices. In the highly concentrated markets at both ends of the farm sector, reduced competition would be expected to alter business behavior in the direction of greater profits and/or lower productivity.

Empirical evidence on this hypothesis is sketchy but some work is underway. Funk and Rice (1978) argued that "The most obvious effect of a supply management marketing board on agribusiness is a transfer of market power from agribusiness sectors to the production sector," but went on to show that hatcheries and feed companies reported higher margins (and pleasure) with boards in Ontario while poultry processors experienced lower margins and dissatisfaction. My own analysis indicates processor and retail margins have risen significantly since the national chicken agency became a nearer reality last year. My feeling is that Funk and Rice did not look far enough; one of their colleagues at Guelph and myself are pursuing this question independently.

The reason for raising these points is to focus on two important aspects of the economic consequences of boards which we have tended to overlook. In addition, to the extent that they are (presumably) unintended impacts, which unfavourably affect the structure, conduct and performance of other important parts of the food industry, they may represent significant information in policy making. Provided more complete information on the food industry including non-producer board effects, perhaps policy makers and farmers would be more inclined to entertain options for derigidifying the existing board structure in agriculture.

But perhaps not; Mr. Whelan has long been a vocal opponent of the kind of economic evidence summarized above. His eloquence appeared in print again in February, 1979: "Critics that charge that marketing boards are inefficient are mischievous and devilish or outright liars." (CP February 17, 1979). The next section examines some of the basis of this assessment.

MARKETING BOARDS IN A POLITICAL AND
ORGANIZATIONAL SETTING

In the second section of this paper, the case was made that marketing board evolution in recent years, namely the extension of regulation and rigidification of significant portions of primary food production, appears to defy the logic of the times. The section above indicates that economic logic and economic evidence generally run contrary to the particular kind of board development that we have seen. But this form of regulation has prospered, it has tightened, and the public and consumer costs of broad activity have increased. What then is required to explain these apparent contradictions?

In a work I think the answer can be stated as - politics. On the surface it appears that the farm lobby has been extremely effective in establishing its case with legislatures, Parliament, and Senate, and other points of impact in the political process. Farmers and farm organizations have increasingly won their battles despite declining actual and relative numbers in a head count. But this is a very superficial explanation of the growth of board activity. The real causes are found partly in the sociology of nations which produces strong sympathy for the farm sector - "agrarian fundamentalism." The search for the origins of this phenomenon is left to the Sociologists and Political Scientists, but we have our share of it in Canada. What I want to attempt, however, is to identify a number of factors from events which have culminated to produce the most active period in agricultural legislation that this nation has experienced. The long development which preceded this section had a purpose: most of these forces have already been mentioned.

Food Price Experience in the 1970's

Farm and food prices in this decade have been dynamic. We have gone from depressed farm prices and incomes in 1969-71 to unprecedented farm prices in 1974-75, and unprecedented food price increases in 1978. These events have fostered, rather than damaged, marketing boards. There are several reasons for this but the predominant reason lies in public reaction to prices and price movements.

To a very significant degree it is price changes which generate public reaction and market noise, rather than price levels as implied by economic performance norms. Consumers, politicians, the media and farmers react when prices change rapidly irrespective of the economic justification for the change. Conversely, there appears to be a quiet acceptance of prices which are known to be too high or too low in economic terms, as long as they remain stable or change at a predictable rate.[3]

Examples are not difficult to find of industrial and manufactured goods, and private and public services which may not meet economic criteria for being at justifiable levels, but which receive little public attention. Similarly, inflation watching and anti-inflation measures are concerned with changes in prices, not with the question of how appropriate price levels are before or after the change.

Enter the regulatory marketing boards. Once past the initial period of adjustment (to higher, more "acceptable" prices), given enough powers, a board can deliver controlled and predictable rates of price increase. Those variable food prices which create problems for consumers when they are rising, and farmers when they are falling, cease to be a problem. Given proper management of the boards, the value of stability will take over and it will be forgotten that prices are too high. This has long gone on in fluid milk (until public hearings became real sources of challenge to regulation[4]); it appears to have occurred in eggs; it appears to be occurring in cheese, butter and other manufactured dairy products.

Growing Pressures to Reduce Government

The 1970's have also been characterized by efforts to arrest the growth of government. Farmers typically have attempted to keep government out of their businesses. Marketing boards, therefore, are the ideal compromise:

Indeed, if programs accomplish the objectives as set out below, they can be considered to be a form of government-sanctioned, producer-administered transfer payment from other affected economic groups to producers. These characteristics, i.e., their relative independence in operation and their lack of dependence on public funds, make them particularly attractive to producers and governments, and undoubtedly account for much of their recent growth in

3 If this proposition is true, again we have a problem with the application of economics to the food industry. Most economists want more, rather than less, competition. But more competition will definitely create some price instability.
4 In Manitoba the process of public hearings on fluid milk pricing will likely soon be replaced by a process of indexing because farmers, the board, bureaucrats, and the Min. of Agriculture find the public debate on price increases unsettling and too "public." This is a natural evolution in the process of public accountability to anyone who understands the public decision-making process.

Canada. (Loyns 1971, p. 38).

Similarly "This concept (direct income transfer to farmers), which implies farmers being dependent on government subsidies, is repugnant to many farmers." (Lane and MacGregor 1979, p. 11). Farmers, like other businessmen, find free enterprise transfers acceptable and government transfers unacceptable.

Anti-inflation Program

There is no need to review the elements of the anti-inflation program initiated in 1975. One aspect was removing structural rigidities in the Canadian economy. While marketing boards would qualify as a government induced market structure rigidity, this aspect of the anti-inflation policy was basically ignored in every area of the Canadian economy. Consequently, to be consistent, it should not apply to marketing boards.

A far more important element which was invoked was price controls, basically a cost-pass-through approach subject to profit and productivity tests. Except for the establishment of threshold profit levels and previous price levels, the question whether precontrol prices were too high or too low did not enter the control mechanisms. In this context, again marketing boards become the model for control. The mechanisms for achieving control within the supply management boards were largely, if not fully, consistent with the efforts of AIB guidelines on prices, and would have been whether or not the boards were scrutinized by AIB. Consequently, this major piece of public policy justified, rather than contradicted, the institution of price regulating marketing boards.

The Federal Minister of Agriculture

When the federal election was called, Mr. Whelan had occupied his Cabinet portfolio in Agriculture for seven years, longer than any other in the Trudeau Cabinet. Mr. Whelan was not only a knowledgeable and staunch defender of agricultural interests, he was a dogmatic defender and promoter of marketing boards. His view of the correct structure for the farm industry was more marketing board control, and actively promoted supply management in, among others, the beef sector. His power base was Ontario, and to a lesser extent Quebec, where import restrictions and provincial self-sufficiency in farm products has considerably political appeal. He was also a skillful power broker in an important area where federal influence was being extended. The Federal Minister of Agriculture, therefore, became a very important catalyst for the developments in market regulation that have been outlined.

216

It would, however, be incorrect to attribute too much
credit for these developments to the person because a Minister
of the Crown does serve at the pleasure of the Prime Minister:
that Mr. Whelan remained in the Agriculture portfolio for seven
years was not entirely, perhaps not even primarily, of his
doing. The influence of the Minister of Agriculture, therefore,
must be viewed in relation to the next point.

Influence of the Federal Cabinet

There are a number of points which might be made here, and
naturally, this factor would not explain the willingness of
provinces to extend board activities. However, three points
will be made which are important to understanding the present
status of marketing boards in Canada. First, it is generally
accepted that the Trudeau era was one of substantially increased Cabinet power and decision-making. Therefore, the growth and activities of marketing boards have explicitly or implicitly or implicitly been sanctioned by the federal Cabinet.
This includes certain activities of provincial boards which may
have been contrary to federal powers but where the federal
government did not choose to intervene. Second, the composition
of the Cabinet, dominated by eastern Canadian members and
heavily influenced by Quebec interests, predictably leaned in
the direction of market regulation which benefited eastern farmers. This is particularly true in dairy and eggs, and it accounts for some of the changes which were made in domestic feed
grain policy. Finally, and probably most significantly, there
was the policy decision made by the Federal Government sometime
in the early 1970's to assure that a greater share of the national pie should be received by the farm sector. This decision likely will not be documented until some of the senior
politicians or bureaucrats write their memoirs but if there was
a policy decision of this sort, it would explain a great deal
of what followed in all agricultural policy and programs at the
federal level in the 1970's.

It is therefore, my basic hypothesis that the growth of
marketing boards, their extension of powers, their operation,
and their relative insulation from adverse economic findings
have to be viewed in this perspective. They have become much
more political instruments for accomplishing income transfer
from other sectors to farmers, and for shifting the balance of
market power more favorably to the farm sector. The role of
boards in the market and the real market functions that boards
perform have become, in the eyes of farmers, boards administrators, farm organizations and the legislatures which permit them
to operate, at best, secondary considerations. I believe it is
much more accurate to describe boards in the present environment

as end in themselves rather than mechanisms for accomplishing certain ends, particularly those marketing ends in which this audience may be most interested. If this hypothesis is valid, then the economic analysis which is applied to boards becomes a palliative for traditional or pure economists, a minor irritant for politicians and farm lobbyists, but it is largely irrelevant as a diagnostic or prescriptive tool. Indeed, some of the analysis serves only to indicate those sensitive areas where marginal changes should be made in order to improve the manner in which boards are seen to be operating. In addition, if the hypothesis is valid, it serves to show how boards have become part of each of the political and belief sets in our contemporary policy instruments. To continually produce economic evidence to illustrate the costs and inefficiencies associated with these instruments acquires, for those holding the beliefs and those who are part of the political establishment, a distinct flavor of irreverence. The gap between economists and those who hold the power in these organizations is large.

The foregoing discussion provides, in my opinion, sufficient reason for the gap to exist between economists and board proponents. But there are two more that require some discussion. The first of these relates to the lack of economic analysis generated by the boards themselves. This creates an inability for economists on the outside to communicate on professional matters with anyone in boards. It is not the case that many of the important boards do not employ economists; in fact there are many economists that work for or close to these organizations. They are, however, much more in operational and management advisor positions than creators of hard economic information, particularly of the public type. In discussing this point recently with a colleague, he described the role of economists within boards as that of the "strategizer." My understanding of the situation would confirm that description as generally accurate.[5]

The second reason for a widening gap between economists and board proponents is far more important and lies directly within the purview of economists themselves; we can do something about this one. It has much more to do with what economists are not doing, than what they are doing on marketing boards. It is a fair observation to state that a relatively large amount of analysis has been done on boards but very little

---

5 It might be noted that our colleagues in the Business Marketing side have even less professional influence on boards than economists. With the exception of advertising campaigns which appear to be increasing in popularity but which appear to have their origins in "Bay Street," it is difficult to find people of this discipline, much less their influence, on marketing board staffs.

has been done on other sources of market power in the food industry, or in fact in other important areas of the Canadian
economy. For example, until Mallen's research on concentration
in food retailing (1976) was published by the Food Prices Review Board, there were only isolated pieces of research on food
retailing. Mallen's study, as significant a contribution as it
is, was as the title states - preliminary. Does the lack of
interest in this $25 billion industry suggest that there are no
problems of structure, conduct and performance? Mallen's results would hardly permit a strong affirmative response to that
question. Similarly, food processing and manufacturing are
known to be highly concentrated in areas, to have significant
levels of "effective protection" from tariffs, and to have significant productivity difficulties in some areas. But are economists, either private or public, looking at these situations?
Judging from the body of literature, the answer would be-not
very actively. Or, there is currently a trial underway in Calgary in which six fertilizer firms are accused of price raising
over the period 1969-1976. Fertilizer (and chemicals which are
even more concentrated and, since 1977, have been protected by
tighter border controls than exist for turkeys or eggs) are important inputs to the modern food production process. They are
ordinary industrial industries which generally have received
little attention from economists in Canada. And the list could
go on, into the labor market, financial institutions, public
utilities and so on. Are pricing arrangements, prices and resource allocations appropriate in these areas or have we simply
failed to consider them? Without answers to these questions,
the criticisms that economists level on marketing boards irrespective of their analytic justification, are seen to be unbalanced and lacking somewhat in credibility. The Food Prices Review Board acknowledged this situation in its Final Report:

> The Board particularly regretted that the abrupt termina-
> tion of its mandate prevented it from making greater pro-
> gress in this key area, particularly with respect to the
> food processing and retailing sectors in which too little
> solid work has been carried out. (1976, p. 39).

CONCLUSION

There is considerably danger that the intent of this paper
may be misinterpreted. What has been attempted is an interpretation of how we arrived at our present status in marketing
board organization in Canada, and an effort to show how economic analysis has severe limitations in its policy prescriptive
application. The intent is not to vindicate the public policy
approach which adds structural rigidities and creates price and
efficiency problems at a time in Canadian economic history when

we must move in another direction if the health of the economy
is to be maintained. Nor is it to vindicate creation of additional economic power bases. It is, however, to suggest that
fine tuning economic analysis and rediscovering the same wheel
cannot be expected to contribute much new information. And it
is to urge colleauges and analysts to devote a much greater
share of their time to other problems of economic structure and
performance which, in the end, are of far greater importance
than are marketing boards. The British Columbia Select Standing Committee provides the last word:

> Supply Control marketing boards cannot be fairly rejected
> unless there is to be a thorough revamping of commercial
> powers in business, professional, and union monopolies
> elsewhere in Canadian Society.

REFERENCES

Agriculture Canada, Marketing Board Statistics, Canada, 1976-77.

British Columbia Select Standing Committee on Agricultre (1978,
    1979), (i) Supply Management and Quota Values in Primary
    Agriculture; (ii) The British Columbia Milk Boards; and (iii)
    Marketing Boards in British Columbia, Volumes I, II, III, IV.

Cattlemen, the Beef Magazine (1978), Editorial (May).

Centre for Studies on Inflation and Productivity (1978), Long
    Term Dairy Policy: Some Queries, (December).

Consumer Research Council (1974), A Report on Consumer Interest
    in Marketing Boards, prepared by J.D. Forbes et al, 1 (Sept-
    ember).

Department of Consumer and Corporate Affairs (1978), Applica-
    tion of Competition Policy to the Food and Agriculture Sec-
    tor, Working Paper No. 2, (July).

Federal Task Force on Agriculture, Canadian Agriculture in the
    Seventies, Ch. 12.

Food Prices Review Board (1976), Final Report, (February).

Funk, T.F. and M.J. Rice (1978), "Effects of Marketing Boards
    on the Agribusiness Sector," American Journal of Agriculture
    Economies, (August).

Grubel, H.G. and R.W. Schwindt (1977), The Real Cost of the B.C.
    Milk Board, The Fraser Institute

Hiscocks, G. (1972), "Theory and Evolution of Agriculture Market Regulation in Canada," in Market Regulation in Canadian Agriculture, Department of Agricultural Economics, University of Manitoba, Occasional Series, No. 3, (May).

Lane, S.H. and M.A. MacGregor (1979), Quotas and Quota Values, School of Agricultural Economics and Rural Extension, University of Guelph, (February).

Loyns, R.M.A. (1971), "A Comparison of Legislative Aspects of Agricultural Market Regulation in Canada and the U.S.," Canadian Journal of Agricultural Economics, 19 (July).

Mallen, B. (1976), A Preliminary Paper on the Levels, Causes and Effects of Economic Concentration in the Canadian Retail Trade: A Study of Supermarket Market Power, Prepared for the Food Prices Review Board, (January).

Martin, L.J. and T.K. Warley (1978), "The Role of Marketing Boards in Stabilizing Commodity Markets," American Journal of Agricultural Economics, (August).

Veeman, M.M. and R.M.A. Loyns (1979), "Agricultural Marketing Boards in Canada," Agricultural Marketing Boards - An Inter - national Perspective, Ballinger Press.

APPENDIX I: PRODUCTS UNDER MARKETING

BOARD JURISDICTION, CANADA, 1976-77

Province	Number of Boards	Products
British Columbia	10	Grains, tree fruits, cranberries, grapes for processing, mushrooms, vegetables, sheep and wool, dairy products, broilers, turkeys and eggs
Alberta	7(+1)	Grains, potatoes. fresh and processing vegetables, cattle, sheep and wool, hogs, dairy products, broilers, turkeys, eggs and fowl
Saskatchewan	6	Grains, hogs, sheep and wool, dairy products, broilers, turkeys and eggs
Manitoba	9	Grains, feed grains and black beans, potatoes and root crops (fresh and for seed), hogs, dairy products, broilers, turkeys, eggs and honey
Ontario	22	Winter wheat, soybeans, seed corn, apples, fresh fruit, tender fruit for processing; grapes (fresh and for processing), asparagus, dry beans, tomato seedling plants, greenhouse vegetables, potatoes for processing, vegetables for processing, Burley and flue-cured tobacco, hogs, dairy products, broilers, turkeys and eggs
Quebec	25	Blueberries, tomatoes, tobacco (cigar, pipe and flue-cured), dairy products, broilers and turkeys, eggs, maple products and wood
New Brunswick	10	Apples, bedding plants, hogs, dairy products, broilers, turkeys, eggs and wood
Nova Scotia	8	Wheat, tobacco, hogs, dairy products, broilers, turkeys, eggs, pullets and wool
Prince Edward Island	6	Potatoes, turnips, tobacco, pedigreed seed, hogs, dairy products and eggs
Newfoundland	1	Eggs

(Continued)

Interprovincial or National

Canadian Wheat Board (CWB)	Wheat, oats, barley for exports (deliveries of rye, rapeseed, flax)
Canadian Dairy Commission (CDC)	Industrial milk and cream
Canadian Egg Marketing Agency (CEMA)	All eggs nationally
Canadian Turkey Marketing Agency (CTMA)	All turkeys nationally
Freshwater Fish Marketing Corporation	Fish, designated freshwater area
Salt Fish Marketing Corporation	Fish, designated salt water area

APPENDIX II: PRODUCERS' RECEIPTS THROUGH MARKETING BOARDS AS A PERCENTAGE

OF FARM CASH RECEIPTS BY COMMODITY, 1975-76 AND 1976-77

Commodity	1975-7[a]			1976-77		
	Farm Cash Receipts	Producers' Receipts Through Marketing Boards		Farm Cash Receipts	Producers' Receipts Through Marketing Boards	
		Value	Percentage		Value	Percentage
	- '000 $ -			- '000 $ -		
Grains[b]	3,325,109	2,977,343	90	3,039,821	2,670,450	88
Oilseeds	387,426	69,600	18	380,594	71,205	19
Fruit	130,497	69,955	54	136,294	79,240	58
Vegetables[c]	407,398	110,968	27	457,704	116,989	26
Cattle and calves	1,817,975	nil	nil	1,963,335	nil	nil
Hogs	886,471	583,363	66	840,166	532,434	63
Dairy Products[d]	1,603,056	1,603,056	100	1,578,048	1,578,048	100
Poultry	419,353	372,123	89	479,547	393,145	82
Eggs[e]	260,165	197,879	76	282,508	225,807	80
Others	791,029	290,714	37	817,019	267,998	33
Total[e]	10,028,479	6,275,001	63	9,975,026	5,935,316	60

[a]Revised

[b]Includes wheat, oats, barley, rye, corn. Canadian Wheat Board participation payments, cash advances and deferred grain receipts.

[c]Includes potatoes.

[d]Includes dairy supplementary payments.

[e]Newfoundland not included.

Source: Agriculture Canada.

THE LAW AND CANADIAN CONSUMERS[1]

J.D. Forbes, The University of British Columbia

ABSTRACT

Consumer law in Canada comprises the common law, statutes, statute law and administrative and regulatory policies and decisions. This body of law evolves in the Canadian political process where consumer interests are balanced with other interests to provide laws in the area of buyer-seller contracts, sales of goods, safety, health and information, trade practices, administrative and regulatory matters, and access and use of the law. Consumers and similar large, latent interest groups have difficulties in having their interests represented in the political process because of problems of organizing and financing these activities. The cases of food policy and competition legislation illustrate the interaction of consumer interests and those of smaller, more powerful interests in the Canadian political process. Consumers have had some successes and some failures in affecting the expansion of consumer law in that pluralistic system.

Au Canada, la loi des consommateurs comprend le droit coutumier, les statuts, la loi écrite et les politiques et décisions administratives et régulatrices. Ce corps de loi évolue dans le processus politique canadien où les intérêts des consommateurs sont contrepeses avec d'autre intérêts, afin de fournir des lois sur les contrats entre acheteurs ét vendeurs, sur la vent des marchandises, sur la sécurité, la santé et l'information, sur les usages commerciaux, sur les questions administratives et régulatrices

[1]The author wishes to thank Susan Burns and S.M. Oberg for their conceptual and editorial contributions to this paper. The research was partially funded by grants from Consumer and Corporate Affairs Canada in 1976 and 1977 (Forbes and Oberg).

et sur l'accès et l'usage de la loi. Les consommateurs et
les grands groupes latents similaires ont de la difficulté à
faire représenter leurs intérêts auprès du processus
politique à cause des problèmes de financement et d'
organisation qu'occasionnent ces activités. Les cas de la
politique sur la nourriture et de la législation sur la
compétition illustrent l'interaction des intérêts des
consommateurs et ceux des interets de groupes moins grands
mais plus puissants auprès du processus politique canadien
Les consommateurs ont remporté quelques succès et quelques
échecs dans l'affectation de l'extension de la loi du
consommateur dans ce système pluraliste.

INTRODUCTION

The rights and the responsibilities of Canadian
consumers are, in large degree, set out in the law affecting
these activities. In recent years consumer protection
under the law has expanded significantly. However, life
as a consumer is not a constant legal battle. Consumers
develop expectations of fairness and justice in the marketplace; sellers learn what is expected of them and the
majority of our transactions take place well within the
range of acceptable legal bahavior. The impetus for new
laws or the modification of old laws takes place at the
margin where conflict arises between consumers and businesses
and governments.

The purpose of this paper is to discuss the major areas
of law affecting consumers in Canada and to describe and
analyze the political process in changing these laws.
Finally, we provide a brief evaluation of the progress of
consumer law in Canada and of the political process using
two examples of that process, food policy and competition
policy.

CONSUMER LAW

Consumer law is an all encompassing term which we have
chosen to represent the laws which have an effect on
consumers. They are legion, they affect every facet of our
activities as a consumer, and what will emerge in this
section is the fact that very often we are unaware of our

rights as consumers and the way in which these rights are guaranteed on the one hand and the ease with which they are eroded on the other.

We have classified law into four components: the common law, statutes, statute law, and administrative and regulatory policies and decisions. The common law is a body of judicial decisions concerning acceptable and correct behavior between parties to an action. It is not set out by the legislatures but builds up through usage and precedent decided by the courts. This particular law is also referred to to as the British Common Law and is generally in use only in North America and the British Commonwealth. In Quebec, as in most of the world outside North America and the Commonwealth, the legal system operates under civil law. In this system all law is codified and very little is left to judicial inter- pretation. Because language, at its best, is ambiguous, there is some judicial interpretation, but any major change to laws in the civil system has to be enacted by legislatures. We devote our time in this paper to describing the common law although there are interesting developments taking place in Quebec in the area as this paper is being written (Quebec Consumer Protection Act 1978).

Where there is no precedent with common law or when legislatures want to change or direct people's behaviour, they have enacted statutes. These statutes may enable completely new types of behaviour, or alter the direction of societies' activities, or may be enacted to change the common law more rapidly than the Courts have seen fit to do. The statutes may also be used to fill in the interstitial areas in the law where the Courts have not chosen to rule.

Statute law is the term used to describe judicial interpretation of statutes. No one really can be certain about the meaning of a law until it has had judicial interpretation, until it has been tested in the Courts. Statutes, because of their normative effect in guiding behaviour, often are interpreted and followed in ways which are assumed to be correct only to have a judicial interpretation dramatically change such behaviour when finally tested in the Courts (Kane, p.2-5).

Administrative and regulatory policies and decisions
is a separate classification we have given to the quasi-
legal and de facto effects of the activities of regulatory
agencies on consumers and their rights. In order to over-
rule or change these decisions it is often necessary to
appeal to the provincial or federal cabinet since there is
no avenue of appeal except to the body itself; this is the
regulatory problem of being judge and juror in the same
action. Activities of the Canadian Transport Commission,
the Canadian Radio and Television Commission, the National
Farm Products Marketing Council, the National Energy Board,
and a host of other regulatory bodies, result in de facto
definition of rights and prescription of rules of behaviour
and are most often the actual consequence of much regulatory
legislation in Canada.

We have grouped the major areas affecting consumers
under seven different headings which we will outline below.
To the lawyer and the knowledgeable layman it will immediately
be apparent that most of the headings are not composed solely
of any one of the four classifications of laws just presented.
Rather, while they may each have evolved from the common law
or from statutes, there is usually a mixture of two or more
of these types in their present form.

The Law of Contract

When we offer to buy and someone offers to sell a good
or service, we have entered into a contractual relationship.
These relationships have been important to consumers over
the years and have been the subject of the development of a
large body of common law as well as the development of
statutes which have changed the buyer-seller relationships
as the complexity of consuming activites expands.

Attitudes reflecting the prevailing philosophy of laissez-
faire of the 19th century held that no person would enter into
a contract that was to their disadvantage. However, as we
move into the 1980's, where one party to a contract for the
supply of goods may be a corporate body whose legal experts
have drawn up contracts in their own favour and the individual
on the other side of the contract may be ignorant of his rights
and sign them away, governments have developed laws of contract
more in line with the realities of our complex marketplace.
Many of these changes are of recent vintage and include legislation on door-to-door selling, undue influence by knowledgeable sellers, unequal bargaining power, fraud, and unconscion-

able contract terms and prices (B.C. Consumer Protection Act, p.5).

Sales of Goods Acts

Sales of Goods Acts make explicit the conditions attached to contracts between buyers and sellers of goods and services. They cover both written and oral contracts, and contain two fundamental conditions of sale: the implied fitness of goods or services for their intended purpose when the buyer can see the good or evaluate service at the time of sale and goods purchased by description in catalogues and advertisements must live up to the description by which they are sold. Each Canadian province and each state in the United States has its own sale of goods act but the basic provisions are similar.

Under this heading come the many laws affecting warranties and guarantees, as well as some of the false and misleading advertising statutes which are generally classified under trade practices but have more to do with truth about the purpose and quality of goods sold. Many legislative changes have occurred in the past ten years in most Canadian provinces to expand requirements for more accurate descriptions of goods and the purposes for which they are intended and to delineate more precisely the nature of warranties and guarantees. (For example, Saskatchewan, Sales of Goods Act, p.6.) The Canadian Broadcasting Corporation commissioned a compilation of information on laws for a consumer self-help pamphlet which summarizes laws in these first two classifications (Trebilcock 1978).

Safety, Health and Information

There is a wide range of laws affecting the safety, health and the provision of information to consumers. The latter includes packaging and labelling rules and regulations, weights and measures, product use, information and many other administrative requirements which provide information for consumers. Health and safety laws include laws instituted for consumer's safety which have such wide ranging application as the packaging of aerosol sprays, seat belt and construction safety legislation for automobiles, building code regulations, fire regulations and the like. Health legislation, again encompasses a wide ranging set of laws dealing with such things as inspection of food, food establishments and food handlers, human and animal quarantines, medical regulation, drug dispensing activities, and the laws on use of hazardous products.

229

Trade Practices

The term trade practices encompasses a wide range of activities in the marketplace between consumers and sellers.
There are two general areas which are covered by trade practice
laws: unconscionable transactions and false and misleading
representation of products. It is generally believed that
these laws came about as the result of increasingly intense
competition by faceless manufacturers and deterioration of the
close and often personal relationships between buyer and the
local seller. While we believe this is a simplistic analysis
of the problem, there is no doubt that most consumers and business persons welcome many of the major elements of Federal and
Provincial trade practices legislation in Canada; among these
are included false and misleading advertising, price discrimination, bait and switch advertising, selling at above advertised price, and pyramid selling.

Administrative and Regulatory Policies and Decisions

While most of us recognize that there are many regulations
which affect us as consumers, few of us recognize the ubiquity
and degree of regulation. Regulation in the province of
Ontario alone encompassed over 292 different provincial regulatory statutes and the resultant regulating bodies (Bresner
et al 1978). Municipal and federal regulatory activities add
considerably to that number. Public utility commissions, communication and energy boards, professional bodies, agricultural
marketing boards, hospital and health institutions, almost any
facet of consumers' existences are touched in one way or another by a regulatory activity. Table 1 presents an illustrative
listing of the federal regulatory legislation, most of which
have direct consumer effects because of the legal rights which
are granted to the regulators in the administration of these
statutes (Doern 1978, pp.1-34) (Phidd and Doern 1978) (Ruppenthal and Stanbury 1976).

There are serious problems in this particular area of
consumer law in representing the consumer interest to ensure
regulation in the consumer interest. The problem is that the
effect of any specific regulation on an individual consumer
is seldom large. Therefore, an individual has little motivation to make sure their consumer interest is taken into account
in the regulatory process. There is then a continual erosion
in the consumer's position in the law because it is in the
interest of the regulated to have the regulators decide matters
in the regulated's best interests. The regulated devote the
time and resources to influencing the regulators. Individual

TABLE 1

FEDERAL REGULATORY LEGISLATION

Agriculture

Agriculture Products Co-operative
  Marketing Act
Agricultural Products Marketing Act
Agriculture Stabalization Act
Animal Disease and Protection Act
Canada Agricultural Products
  Standards Act
Canada Dairy Products Act
Canada Grains Act ·
Canadian Dairy Commission Act
Canadian Wheat Board Act
Cheese and Cheese Factory
  Improvement Act
Farm Products Marketing Agencies
  Act
Feeds Act
Fertilizers Act
Fruit, Vegetables and Honey Act
Grain Futures Act
Hay and Straw Inspection Act
Inspection and Sale Act
Livestock and Livestock Products
  Act
Livestock Feed Assistance Act
Livestock Shipping Act
Maple Products Industry Act
Milk Test Act
Pest Control Products Act
Plant Quarantine Act
Seeds Act
Western Grain Stabalization Act

Fisheries

Freshwater Fish Marketing Act
Coastal Fisheries Protection Act
Federal Fisheries Act
Fish Inspection Act
Fisheries Prices Support Act
North Pacific Fisheries Convention
  Act
North Pacific Halibut Fisheries
  Convention Act
Northwest Atlantic Fisheries
  Convention Act
Saltfish Act

Communications

Broadcasting Act
Radio Act

Energy

Atomic Energy Control Act
Dominion Water Power Act
National Energy Board Act
Oil and Gas Production and
  Conservation Act
Petroleum Administration Act

Transportation

Aeronautics Act
Atlantic Region Freight Assistance
  Act
Canada Shipping Act
Department of Transport Act
Government Harbours and Piers Act
Harbour Commission Act
Motor Vehicle Transportation Act
National Harbours Board Act
National Transportation Act
Navigable Waters Protection Act
Pilotage Act
Railway Act
Railway Relocation and Crossing Act
St. Lawrence Seaway Authority Act
Transport Act

Financial Institutions and Markets

Bank Act
Canadian and British Insurance
  Companies Act
Foreign Insurance Companies Act
Loan Companies Act
Pension Benefit Standards Act
Trust Companies Act

Environmental Protection

Artic Waters Pollution Prevention
  Act
Canada Water Act
Canada Wildlife Act
Clean Air Act
Environmental Contaminants Act
National Parks Act
Northern Canada Power Commission
  Act
Northern Inland Water Act
Ocean Dumping Control Act
Territorial Lands Act

Health/Safety/Fairness/Information

Cold Storage Act
Consumer Packaging and Labelling Act
Corporations and Labour Unions
  Return Act
Department of National Health and
  Welfare Act
Electricity Inspection Act
Food and Drug Act
Gas Inspection Act
Hazardous Product Act
Heat and Canned Foods Act
Meat Inspection Act
Motor Vehicle Safety Act
Motor Vehicle Tire Safety Act
Narcotic Control Act
National Trade Mark and True Labelling
  Act
Precious Metals Marking Act
Quarantine Act
Radiation Emitting Devices
Textile Labe'ling Act
Weights and Measures Act

Occupational Health/Safety/Fairness

Canada Labour Code
Explosives Act
Fair Wages and Hours of Labour Act

Framework Legislation

Anti Inflation Act
Bankruptcy Act
Canada Business Corporation Act
Canada Corporation Act
Combines Investigation Act
Copyright Act
Criminal Code
Foreign Investment Review Act
Industrial Design Act
Patent Act
Statutory Instruments Act
Trade Marks Act

Source: W.T. Stanbury, Possible Areas of Research: Economic Council of Canada
  Reference on Regulation, Economic Council of Canada, mimeo, July 24,
  1978, Appendix I.

consumers have neither the resources nor the motivation to influence the regulators and, in many cases, the consumer has not
been allowed access to the regulatory process. While on an
individual level any loss in consumer interest and rights may
be small, in the aggregate, over all consumers and over all the
areas of consumer's life which are regulated, consumer rights
have been eroded.

A recent example of the problem can be illustrated with the
advanced booking charter fares decision of the Canadian Transport Commission. The Canadian Transport Commission ruled that
they would not allow low cost advance booking charter fairs
for scheduled Canadian airlines. The only avenue of appeal to
this decision was to the Cabinet. Had the Consumers' Association of Canada not acquired the technical expertise and detailed facts about the situation, and appealed to the Cabinet, who
finally overruled the CTC, consumers would not have had access
to these low cost fares (Consumer Association of Canada 1978).
This type of appeal activity is completely outside of the capabilities of an individual consumer. The whole range of
regulation, its positive and negative affects, and its effects
on the Canadian economy are the subject of a large study now
underway at the Economic Council of Canada (Economic Council
of Canada 1978).

Access and Use of the Law

Finally, if the law is to be effective in defining the
rights of consumers, there must be access to the courts and
effective means of using the law to this end; the right to
standing or locus standi and class actions are the two major
issues in this area.

If an individual is being very specifically damaged, then
that individual has a right to sue for redress in the courts.
However, the complications arise where the interests of
consumers as a whole are prejudiced but no particular individual is being hurt more than any other, and the individual hurt
is small. In this case, we in Canada have to rely on the
Attorney General to sue on behalf of the public. However, it
has often been difficult to prod the Crown into action, especially if the action challenges government policy. Consumers
and consumer groups need to obtain rights to "stand" before
the courts and regulatory bodies to present their cases. While
too technical to discuss here, consumer rights to stand have
been enlarged upon in recent court decisions (Johnson 1975,
pp. 137-160).

Another important tool in using the law to the interest of
consumers is the ability to band together as a group when many

people are damaged or perceive an erosion of their interests. One individual consumer suing Ontario Hydro or General Motors is a pretty uneven contest. Thirty thousand individuals in the same action greatly reduce the power imbalances in these types of proceedings. The small can fight the large.

The types of situations which are suitable to the use of the class action include those where proof of fact and damages is often difficult and expensive, where laboratory tests and expert witnesses are needed, where an individual cannot afford to bring suit, either because of the cost of the action itself or because the damage to any individual is small and where there is a risk of losing and incurring the total legal fee of both parties to the dispute. In a class action in British Columbia, British Columbia was forced to pay interest on all deposits for guarantee of hydro services (Chastin vs B.C. Hydro Power Authority 1972, pp. 443-449).

These major areas of the law affecting consumers, the law of contract, sales of goods act, safety, health and information trade practices, administratative and regulatory policies and decisions, and access to and use of the law evolve from a political process. The next section of the paper describes the political process in which Canadian consumer law is conceived, given birth, and nurtured.

THE POLITICAL PROCESS OF CONSUMER LAW

The Canadian system of parliamentary democracy has unique implications for the process which results in consumer law. Concentration of decision-making power in cabinets at the federal and the provincial level, a system of loose federalism, historical evolution of accepted modes of behavior, and some deep political cleavages all contribute to this uniqueness and to the development and application of consumer laws.

The overriding characteristic of this political decision-making system is the division of power between two groups, the politicians, in particular the Cabinet ministers, and the senior bureaucrats through their influence both on their minister's power and on the drafting of legislation. At the other extreme of the power continuum is the minimal effect of individual members of Parliament. MP's in the party in power have some influence on Cabinet through the party caucus, but MP's in the opposition parties have relatively little power. Since the use of parliamentary committees to design legislative proposals is not used in the Canadian system, individual MP's cannot achieve the influence which the powerful committee system in the United States Congress conveys on their legislators

(Presthus 1973) (Neilson and McPherson 1978).

It is difficult to underestimate the power of the bureaucracy in influencing legislation at both the federal and provincial level. Although the balance of our discussion will focus on the federal situation, the power of provincial bureaucrats follows the federal situation quite closely (Presthus 1973) (Neilson and McPherson 1978).

The senior bureaucracy in Ottawa is composed of a highly skilled group of administrators and policy formulators who provide a continuity not provided by Cabinet ministers who are periodically shuttled from one ministry to another. The bureaucrats' power derives from their continuity, from the resources to analyze and develop legislation, from their formal and informal information and power relationships with other bureaucrats and from their understanding of how to make the system work. No individual Cabinet member nor group of Cabinet members are capable of understanding the many and complex issues which come before Cabinet. They therefore have to depend upon bureaucrats in their ministry to provide them with well thought out legislation and with opinions and positions on legislation being introduced by other Cabinet ministers.

The typical pattern of the development and passage of a piece of legislation begins when the minister becomes convinced that there is a need for new or revised legislation. The ministry or ministries involved, through the bureaucrats and through interdepartmental committees, develop a piece of legislation which is presented to the Cabinet. If it is approved by Cabinet, it is sent to Parliament for first and second reading and discussion in the House of Commons. After second reading it is sent to the appropriate Parliamentary and Senate Committee for hearings. Changes, usually minor, may be made in the committees, and the legislation is then given final reading and discussion in the House. If it is approved by the House, it is then sent to the Governor General for Royal Assent and is proclaimed as law.

Most bills are voted on along party lines and it is rare that an opposition bill is given substantive consideration or that the members are released by the party whips to vote freely on the legislation. Because Parliamentary Committees are not brought into the legislative process until after second reading of the legislation in the House of Commons, any major changes at that time would be an embarrassment to the government. That being the case, substantive changes in legislation sent to committees are the exception rather than the rule. Changes at this point are difficult for interest groups, such as consumers, to accomplish and usually require a much greater expenditure of resources than if influence had been made early in the process, during the design of the legislation.

In conclusion it is more effective and least divisive for interest groups to influence the design of legislation either through the access to bureaucrats in its preparatory stages or directly to the Cabinet Minister who will introduce it to Cabinet. Even though legislation has not received public scrutiny when it reaches Cabinet, any major change at this point is highly improbable without major delays and redrafting because of the wide ranging consultative process in its life before arriving at Cabinet. This consideration, plus the costs of concensus in Cabinet on controversial and complex legislation which have large components of political tradeoffs (i.e., involve conflicting interests of several Cabinet portfolios) all contribute to the general desire to restrict major change once legislation reaches Cabinet.

The logical conclusion from this type of political decision-making process is that if laws favorable to consumers and restrictive to other interests are to be promulgated, organizations must be designed to have the concepts and justification for their inclusion presented to influential Cabinet members and bureaucrats before and during the development of legislation. This is what other effective interest groups have done and consumers are following suit (Presthus 1973) (Aucoin 1975).

Deep Socio-Political Cleavages

Overriding all Federal government decision making are the deep political and geographic cleavages of Canadian society. Of these, the East-Central-West cleavage is prominent and has evolved from immense differences in economic structure, resource endowment, population density and history of the three regions. Second, the devisiveness of the two major cultures, French and English, combined with the unique character of the Canadian constitution and federalism, ofttimes completely overrides consumer as well as many other interest groups' considerations in the political process.

The Canadian political process is often dominated by political tradeoffs among the interests of the deep geographic and cultural cleavages. What is important for our purpose here is to recognize that consumer interests and laws may be submerged in the accommodation of these other interests even if the consumer interests are legitimate and even if they are recognized as such by the politicians (Presthus 1973) (Lijphart 1968). Dairy policy, discussed below, is a prime example of one such case.

235

Interest Group Accommodation

Presthus sees interest group representation in Canada characterized by an elite group of **individuals and organizations** presenting information to senior bureaucrats, to influential politicians (mainly, but not exclusively, Cabinet ministers), and to the public media to develop public opinion and have their interests represented. There is no doubt that in this representation activity, especially in the economic area but also in other areas of government concern, a small clique of "old boys" who are, or have been, the major influentials has characterized the Canadian system (Porter 1965) (Clement 1975) (Newman 1975) (Presthus 1973). Although much of this old-boy network exists today, in the 1960's the federal government instituted a number of changes whose goal it was to open up the political system to interest groups that had, hitherto, been denied access. Aucoin believes that this development has "provided for more information, more expert opinion, a greater clarity in the dimensions of policy issues and a greater degree of participation in the policy-making process. Having stated this, one should point out, however, that the changes are relative in degree and, in many cases, difficult to evaluate." (Aucoin 1975).

The major interest groups participating in the political process to develop consumer laws include the Consumers' Association of Canada, an organization of 100,000 members whose objectives are to represent the interests of all Canadian consumers, and who have been active since 1947 in this area both federally and provincially; the Public Interest Advocacy Centre, a small federally funded group providing legal advice and counsel to public interest groups, most of whose objectives have significant consumer interest components; the National Anti-Poverty Association, a group representing low income Canadians, again whose objectives and goals are often of the consumer interest variety; and smaller, more narrowly focused interest groups such as the Automobile Protection Association which lobbies for improved performance and safety in automobiles (Forbes 1979, forthcoming).

The interest groups that are important in consumer law are not just those who are in favor of the legislation but groups who may be opposed to the legislation. Consumers are also interested in laws whose main effects are on other interest groups, for example business, and where consumers may be in opposition to some of the elements of the legislation because it may diminish the consumer's interest in favor of the special interest group. The government also plays this dual role: in the case of Consumer and Corporate Affairs Canada, the primary

236

role is to institute consumer related legislation and secondly to represent the consumer's interests in interdepartmental committees when legislation is being drafted which will have an effect on consumers even though it may be through another government department.

The study of all aspects of the interaction of government and interest groups in the development of consumer law is fascinating but of too wide a scope for detailed discussion in this paper. However, two case studies illustrate the most important elements of that process.

THE TALE OF TWO LEGISLATIVE SAGAS

The study of two policy areas, food and agricultural policy and competition policy, were selected to illustrate the political process in the evolution of consumer law. The first case, food and agricultural policy, illustrates the indirect effect on consumers of laws designed to benefit one segment of society and displays elements indicative of the socio-economic cleavages within Canada. The second case, competition policy, illustrates the difficulty of changing laws when politically and financially strong special interest group powers are threatened. Large, latent interest groups like consumers face a difficult task under these circumstances.

Food and Agriculture Policy

In order to fully comprehend the evolution of the legal and administrative policies relating to food and agriculture policy as they relate to the consumer, it is necessary to briefly state the goals and policies which comprise this policy. The stated goals of Canadian agricultural policy is to ensure income adequacy and stability plus an equitable distribution of income to all farmers, large and small, east and west.

The major tools used in the pursuit of these goals include the provision of equal access by all producers to the market for their products, direct and indirect subsidation of transportation and basic inputs to the production process, price setting, supply restriction, import controls, market development and income stabilization. The drift of agricultural policy in the past ten years can be characterized as a move away from market determination of prices and resource allocation to complete regulation of the agriculture sector (Veeman and Veeman 1976, 1978). That move is not complete, of course, but an illustration of how far it has gone is the fact that production of milk in Canada is almost at the point of complete government control notwithstanding that the resources are owned by individual producers. The returns to those resources and the amount that they can produce is completely determined by national and provincial regulation. On the other hand, manipulation of price and supply can only go so far because the two major subsectors of agriculture, grains and meats, are closely tied to world markets and wheat is a significant and important foreign exchange earner for the Canadian economy.

The consumer content and effect of these legislative and regulatory policies is large even though indirect. One of these indirect effects is that of income transfers from consumers to producers. The largest transfer is in dairy policy which costs consumers and the country in the neighborhood of $1 billion yearly. Direct government subsidy payments amounted to $200-$450 millions annual over the past five years for the cost of manufacturing milk (that milk used for the production of butter, cheese, skim milk powder, and other manufactured dairy products). About sixty percent of these payments go to Quebec dairy farmers and, because of the national unity problem, change can be politically explosive. Indirect subsidies, through import exclusion of all but a small portion of manufactured dairy product requirements, contribute to the balance of this cost (Loyns 1977, forthcoming) (Veeman and Veeman 1974). In addition, provincial milk boards have set prices at a level above real market prices to add an estimated tens of millions of dollars to this national subsidy amount (Grubel and Schwindt 1977) (Barichello 1977) (Broadwith, Hughes and Associates 1978). The institution of national and provincial marketing boards in the 1960's and 1970's has, in those cases where boards have exercised price setting and supply restriction powers, resulted in an additional direct consumer-producer subsidy in the range of $30-100 million annually. These subsidies are composed mainly of those to eggs, broilers and turkeys.

The consumer concern is not that large resource transfers are being made to producers (governments make large transfers among other groups within the society), but rather that much of the control of the transfer of this money is delegated to the self-interested producers without adequate consideration of the effects of these transfers on consumers. Consumers have neither the guaranteeed right of access to any of the marketing control groups nor to an independent adjudicating authority. Almost invariably, access is to the board that made the original decision, so one appeals to the judge who is also the defendant (made the original decision) (Forbes 1976) (National Farm Products Marketing Council 1976). The goal for consumers in agricultural and food policy then was to obtain recognition and guarantee of rights of participation and influence in that policy.

A combination of rapidly escalating food prices, media highlighting of the general concern over these price increases, activities by interest groups, such as the Consumers' Association of Canada, several independent analyses of marketing boards and their use of power, and some independent analysis by the Treasury Board of the effects of Canadian dairy commission manufacturing milk policy resulted in two developments which were critical in providing the impetus for a change from agriculture policy to a national food policy and aided consumer legitimation in the process. The government appointed a Food Prices Review Board in 1974 which provided an objective and independent analysis of the effects of agricultural policy laws. These reports have stood the test of time and have been remarkably accurate in predicting not only the effects of various agriculture policies but their future development. Their final report, Telling It Like It Is, is a significant agricultural and food policy document, the only one since the publication of the Task Force Report on Agriculture in 1970.

The second occurrence in the move from a strictly agricultural to a broad food focus was the establishment of a Food Policy Group which provided within Consumer and Corporate Affairs Canada the resources and expertise to represent consumer food interests on interdepartmental committees. This group functioned not only to evaluate proposed legislation in the area but also to provide a watchdog function over the application and administration of existing legislation, including the activities of the National Farm Products Marketing Council and the national marketing boards under the organization's administrative aegis.

In 1978 a policy document entitled A Food Strategy for Canada was published as a joint effort of the Food Policy Group in Consumer and Corporate Affairs and Agriculture Canada (Agriculture Canada and Consumer and Corporate Affairs Canada 1977). This was followed by a large policy conference in February 1978 where representatives of the producing, processing, distributing, and retailing sectors of the food industry and consumers got together and tried to develop position papers on food strategy (Agriculture Canada and Consumer and Corporate Affairs Canada 1978) (Skogstad 1978). As a result of the Food Strategy Conference, a system of interdepartmental committees has been established to redress the preponderance of agricultural interests in the policy process (Interdepartmental Steering Group on Food Strategy 1978 and 1979).

Food strategy is illustrative of the process of the evolution of consumer related laws and administrative procedures described previously. The statutes under which these policies are administered provide a wide range of discretion

239

for both the ministers involved, the Cabinet, and the administrative and regulatory agencies such as the Canadian Dairy
Commission (C.D.C.), the Canadian Wheat Board (C.W.B.) and the
National Farm Products Marketing Council, which **administer**
major portions of the activities which are subsumed under a
food strategy.

The Cabinet, the Cabinet Ministers, and especially the
Minister of Agriculture, appoint members to the regulatory
bodies in the food sector and approve the major decisions by
the C.D.C. and the C.W.B. Since the political ramifications
of these two boards are so wide ranging, it is doubtful that
Cabinet will want to release any of this power. Therefore, the
Minister representing **consumers, needs continuing expertise and**
resources to understand the implications of Cabinet decisions
affecting food as well as to monitor activities of the National
Farm Products Marketing Council, the national regulatory body
for marketing boards, which remains highly biased in favor of
the agriculture sector (Forbes 1976).

The probability of changes in food policy laws favourable
to consumers is low but they are probably not needed if consumer interests can be more effectively represented and public
accountability and regulation increased. This brief description of the food strategy system and its evolution provides
good examples of where regulatory **decisions** and procedures
assume the legal and controlling power of laws, of some significant regional and linguistic cleavage problems restricting
the scope of alternatives for politically **acceptable** short-run
change, of politically effective special interest groups (agricultural producers) effectively directing the evolution of
laws in a direction which is , in some degree, against the
interests of consumers and other special interest groups (some
processors of food products), and of restrictions of access to
the regulatory agencies and to regulatory information. We now
look at an example where laws and changes to laws are the prime
avenue to change.

Competition Laws

The events surrounding the attempt to change Canadian
competition legislation so as to better serve the interests of
consumers is illustrative of several important problems in consumer law and the political process. First, the process of
change is long, in this case over ten years with a stormy history that is by no means over. Second, the issues are complex
and difficult to understand. Third, the life of the bill illustrates the asymmetry of the representation of powerful
interests compared to those of consumers and the general public.
Fourth, it illustrates the dedication of a small group of bur-

FIGURE 1

THE PROVISIONS AND INSTITUTIONAL RELATIONSHIPS OF BILL-256

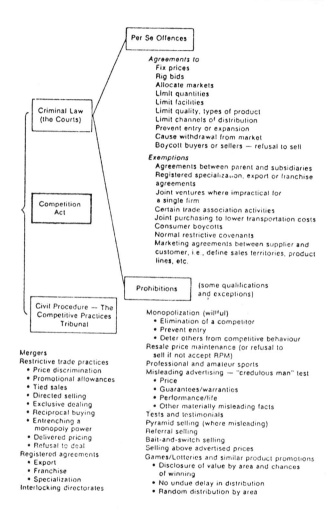

Source: G.B. Reschenthaler, "The Proposed Competition Act of 1971: Ascendency
of the Consumer Interest", Chapter 7 in W.T. Stanbury, Business Interest and the Reform of Canadian Competition Policy 1971-1975,
Carswell/Methuen, Toronto, 1977, p. 77.

eaucrats, academics and consumer organizations in keeping the
issue alive (Stanbury 1977) (Stanbury and Cook 1978, p.36).

The issues are complex but, at the expense of oversimpli-
cation, the bureaucrats who have to enforce competition legislation wanted to accomplish several things with the revamping
of the Combines Investigation Act. First, they wanted to take
the interpretation of the legislation out of the courts and
into a tribunal which would not be constrained by court procedures and legal precedent in deciding the competitive effects
of economic matters. The courts are unsuited to handling the
determination of economic matters. Secondly, they wanted to
give to the courts a law which would be sufficiently specific
to allow relatively easy determinaion of per se offenses (agreements to monopolize or restrict competition through activities
such as price fixing, bid-rigging, allocating markets, etc.)
and prohibitions (such as monopolization, resale maintenance,
and some trade practices). The extent of the types of regulations involved and the division of jurisdiction between the
courts and the proposed Competitive Practices Tribunal, as
introduced to Parliament on June 29, 1971, is outlined in
Figure 1. It is evident that Bill C-256 was one which could
have had a significant impact in all areas of Canadian business.

A contributing factor to the discussion and confusion surrounding Bill C-256 and its decendants was the complexity of
the issues and the difficulties of forecasting the outcomes if
the legislation was invoked. How does one measure the degree
of competition? Are the levels of competition in Canada relatively low? What technology levels and sizes of firms are
needed for maximum efficiency? What levels of competition can
we expect in a country of only 23 million people? On the other
hand, there is little doubt that many of the restrictive
practices, such as market allocation, bid-rigging, resale
price maintenance, and other restrictive practices take place
almost daily in the Canadian economy and are anti-competitive
per se. Yet, enforcement of many of the proposed provisions
could only have resulted in an increase in competition without
any detriment to the Canadian economy. The discussion which
follows, however, does not treat the substantive issues but
focuses on the political process which has surrounded the
history of the legislation.

The immediate history of the competition policy legislation started in July 1966 when the Economic Council of
Canada was asked to prepare a report about who should have
responsibility for enforcing competition policy in Canada. The
response to this report was published in July of 1967 under the
title Interim Report: Consumer Affairs and the Department of
Registrar General. Two years later, in July 1969, following an

242

extensive investigation, the Economic Council published a major policy document, Interim Report on Competition Policy, which was the basis for drafting the Competition Act, Bill C-256 (first reading on June 29, 1971). A large number of symposia, public and private meetings between interest groups, bureaucrats, and the government, and much discussion in the media ensued. Bill C-256 died on the order paper when the government was dissolved in the fall of 1972.

A year later, in November 1973, Bill C-227, now called Stage I, containing mainly the trade practices portions of the original amendments to the Combines Investigation Act, was introduced by the government. The very contentious issues of mergers, monopolies, and especially the administrative powers of the Competitive Practices Tribunal, were to be saved until Stage II. Over the next fifteen months hearings by the House Standing Committee on Finance, Trade and Economic Affairs and by the Standing Senate Committee on Banking, Trade and Commerce received many briefs on Bill C-227. Ministers and senior bureaucrats met publicly and privately with interested groups on the bill. The second amended bill, Bill C-2 (great grandchild of C-256, out of C-227 and C-7) received final reading in October 1975 and became law on January 1, 1976.

In between the time that Bill C-256 died on the order paper in the fall of 1972, and March 1977 when Stage II amendments were given first reading in the house (Bill C-42), many studies and many alternative proposals were commissioned from academics and lawyers by the Department of Consumer and Corporate Affairs. These studies were released starting in May 1976. In June 1977 hearings on Bill C-42 were held by the House of Commons Standing Committee on Finance, Trade and Economic Affairs. In August of that year the House Committee presented its report, Proposal for Change. In November of 1977, Bill C-13, a 70 revision change of Bill C-42, was given first reading in the House. The major changes included provisions for an appeal to Cabinet on decisions of the Competition Board (the name now given to the originally proposed Competition Practices Tribunal), the exemption under the act of any anticompetitive practices by agricultural marketing boards, and a weakening of the 'tests of efficiency' and of the joint monopolization provisions. Now termed the Competition Act, it and all of its provisions died on the order paper in the summer of 1978 and have never been reintroduced (Stanbury and Cook 1978, p. 36).

"Almost from the (introduction of Bill C-256) the atmosphere 'was' overladen with hostility and invective in the attacks on the bill and its underlying principles. And these assaults have not been limited to the expression of intellect-

TABLE 2

INTEREST GROUP PRESENTATIONS ON
COMPETITION POLICY, 1971-73 and 1977*

Category	C-256 1971-73	C-42 1977	Total
Individual business firms and trade organizations	161	81	242
Governments/Regulatory Agency	4	0	4
Farm organizations, marketing boards, provincial governments or departments	0	40	40
Professional associations	12	0	12
Consumer organizations	2	2	4
Lawyers (on own behalf)	10	5	15
Academics	6	8	14
Individuals	1	8	9
Other	1	3	4
	197	147	344

* Compiled from W.T. Stanbury, Business Interests and the Reform of Canadian
Competition Policy, 1971-1975, Carswell/Methuen, Toronto, 1977, p. 114 and
W.T. Stanbury and Stephen Cook, "Competition Policy: The Retreat Begins",
Canadian Consumer, Consumers' Association of Canada, February 1978, p. 36.

ual differences. They have been punctuated by emotionalism
and vituperation." (Buchwald 1972, p. 10).

The interests of business firms and other regulatory
bodies created wide ranging discussions and resulted in much
press coverage and the submission of many briefs to the government. An illustration of the asymmetry of the representation
of interests when powerful groups in society are threatened is
no where better demonstrated than in the representations on
reforms to the competition legislation. The presentations made
over the six year period between 1971 and 1977 are presented
in Table 2.

Fully 70 percent of the submissions on the bill were made
by individual business firms and trade organizations, and
except for one or two instances, were negative in their presentation (Stanbury 1979). Bill C-42 was introduced with legislation which would include within the provisions of the legislation agricultural marketing boards whose restrictive practices had begun to create widespread concern. It is interesting that the agriculture lobby can, with great effectiveness,
bring out its members. And they should have been justifiably
concerned because, among the practices which supply management
marketing boards and their national counterparts use, are price
fixing, market allocation, limits to production and supply,
limits to facilities for production and distribution, limits
to channels of distribution and prevention of market entry or
expansion. It is evident that those groups with a direct and
financial interest, those groups who have monetary and technical
legal expertise to prepare briefs, rallied to the threat of
their interests.

Of equal interest, is the fact that only four briefs were
presented by consumer organizations. This is not surprising
given that consumer organizations are historically poorly
funded and lacking in the technical expertise which informed
comment on complex legislation requires. However, this number
underestimates significantly the presentations made on behalf
of the public and the consumer interest. The Economic Council
of Canada in its reports and the Department of Consumer and
Corporate Affairs had commissioned many background studies on
proposals for the legislation. The preponderance of these
recommendations put forth the consumer and public interest
viewpoints.

The political realities were such that the government was
forced to revise the legislation in all of its forms. There is
no indication that Stage II will be reintroduced in the immediate future. That such controversial legislation has been
introduced into the Parliament at least twice, against very

strong political odds, should be sufficient evidence for the most demanding judge that the Department of Consumer and Corporate Affairs is convinced that this legislation is necessary to maintain a competitive Canadian economy. For those who want to delve further into the **history** of the legislation they will find the corpse of at least one Minister of Consumers and Corporate Affairs and evidence of the expenditure of large amounts of funds by business, agriculture and trade organizations to lobby for the prevention or to drastically alter the conditions of the legislation.

Competition policy is indeed a good example of a long term, complex issue whose results are most likely to benefit individual consumers. However, the asymmetry of representation when the powerful interests are threatened inundates the legislation and, except for the dedication of a small group of people who are convinced of its need, the public and consumer interest is subsumed in the political realities. The pluralist process is working but the scales are balanced against large latent interest groups. However, one doubts that this legislation will remain buried forever, but one also must not be too hopeful of an immediate resumption of the political battle.

SUMMARY AND CONCLUSIONS

Consumer law, comprising four components, the common law, statutes, statute law, and administrative and regulatory policies and decisions, form a complex maze which define the rights of individuals in their roles as consumers in Canada. There have been significant, positive increases in the rights of consumers in the area of the law of contract, the sale of goods for their proported purposes, and safety, health and information. In addition, passage of Stage I of the Competition Act in January of 1976, plus provincial trade practice legislation, has significantly strengthened the government and the individual consumer's ability to obtain fair play and redress in the market-place. Access to regulatory bodies is also more open than previously.

However, the consumer interest is difficult to represent when the interests of powerful, well organized groups in society are threatened. In the final analysis the development of consumer law takes place within the political process and two case studies, the evolution of Canadian agriculture and food legislation and the ongoing saga of revisions to competition law, illustrate the political process of consumer law and the difficulties of ensuring representation of consumer interests in the fact of powerful special interest groups in a democratic country.

246

REFERENCES

Agriculture Canada and Consumer and Corporate Affairs Canada (1977), A Food Strategy for Canada, mimeograph, Agriculture Canada and Consumer and Corporate Affairs Canada.

Agriculture Canada and Consumer and Corporate Affairs Canada (1978), "Position Papers of the Food Strategy Conference," mimeograph, Agriculture Canada and Consumer and Corporate Affairs Canada.

Aucoin, Peter (1975), "Pressure Groups and Recent changes in the Policy-Making Process," in Pressure Group Behavior in Canadian Politics, A. Paul Pross, ed., Toronto: McGraw-Hill Ryerson Ltd.

Barichello, Richard R. (1977), "An Economic Analysis of the Dairy Farm Income Assurance Program," unpublished, Vancouver: Department of Agricultureal Economics, University of British Columbia.

Bresner, Barry and Timothy Leigh-Bell with J. Robert, S. Pritchard, Michael J. Trebilcock and Leonard Waverman (1978), "Ontario's Agencies, Boards, Commissions, Advisory Bodies and other Public Institutions: An Inventory (1977)," in Government Regulation: Issues and Alternatives 1978, Toronto: Ontario Economic Council.

British Columbia (1976), Consumer Protection Act, Section 9, 10 and 11.

Broadwith, Hughes and Associates (1978), "The Ontario Milk Marketing Board: An Economic Analysis," in Government Regulation: Issues and Alternatives 1978, Toronto: Ontario Economic Council.

Buchwald, Harold (1972), Annual Report 1971, Canadian Consumer Council, Ottawa: Queen's Printer.

Chastain v. B.C. Hydro and Power Authority (1972), Dominion Law Reports 32 (3d), 443-459.

Clement, Wallace (1975), The Canadian Corporate Elite, Toronto: McClelland Steward Ltd.

Consumers' Association of Canada (1978), "Report on the Regulated Industries Program 1977-1978," unpublished, Consumers' Association of Canada.

Doern, G. Bruce, ed. (1978), The Regulatory Process in Canada, Toronto: MacMillan of Canada.

Economic Council of Canada (1978), Regulation Reference: A Preliminary Report to First Ministers, Document: 800-9/004, and updates, Ottawa.

Forbes, J.D. (forthcoming), "Influence Groups in Canadian Consumer Policy," Canadian Marketer.

_____ (1976), "Insuring Public Accountability and Consumer Interest in Regulatory Agencies in the Food Industry," Vancouver: Working Paper No. 399, Faculty of Commerce and Business Administration, University of British Columbia.

_____ and S.M. Obert (in process), Consumer Interest: Definition and Dimensions.

Grubel, H.G. and R. S. Schwindt (1977), The Real Cost of the B.C. Milk Board, Vancouver: Fraser Institute.

Interdepartmental Steering Group of Food Strategy (1978), "Recent Developments in Food Strategy," mimeograph, Ottawa: Interdepartmental Steering Group on Food Policy.

Interdepartmental Steering Group of Food Policy (1979), "Summary of Developments in National Food Strategy," mimeograph, Ottawa: Interdepartmental Steering Group on Food Policy.

Johnson, John M. (1975), "Locus Standi in Constitutional Case after Thorson," Public Law, 137-160.

Kane, T. Gregory (1975), A Study on Law Reporting in the Commonwealth, London: Commonwealth Secretariat, Malborough House.

Lijphart, Arend (1968), The Politics of Accommodation, Berkeley: University of California Press.

Loyns, R.M.A. (Forthcoming), "Marketing Boards: The Irrelevance and Irreverence of Economic Analysis," Macromarketing: A Canadian Perspective, Donald N. Thompson, Patricia Simmie, Louise Heslop and Stanley J. Shapiro, eds., Chicago: American Marketing Association, 201-230.

National Farm Products Marketing Council (1976), Proceedings of the Public Hearings: Canadian Egg Marketing Agency's Pricing Formula, Vol.I-V plus Summary and Conclusions, Ottawa.

Neilson, W.A.W. and J.C. MacPherson, eds. (1978), The Legislative Process in Canada: The Need for Reform, Institute
for Research on Public Policy, Toronto: Butterworth.

Newman, Peter C. (1975), The Canadian Establishment, Toronto:
McClelland and Stewart Ltd.

Phidd, Richard W. and G. Bruce Doern (1978), The Politics and
Management of Canadian Economic Policy, Toronto: MacMillan
of Canada.

Porter, John (1965), The Vertical Mosaic, Toronto: University
of Toronto Press.

Presthus, Robert (1973), Elite Accommodation in Canada,
Toronto: Macmillan.

Province of Quebec (1978), Consumer Protection Act.

Ruppenthal, Karl M. and W.T. Stanbury (1976), Transportation
Policy: Regulation, Competition and the Public Interest,
Vancouver: the Center for Transportation Studies, University
of British Columbia.

Saskatchewan (1977), The Consumer Products' Warranties Act.

Skogstad, Grace (1978), "The Farm Products Marketing Agencies
Act and the Food Policy Debate: Case Study of Meeting of
Agricultural Policy," Paper presented at the Fiftieth
Annual Meeting of the Canadian Political Science Association,
London, Ontario.

Stanbury, W.T. (1977), Business Interests and the Reform of
Canadian Competition Policy 1971-1975, Toronto: Carswell/
Methuen.

_____ (May 1979), Personal communication.

Stanbury, W.W. and Stephen Cook (1978), "Competition Policy:
The Retreat Begins," Canadian Consumer, February, 1978.

Trebilcock, M.J. (1978), Help: Handbook of Consumer Rights
in Canada, Toronto: Marketplace, Canadian Broadcasting
System.

Veeman, M.M. and T.S. Veeman (1976), "Direction of Canadian
Agricultural Policy," in Canadian Society of Agricultural
Economics Proceedings 24, 78-90.

Veeman, M.M. and T.S. Veeman (1974), "The Impact of Federal
Dairy Policies and Provincial Milk Boards on Canadian
Consumers Council, Ottawa: mimeo.

Veeman, Terrence S. and Michele M. Veeman (1978), "The Changing
Organization, Structure and Control of Canadian Agriculture,"
in American Journal of Agricultural Economics, Vol. 60,5,
759-768.

CONSUMER PRODUCTS WARRANTIES:
PERSPECTIVES AND ISSUES[1]

John R. Kennedy, The University of Western Ontario
Michael R. Pearce, The University of Western Ontario
John A. Quelch, The University of Western Ontario

ABSTRACT

The paper provides the reader with an introduction to
consumer products warranties from a number of perspectives:
consumers, brandowners, and government policymakers responsible for the formulation and administration of the social
rules within which Canadian warranty systems operate.

Two themes appear throughout the article. One is the notion of a square deal for all parties having a stake in consumer product warranties. The other is the actual warranty of
a fictionalized company entitled Homeline Appliances. The
two themes are used as background in the development of understanding of the basis of warranty in law, the difference
between implied and express warranties, the problems occurring
under "traditional" law, recent changes in Canadian consumer
products warranty law, and the complex problems faced by a
brandowner in establishing an express warranty offer delivery
system.

The final section of the paper is a brief exposition of
four major current issues which the authors believe must be
addressed to ensure meaningful and lasting improvements in
Canadian consumer products warranties.

Cet article est une présentation des garanties qui ac-
compagnent certains produits de consommation et fourni au
lecteur une quantité de perspectives: celles des consommateurs, des propriétaires de marque de fabrique et aussi
celles des responsables de la politique gouvernementale pour
la formulation et l'administration des normes sociétaires,
sous lesquelles fonctionnent les systemes de garanties au
Canada.

Deux thèmes epparaissent tout le long de l'article. L'un
est l'idée du procédé qui se veut honnête envers tous ceux qui

---

1 This paper is an outgrowth of research undertaken with the
support and funding of the Federal Department of Consumer and
Corporate Affairs.

ont des intérêts en jeu dans les garanties de produits de consommation. L'autre discute de la garantie actuellement offerte
par une compagnie fictive, appelée "Homeline Appliances". Ces
deux thèmes sont utilisés comme arrière-plan dans le développement de la compréhension des fondements de la garantie en
loi, de la différence existant entre les garanties implicites
et les garanties énoncées, des problèmes qui surviennent à
cause des lois "traditionnelles", à cause des récents changements apportés à la loi sur les garanties de produits de consommation et aussi à cause des problème auxquels doit faire
face le propriétaire de marque de fabrique lorsqu'il tente
d'établir un système d'offre de garantie énoncée.

L'article se termine par une brève exposition des quatre
problèmes majeurs actuels qui, les auteurs le croient ferme-
ment, doivent être abordés afin d'assurer des améliorations
significatives et durables aux garanties des produits de consommation canadiens.

INTRODUCTION

Most of us are quite familiar with product guarantees and
warranties. These are the cards, certificates, and letters
that we discover when we open the carton, the oven door, the
glove compartment and so on. In fact, most of us pay little
attention to these documents - until there is a problem with
the product. Then, we like most consumers, try to unscramble
the legal jargon to find out whether our problem is covered or
not "under warranty." At that point, post-purchase for most of
us most of the time, many problems with warranties become all
too apparent. It is at this point that consumer dissatisfaction with the product may be aggravated by consumer dissatisfaction with the market system (retailer, distributor,
manufacturer, and government protection agencies).

Consumer dissatisfaction with durable products has traditionally been noteworthy. There are, of course, many ways to
measure consumer satisfaction/dissatisfaction. The best ways
are the most expensive and time consuming and therefore generally least available to public policy makers and business
executives. Both groups respond best to expressions of complaint from their respective market audiences - voters and customers. On a national basis, complaints received by Box 99 are
often used as an indicator of consumer concern by policymakers.
There are several problems with Box 99 data, but they do allow
rough estimates of dissatisfaction over time. In fiscal year
April 1, 1974 - March 31, 1975, complaints about guarantees and
warranties constituted 3 percent of the total complaints received by Box 99 in Ottawa and regionally. During fiscal year

TABLE 1

COMPLAINTS RECEIVED BY BOX 99
JANUARY-JUNE, 1978

| Category | Number of Complaints | | | |
	Guarantees and Warranties	Quality	Repairs and Servicing	Total all Complaints for Category
Appliances	142	178	258	1,261
Motor Vehicles	703	899	1,548	5,229
Real Estate	177	324	309	5,784

1978-79, the rate was close to 5 percent of the total complaints received. More specifically, the three key areas of warranty complaint are in appliances, motor vehicles, and real estate. There is some question as to the categorization of complaints amongst "guarantees and warranties", "quality", and "repairs and servicing". Table 1 reports some complaint totals for Box 99 from January - June, 1978. These numbers should be viewed in the context of a total complaint load of 28,228.

Such figures are not conclusive, nor do they indicate regional concerns. Nonetheless, study after study has reached the same conclusion: warranties are of sufficient concern to consumer-voters to constitute a political issue. This conclusion is no less true in Canada than it is in the United States and other developed economies. Consumer advocates and governments have been very active recently in proposing, studying, and imposing changes on the warranty systems for consumer products.

We have spent the past year examining these trends and the issues which have emerged. We have looked at several viewpoints: consumers, retailers, manufacturers, government officials. Our purpose is to share with you some of our learning and observations regarding the issues in the consumer products warranty field.

Warranties are an exceedingly complex topic; we do not pretend here to cover all aspects of this field. We will briefly examine what, in general, warranties mean to consumers, members of the business community, and public policy officials. Then, a lengthier discussion of existing and new law will follow, leading to an examination of the implications of such law for consumers, business and government. Our sources are varied,

253

ranging from legislation to focus groups with consumers and personal interviews with business executives in the automotive and appliance industries in Canada and personal interviews with government officials.

WHAT DO WARRANTIES MEAN?

In order to help the reader, we will continually refer to a sample warranty from a mythical company entitled Homeline Appliances. In fact, while the company is fictional, the warranty was taken from an actual manufacturer in Ontario. Although the warranty for Homeline, shown as Exhibit 1, is for appliances, in most respects it could be for any other consumer durable.

The Homeline warranty is a product warranty, as distinct from a store guarantee such as "satisfaction or your money refunded." In law, only the word warranty exists so we will not use the word guarantee any further.

How would a consumer, poised to purchase an appliance, react to this warranty? Our focus group research has shown that consumers might react in one or more of several ways, including:

-feel reassured by the mere existence of a warranty, no matter what it said, because someone stands behind the product

-believe that the "tested" statement was additional evidence of product quality

-notice particularly the 90 day stipulation, but not think much about it, or wonder why only 90 days, if other manufacturers offered longer protection

-believe that the warranty offered some protection against economic loss if the product was defective in some way

-not understand most of the legal phraseology.

One might say that the warranty was partial evidence to the consumer that he was going to get a "square deal." However, the most likely reaction is none of the above except noticing that a warranty existed - period. Instead, most consumers will neither ask about nor read the warranty pre-purchase.

On the whole, however, a warranty offers risk protection

EXHIBIT 1

<u>HOMELINE WARRANTY</u>

Please fill in this card and return to us immediately in order
to obtain full warranty protection.

PURCHASER_____ DEALER _____

ADDRESS_____ ADDRESS_____

PROVINCE _____ PROVINCE _____

MODEL NO._____ SERIAL NO._____ PURCHASE DATE_____

---------------------- t e a r   h e r e ----------------------

We hereby warrant that the appliance bearing the model and
serial numbers listed above has been thoroughly tested and approved as being of high standard of quality and free from defects in materials and workmanship. We agree to replace without charge for parts or labour any part or portion thereof
which proves to be defective in either material or workmanship
within a period of 90 days from date of purchase, provided
that notice of such defective part is given to Homeline
Appliances' nearest sales or service outlet within the said
period of 90 days. No further or other warranty expressed or
implied in connection with the sale of this appliance is given
and our sole liability consists in replacing defective parts
or portions as aforesaid. We shall not be responsible for any
special indirect or consequential damages arising in any manner
whatsoever. This warranty is for the sole benefit of the original purchaser. Our responsibility ends in case the purchaser
resells this appliance, makes any changes in this appliance,
adds any parts or devices not of our manufacture, or fails to
comply with the operating instructions provided with this
appliance.

_____

to the consumer, protection against breakdown in product performance resulting in economic loss due to seller fault for a
specified period of time. Notice that breakdown in product
performance resulting in personal injury or property damage is

product liability - a separate although related topic as we shall see.

What does the Homeline warranty likely mean to Homeline and its trade channel members? We have discovered manufacturers and retailers have different intentions in mind when offering warranties; therefore, Homeline may have some or all of the following motivations:

-to ensure that the product is delivered to the consumer in proper working order; that is, not defective in parts or workmanship for a specified period of time

-to limit legal liability; that is, to limit responsibility by time period, dollar commitment, and so on (for example 90 days, no other warranty express or implied shall apply, no indirect or consequential damages, original purchaser, an no product modifications)

-to clarify responsibility amongst consumer, dealer, manufacturer in the event of a product problem (who fixes, who pays)

-to induce purchase by offering better risk protection than competitors

-to establish a feedback system to improve product design, manufacturing quality, delivery, and so on.

In other words, the honest business person is offering what he thinks is a square deal. However, often business perception of good value for the purchase price differs from consumer perception of good value - the "square deal" offered is not square as far as the consumer-voter is concerned. Government officials - and we include public policy officials and members of the judiciary - are concerned with equity in the buyer-seller relationship. In short, is the Homeline warranty a fair promise and, importantly, is that promise delivered to consumers? This brings us to an examination of relevant law.

ONTARIO WARRANTY LAW

Warranty law is a provincial matter because it deals with property rights. This means that in Canada alone there are ten streams of legislation and case law. Accordingly, our intent here is to simplify Canadian warranty law as it exists today. We'll look most closely at Ontario law as an example of typical Canadian warranty law.

Warranty law is sales law. By definition, a sale is a contract by which goods are transferred from seller to buyer. Sales law has developed over a long period of time as common law both in England and North America. In 1893, England codified common law principles in a Sale of Goods Act. Canadian provincial laws followed shortly thereafter, almost on a word for word basis. In the United States, the Uniform Sales Act was patterned after the English law. Later, the Uniform Sales Act was replaced by the Uniform Commercial Code.

Such laws contain lengthy provisions about contract formation, breach of contract, and remedies for breach of contract. For example, a study of sale of goods law reveals that for a contract to be enforceable there must be offer, acceptance, intention, capacity, sufficient certainty of terms, and consideration (money, for instance) transferred from the buyer to the seller. Each of these words has specific meaning in law. Further, one would learn that the elements of a contract may include: (a) agreement between the buyer and seller; (b) general custom (trade practice) and (c) statutory rules. Rather than dwell on this, it is important to realize that the basic premise underlying sales of goods law was that both buyers and sellers were entering into the contract with relatively full knowledge of the circumstances and on approximately an equal footing.

With the preceding as background, let us examine the Homeline warranty in light of the Ontario Sale of Goods Act (R.S.O. 1960, c 358).

Under the Ontario Sales of Goods Act, an important distinction is made between "condition" and "warranty." A condition is a major or essential term of a contract, breach of which relieves the injured party from further duty to perform the contract if he so elects. A warranty is a less important or non-essential term, breach of which does not relieve the injured party from the deal, although he may sue for damages. This distinction is important because it determines the nature of the remedy available to the injured party. In other words, breach of warranty by the seller entitles the buyer to claim damages, or get the product repaired or replaced, but does not entitle him to rescind the contract and get his money back. This distinction is artificial according to some experts, and worse, is always determined on a situation-specific basis. This means the average buyer is highly unlikely to know what remedies he is entitled to in the event of product problems. We will use the term warranty henceforth.

Another distinction is made in the law between implied and express warranties. Implied warranties refer to promises the seller is always presumed to have made to the buyer, even if nothing was said about those promises. At one time these presumed promises could be disclaimed in many jurisdictions by saying so in a written statement. In short, implied warranties are statutory rights given the buyer by law. Express warranties refer to statements of reassurance about product quality and performance made by the seller that can be construed as inducements to purchase. Traditionally, such statements were only binding if made in writing - something called the parol evidence rule disallowed statements made verbally. This rule has been relaxed in judicial practice. In short, the Homeline warranty we have been using as our example is an express warranty.

The Ontario Sale of Goods Act confers seven implied warranty rights on the buyer. The explanations provided below are by no means complete description:

-title - seller has right to sell the product

-quiet possession - no interruption of physical possession and enjoyment

-freedom from encumbrance - undisclosed third party does not have a claim

-fulfillment of description - goods correspond with description provided

-sale by sample - goods received correspond with sample seen by buyer

-fitness for particular purpose - purpose for which the buyer wants the product is clear and the buyer relies on the seller's judgment

-merchantability - "The condition that goods are of merchantable quality requires that they should be in such an actual state that a buyer fully acquainted with the facts and therefore knowing what hidden defects exist and not being limited to their apparent condition would buy them without abatement of the price obtainable for such goods if in reasonably sound order and condition and without special terms" (Bristol Tramways v. Fiat Motors).

These implied rights provide the buyer with the basis to claim for product failure damages, consequential damages, or personal injury. They are extended to the buyer who is in privity of contract with the seller. Privity refers to the direct contractual link between two parties, such as between a

258

consumer and a retailer. Generally speaking, consumers do not have privity of contract with wholesalers and manufacturers. However, in personal injury cases, the courts have frequently set aside the need for privity of contracts and permitted purchasers to pursue the manufacturer or wholesaler directly.

As mentioned previously, sellers of consumer products in Ontario were allowed for some time to limit their obligations under implied warranty law by the use of disclaimers. Homeline's warranty contains the sentence: "No further or other warranty expressed or implied in connection with the sale of this appliance is given and our sole liability consists in replacing defective parts or portions as aforesaid." An amendment to the Ontario Consumer Protection Act (1971, c 24 s.2) now makes such disclaimers for consumer products void in law; that is, they are not binding. Notice that disclaimers are not prohibited, thus permitting Homeline to give consumers the impression that implied rights have been limited.

The Sale of Goods Act does not stipulate what must be said in an express warranty. This is particularly noteworthy in view of the disclosure of relevant information approach taken by the U.S. Magnuson-Moss Warranty - Federal Trade Commission Improvement Act of 1975.

Overall, then, the Homeline warranty is legal under existing Ontario Sale of Goods law. There are sections, such as the disclaimers, which are on the margin or not binding, but nonetheless the warranty is legal. The important question, however, is whether it represents a "square deal" for all parties. In short, is it a meaningful promise by Homeline, is the promise delivered to consumers and, perhaps more important, what role should governments play if there are differences of opinion between Homeline and consumers as to the equity of the promise, delivery against that promise, or both?

GOVERNMENT CONCERN

There was increasing government concern during the 1960's and early 1970's in both Canada and the U.S. that the consumer was not getting a square deal, and that consumer goods industries were exposing consumers to both high average risk of economic loss and high individual risk of economic loss. There was particular concern with respect to high purchase price consumer durables such as automobiles, mobile homes, household appliances, and pianos. The manner in which risk of economic loss was being shifted to consumer were many and varied. They include:

-products designed for short economic life
-frequent product failure
-inavailability of parts and service
-products not repaired properly
-products not repaired quickly
-verbal promises made prior to purchase, but later limited
  or deleted in written legal contracts
-full information disclosure not made prior to purchase
-consumer understanding of information masked by use of
  legal terminology and/or fine print
-insufficient competition in the provision of after-sale
  protection against economic loss
-onerous consumer requirements to gain access to warranty
  service
-refusal of valid warranty claims.

There were widespread public evidence and allegations that express warranties were not being used by warrantors as meaningful promises to consumers, but were being used to shift risk of economic loss onto consumers through inappropriate coverage provisions and the use of disclaimers to severely limit consumer recourse in law. Further, warrantors were said to be using their position as arbitrators in disputes with consumers over delivery of the promise to shift further economic loss onto the consumer.

There was also growing awareness and concern within the law profession and government that the law itself was an impediment in the achievement of equity between consumers and warrantors. The reality of a consumer society was that the basic premise underlying sale of goods law of equality of footing between buyer and seller did not hold for most consumer sales. Further, many warranties were given by an organization other than the one which made the sale to the consumer, yet contract law confined consumer recourse to the seller. Consumer, in addition, meant the person who purchased the product, and not an individual who might own the product by virtue of having received it as a gift.

STATUTORY CHANGES

Based on concern by the legal profession with existing law and expressed dissatisfaction by consumer-voters, governments throughout North America have reacted with changes in warranty law. We will confine our discussion to major changes in Canadian statutory law even though a comparison with the U.S. Magnuson-Moss Warranty - Federal Trade Commission Improvement Act is a meaningful endeavour.[2]

One very visible foundation for statutory change in
Canada is the Ontario Law Reform Commission Report on Consumer
Warranties and Guarantees in the Sale of Goods, released in
1972. This major study concluded with suggestions for sweeping
changes in statutory law. The following excerpt gives the
flavour of the report:

> Apart from the more specific analysis to which some
> portions of this Act will be subjected in the following
> chapters of this report, its principal shortcomings can
> be said to be these. It proceeds from the fictitious
> premise that the parties are bargaining from positions of
> equal strength and sophistication and it uses concepts to
> describe and distinguish between different types of ob-
> ligations that are not obsolete and difficult to apply.
> In supplies a framework of remedies for breaches of the
> seller's obligations that are unrelated to practical
> realities. Especially serious is the Act's preoccupation
> with the bilateral relationship between the seller and
> the buyer, which totally ignores the powerful position of
> the manufacturer in today's marketing structure. This
> results, at least in the Anglo-Canadian law in shielding
> the manufacturer from contractual responsibility to the
> consumer. By the same token the law has largely ignored
> the impact of manufacturers' express warranties and the
> defects in their contents and administration. Finally,
> our sales law is private law and it has failed to provide
> any meaningful machinery for the redress of consumer
> grievances. This last weakness is perhaps the most ser-
> ious of all weaknesses, for as has been frequently ob-
> served, a right is only as strong as the remedy available
> to enforce it. (OLRC Report, p. 23)

The Ontario government issued a Green Paper on Consumer
Product Warranties in Ontario in August, 1973 seeking comments
from interested parties on the proposals submitted to it by the
OLRC. Some of the proposals which the Ontario government
found most contentious in the view of the business community
were as follows:

-An implied warranty that the goods (including where
appropriate, the individual components of the goods)

---

2 For a good introduction, see Feldman, L.P. "New Legislation
and the Prospects for Real Warranty Reform" in Consumerism
edited by Aaker and Day, Free Press, Third Edition, 1978,
pp. 154-183.

shall be durable for a reasonable period of time, having regard to all the surrounding circumstances of the sale.

-An implied warranty that spare parts and reasonable repair facilities will be available for a reasonable period of time with respect to goods that normally require repairs. (OLRC Report, p. 156)

According to one official in the Ontario government, the business reaction to the durability rule was virtually unanimous: they did not like the uncertainty "reasonable" created and wanted a specific list of "circumstances of the sale" that would bear on an interpretation of the word reasonable.

In 1976, Bill 110 got first reading in the Ontario legislature. This bill, "An Act To Provide For Warranties In The Sale Of Consumer Products," put legal form to the majority of the OLRC Report recommendations. In our view, the departures from those recommendations were relatively minor, for example, here is the "durability" section:

4. There is an implied warranty by the manufacturer and retail seller jointly to the consumer of a consumer product that,

    (a) the consumer product and its components will perform for a reasonable length of time, having regard to the price and all surrounding circumstances; (Bill 110, Ontario, 1976)

As of 1979, the Ontario government has not pursued Bill 110 beyond first reading and is still studying the entire area of warranties.

On May 10, 1977, the government of Saskatchewan passed its Consumer Products Warranty Act. This act contains much that looks familiar to a student of the OLRC Report. The implied warranty rights (statutory rights) of title, quiet possession, freedom from encumbrance, sale by sample, fulfillment of description, and fitness for purpose have been retained, updated, and (in the view of some) clarified. To these implied rights have been added a section on durability and a section on spare parts and servicing facilities (see Exhibit 2 for a partial text). A close reading reveals a difference from the Ontario version: in Saskatchewan the retailer appears to be legally liable whereas in Ontario both the manufacturer and retailer share liability. In fact, a later section (s. 13) in the Saskatchewan Act extends responsibility to the manufacturer, under a specified set of circumstances.

EXHIBIT 2

EXCERPTS FROM SASKATCHEWAN'S CONSUMER PRODUCTS

WARRANTIES ACT, 1977 - STATUTORY RIGHTS -

11. Where a consumer product is sold by a retail seller, the
following warranties shall be deemed to be given by the
retail seller to the consumer:

(7) that the product and all its components shall be durable for a reasonable period of time, having regard to all
the relevant circumstances of the sale, including the
description and nature of the product, the purchase price,
the express warranties of the retail seller or manufacturer, the necessary maintenance the product normally
requires and the manner in which it has been used;

(8) where the product normally requires repairs, that
spare parts and reasonable repair facilities will be
available for a reasonable period of time after the date
of sale of the product.

It is also interesting to note that the Saskatchewan Act
confers rights on the consumer purchase plus anyone who re-
ceives the product as a gift or subsequently repurchases the
item during the time period "reasonable" is interpreted to
cover. Further, unlike the existing Ontario provision that
voids disclaimers, Saskatchewan prohibits them outright.

The Saskatchewan Act includes an extensive section (s. 17)
on express warranties. There are rules regarding what information an express warranty must contain and what information or
statements must not be contained (Exhibit 3). These rules are
quite similar in many ways to the information required by the
Magnuson-Moss Act. One major difference, however, is that the
Saskatchewan Act does not require full disclosure pre-purchase.

Another extensive section of the Saskatchewan Act includes
several provisions for remedies in the event of breach of
warranty rights. These remedies range from the traditional
civil suit in small claims or divisional court to new powers of
mediation and non-judicial arbitration. This section is undoubtedly intended to ensure that warranty promises are indeed
delivered to consumers.

Finally, the Saskatchewan Act provides for extensive rule-
making authority by the government. This authority allows

product category specific application of or exemption from specific regulations.

Other provinces have made statutory changes as well. New Brunswick passed its Consumer Products Warranty and Liability Act in July, 1978. Quebec also passed the Quebec Consumer Protection Act in 1978 which contains 20 sections relevant to consumer warranties. Both acts have much in common with the Saskatchewan Act and at first glance one might conclude that the Saskatchewan Act is being used as a model statute. This, however, would not be the complete perception of the senior civil servants in the provinces. For example, the N.B. Act does not outline in detail what information must be included in an express warranty. The N.B. Act does, however, include a section on product liability. This provision introduces the concept of "strict liability" to N.B.: the person suffering loss does not need to prove negligence or establish he has a contract with a seller in order to claim damages. Instead, he has to prove he suffered a loss because of design fault, workmanship, or materials and that that resultant loss was reasonably foreseeable. As another example of difference, the Quebec Act provides for warranties on used products sold by dealers. Each act has generated much comment and study, but little is known yet how each will be administered or interpreted by the courts.

Overall, three provinces have passed revised statutes dealing with warranties. As of mid-1979, only one of these provinces, Saskatchewan, has proclaimed their legislation in force, a term which means the date on which the act becomes the law. These changes have been greeted with enthusiasm by some and intense opposition by others. Meanwhile, all provincial authorities are examining proposals for change. It remains to be seen if the new directions taken by Saskatchewan, New Brunswick, and Quebec will be followed by the rest of the provinces.

BUSINESS RESPONSE

Businessmen were very aware of, and in some case reluctant participants in the public airing of concerns in the 1960's and early 1970's that business was too often not providing their customers with a square deal. And they are aware of the public airings that continue to this day. Many organizations responded by making improvements in the quality of their delivered products, in their selling operations, in their warranty offers, or in the quality of their after-sale service operations. Other organizations made little, if any, change in their operations. These included those firms whose business practices result in the continuing public airings of concern,

264

EXHIBIT 3

EXCERPTS FROM SASKATCHEWAN'S CONSUMER PRODUCT
WARRANTIES ACT, 1977 - EXPRESS WARRANTIES -

17.--(1) Nothing in this Act shall prevent a warrantor from
giving additional written warranties in addition to
the statutory warranties set out in section 11.

(2) Any additional written warranty shall contain:

(a) the name and address of the warrantor;
(b) the parts of the consumer product covered by the
warranty;
(c) the duration of the warranty;
(d) the conditions that the person claiming under
the warranty must fulfill before the warrantor
will perform his obligation under the warranty;
(e) the costs, if any, that must be borne by the
person claiming under the warranty;
(f) a statement that the provisions of the additional written warranty are in addition to and
not a modification of or subtraction from the
statutory warranties and other rights and remedies contained in this or any other Act;
(g) the procedure a person claiming under the warranty has to follow for the presentation of a
claim under the warranty;
(h) the name and address of the repair facility that
the consumer product is to be sent to for repair
or that a request is to be sent to for repair of
the product in the home of the person claiming
under the warranty.

(3) No additional written warranty shall contain any
provision:

(a) that makes the warrantor or his agent the sole
judge in deciding whether or not there is a valid
claim under the warranty;
(b) that purports to exclude or limit any express or
statutory warranty or any of the rights or remedies contained in this Act;
(c) that makes a claim under the warranty dependent
on the consumer product being returned to the
warrantor, when it would be unreasonable to so
return the product;
(d) that limits the benefit of the warranty to the
consumer and that excludes or in effect excludes
persons mentioned in subsection (1) of section 1
from receiving the benefit of the warranty; or
(e) that is deceptively worded.

as well as the many others who believed that they had been providing, and were continuing to provide their customers with a
square deal.

At the same time, some members of each of these groups began expressing concerns of their own. They said some consumers'
idea of a square deal in terms of product, performance protection, and quality of service would cost more than those same
consumers were willing to pay. Some consumers expected performance protection, even though they did not properly maintain
the product or abused it in operation.

There have been views expressed as well about the new legislation. They range from the view that the legislation is un-
necessary, through concern that the legislation might result in
court judgments creating large liability for products previously sold, to the view that the legislation is functional
and worthwhile.

In this context, let us return to our Homeline example.
Based on changes in Saskatchewan, the Homeline warranty may be
challenged on several grounds:

-the 90 day warranty period,
-the disclaimer of implied warranty rights,
-the disclaimer regarding owners subsequent to the original purchaser, and
-failure to comply with section 17 rules regarding content
of express warranties.

Similarly, we could examine Homeline relative to New Brunswick
or Quebec. In each instance, it becomes quite obvious that
Homeline is probably not within the letter of the law and is
certainly not within the spirit of the law. Therefore, rather
than detail these deviations, it is more appropriate to examine appropriate changes in Homeline's approach to provide a
better warranty.

HOW MIGHT HOMELINE GO ABOUT SETTING
A SQUARE DEAL WARRANTY OFFER?

A Homeline manager, given responsibility for establishing
a new "square deal" warranty will not have an easy job. He
knows that his company's products are such that consumer use is
accompanied by physical product wear. Conceptually, a year's
production of one product can be thought of as having an average expected economic life expressed in usage, and a minimum
and maximum expected life. The average amount of usage associated with the economic life of the product will be

determined by the performance capabilities of the machine, conditions of use, style of consumer use, the level and quality of product maintenance and repairs, and a number of factors associated with consumer resources and needs in the future, together with future market offerings and costs. To the extent that there is variation in any of these factors, there will be a difference between minimum and maximum product life. The economic life of the year's production of the product could be expressed as a curve, with the total area under the curve representing the year's production. However, even if our manager had good knowledge of the performance capability of the machines under some testing standard, he would still have only a rough approximation of the true curve. However, he does know that the products below the average will be heavily weighted on some combination of those weakest in inherent performance capability, those used under severe conditions, and those abused and/or poorly maintained.

What is consumer perception of a square deal at the time of purchase of a machine? It is likely to include some notion that the average economic life, whatever it is, represents value for the purchase price. It is likely to include also an offer of compensation in the event of product failure. However, it is not likely to include compensation up to the average length of product life, because this would mean subsidization of those customers who abused or misused their products. Consumer perception of a square deal on this dimension is more likely to be compensation for a machine that breaks down with very little use, or wears out quickly within "reasonable" conditions of use, style of use, and maintenance. That is, the consumer is likely to include in the idea of a square deal, protection against the risk of economic loss caused by factors out of his or her control.

It is to Homeline's advantage to provide this risk protection as an inducement to the prospective buyer. The inducement is twofold. First, the higher individual buyer risk of product failure is lowered by spreading the cost of product failure over all buyers. Second, the existence of the risk protection is likely to influence the prospective buyer's idea upward of what that unknown average economic life of the product is.

However, there remains for our Homeline manager the task of determining how best to communicate the offer of risk protection to prospective buyers, and how best to set up and administer within the distribution system a method of providing service against the offer fairly and at reasonable cost. The two are interrelated, as we shall see.

267

If the offer is expressed as compensation for defective material and workmanship (fault), there must be sufficient expertise in the distribution system to assess products on these dimensions. To the extent that such expertise is above a very minimum level, it will be both difficult and expensive to get the expertise distributed widely and evenly throughout the distribution system. The alternative of concentrating expertise will result in delays in decisions which will be resented by consumers.

In either approach, individual product judgment decisions must be made. Those refused compensation with this kind of system are likely to be unsatisfied for one or more reasons:

-The buyer is unlikely to understand decisions based on technological considerations, and regard them as unfair or irrelevant.

-The buyer may perceive that the person making the decision has a financial interest which influenced the decision.

-The reason given for refusing compensation is most likely to be product abuse, misuse, or lack of maintenance. The buyer is not likely to perceive himself/herself as an atypical product user.

A second way of expressing the offer is compensation for any buyer within a given period of time (no fault). This reduces the requirement for expertise and related costs in the distribution system. However, there are some new problems for our Homeline manager. The shift to time from usage has altered the economic life curve. Products below the average on a time curve will include not only those that were defective, those that were used in severe conditions, and those that were abused or poorly maintained, but those products which were used frequently and their full-value economic life used up. Further, there may be some products above the average which are in fact defective, but the defects do not surface because the product was used very little.

It should be apparent that the decision on a time period is not an easy one. The shorter the time period set, the more likely it is to exclude buyers who have a defective product. The longer the time period, the more the buyers to the right of that time line are subsidizing buyers who used up the economic life of the product quickly or who misused or poorly maintained the product. For Homeline however, lengthening the time period likely will influence prospective buyers' assessment of the average economic life of the product.

Whatever the time period decided upon, a further decision must be made as to whether exceptions will be allowed in cases where requests for compensation are made after the stated time period. If this second option is selected, the problems and costs associated with expertise and individual decisions (fault) again must be faced, together with dissatisfaction on the part of those customers refused compensation. Similar problems, costs, and consumer dissatisfaction will result if a decision is made to exclude from compensation those who abuse products within the stated time period.

Finally, the Homeline manager must take into account that in certain provinces, a court, on application of a consumer, might order on the basis of implied warranty that the firm proved coverage beyond the fixed time period stated in the express warranty.

There are also some issues related to the shift to records as the basis of the decision. If the onus is on the buyer to produce the records, and those records are not available, many buyers will be dissatisfied because of their belief that compensation has been denied on a technicality totally divorced from product performance. On the other hand, if Homeline assumes responsibility for the keeping of records, there are administrative costs, which increase disproportionately as the time period is extended.

An idealized sequence of the steps that the preceding suggest should be followed by the Homeline manager in the establishment of warranty are:

1. Determination of the magnitude of the consumer risk created by Homeline through the delivery to the buyer of a product that is defective. Ideally, this should include information on both the average risk and frequency distribution of the amount of risk to which individual buyers might be exposed.

2. Development of alternative warranty offers. These will include combinations of fault, no-fault, and compensation coverage.

3. For the appropriate warranty offers, determination of the magnitude of the potential liability created, beyond that of risk created by Homeline, by virtue of the way the offer is expressed.

4. Dollar, time and psychic costs incurred by both buyers and Homeline in the operation of the alternative compensation systems.

5. Selection of the warranty offer which best meets <u>both</u> of the following criteria:

   (a) The minimization of individual consumer product risk, cost, and consumer costs in obtaining compensation.

   (b) The minimization of incremental product costs by compensation costs beyond Homeline created product risk and costs associated with the operation of the compensation system.

Three things should be noted in this sequence. First, many of the costs are difficult to estimate without information based on historical events. Second, the relevant costs will vary widely across product classes and even among variations in models within a product class. Third, it should be explicitly recognized that the two criteria in Step Five are conflicting, and that tradeoffs must be made between minimizing individual cost risk and costs averaged over all buyers. Tradeoff problems will be minimized in a system that contains both a component of no-fault and a component of fault.

More could be said about the business response possibilities and the issues raised as a marketer re-examines his warranty offer and delivery system. We feel, however, that four general issue areas stand out as one looks at the quest of consumers, business, and public policy officials to obtain "square deal" warranties. We believe these issues must be addressed in order to make any meaningful and lasting improvements in warranties in Canada.

MAJOR CURRENT ISSUES

The Semantics or Meaning of the Law

The new laws create uncertainty for both businessmen and consumers until there has developed some body of case law through judgments. Much of the uncertainty arises from the use of the word "reasonable" in the legislation. Here, it is clear that the intent of the law is to have the courts decide what reasonable is, given the circumstances of the situation. However, there are other words and phrases in the legislation where intent is not so clear, and which could vitally affect the interpretation of the word "reasonable". Section 17-(1) of the Saskatchewan Act (see Exhibit 3) states that "Nothing in this Act shall prevent a warrantor from giving additional written warranties in addition to the statutory warranties set out in section 11."

The words "additional" and "in addition to" can be interpreted as running either concurrently or consecutively with the
statutory warranties, and is the kind of problem that could be
minimized by improved draftsmanship and/or through a clear
statement of intent. A similar kind of problem occurs with the
use of the word "durable" (Section 7, Exhibit 2). For those
products which normally require maintenance and repairs, does
durability mean functional reliability (the product works) or
functional longevity (the product works over a long period of
time)? If it means functional longevity, what are the implications for who bears the responsbility and cost for maintenance and repairs over that period of time?

The Thrust of the Law

The semantic ambiguities described in the previous section
lead to some general uncertainty as to the thrust of the law.
If the emphasis should be placed on concurrent express warranties and/or functional reliability, this would indicate that
the preponderance of problems related to the consumer getting a
square deal relate more to the delivery of defect-free products
and the prompt after-sale service of those problems that arise.
However, if the emphasis should be placed on consecutive warranties and/or functional longevity, this would indicate that
the preponderance of problems relating to the consumer square
deal relate much more to the long-run performance capabilities
of products in the market place.

Alternatives to Statutory Law

To what extent are there alternatives to statutory change
to improve warranty offer and delivery? One interesting development in this regard are service contracts, variously named
as extended protection plans, maintenance contracts, and so on.
These offers are additional to the standard warranty, generally
different in problem coverage, and are paid for independent of
product purchase price. They are not extended warranties in
law, but rather insurance policies against varying kinds of
product breakdowns in the post-warranty period. These service
contracts have several virtures: (a) they are optional and in
some instances terms can be varied, (b) they are paid for in-
crementally so some decision as to the value of protection offered is required of the consumer, and (c) being separate to the
product contract, they are sold on their own merits. At the
same time there are shortcomings in that the inter-relationship
of implied warranties, express warranties, and service contracts has not been clearly established. Further, most consumers are likely to regard service contracts as an extended
warranty option, comparable to physical product options, but
will have relatively more difficulty in assessing the relative

271

value of this risk protection option.

Very much related to variations in risk protection offered are variations in means to ensure such promises are delivered. Statutory changes dependent upon court enforcement are unlikely to provide meaningful improvements in equity for the consumer. First, the real costs (monetary, psychic, and time) of going to court on a warranty issue may far outweigh potential redress. Second, systematic product failure, especially after the expressed warranty period, is not adequately handled under the court system. For these reasons, more attention and creativity must be given to the methods of dispute resolution and decision enforcement. For example, if speed and cost (efficiency) are recognized as highly desirable in dispute resolution, then non-judicial decision-making certainly appears necessary. However, industry self-regulation or government appointed mediators/arbitrators may lack in effectiveness of enforcement what they appear to offer in efficiency of decision-making. In other words, multiple systems congruent with consumer behavior patterns and business realities will undoubtedly be required. Such variations undoubtedly will make it less likely that all decisions made will be congruent with one another: flexibility will mean less assurance that "equity" will be interpreted consistently. Much meaningful work remains to be done to identify and assess alternatives to statutory changes, leaving aside evaluation of statutory changes. Marketing academics certainly could contribute much in this respect by combining their knowledge of consumer behavior and their understanding of marketing practice.

Better Understanding Among Consumers, Governments and
    Businesses

Perhaps the most important issue to be resolved is a better understanding among consumers, governments and businesses than now exists that, while each has a stake in getting their own versions of a square deal, the common goal should be the offer and delivery of what is a square deal for all parties simultaneously.

CANADIAN MARKETING MANAGEMENT
IN A CONSERVER SOCIETY

George H. Haines, University of Toronto
G.J. Leonidas, University of Toronto
M.S. Sommers, University of Toronto

ABSTRACT

This paper comments on some of the anticipated implications
of the "conserver society" for marketing management. The purpose
throughout is to show the kind of macro issues with which Canadian marketing management must deal and to underscore some of
the obvious and less obvious implications inherent in these issues.

The first part of the paper discusses the reality and the
urgency of the limits to growth theorem and what it means for
Canadian marketing management in dealing with the whole concept
of conserverism and conserver societies. The second section ad-
dresses the question of Canada in the world order, with respect
to Canada's ability to deal with global versus regional problems and associated business and industrial consequences. The
third section discusses some of the ways Canadian marketing management may deal with international and national problems. The
fourth section examines some of the management decision areas of
business operations and the manner in which conserver concepts
may be implemented, within the context of the limits to growth
arguments and national and international realities.

Cet article se permet de commenter certaines mises en cause
prévues dans la "société de conservation" au sujet de l'administration du marketing. Le but de cet article est de démontrer
le genre de macro-questions que l'administration du marketing
canadien doit traiter et de souligner quelques unes des implications évidentes et d'autres moins évidentes, propres à ces questions.

La première partie de cet article discute la réalité et
l'urgence de limiter le théorème d'extension et ce qu'il signifie pour l'administration du marketing canadien en se rapportant
à l'idée générale de conservation et aux sociétés conservatrices.
La deuxième partie de l'article commente la place que détient le
Canada au niveau mondial, en ce qui concerne sa capacité de
s'occuper de problèmes globaux et non régionaux et de faire face

aux conséquences associées aux commerces et industries. La troisième partie discute de certaines facons par lesquelles l'administration du marketing canadien peut traiter les problèmes internationaux et nationaux. La quatrième partie examine quelques une des décisions d'administration des opérations commerciales et la manière possible d'intégrer des idées de conservation dans le contexte de limitation de l'extension et dans les réalités nationales et internationales.

When reviewing a good deal of what has been said and written about limits to growth, conservation, waste, new futures, etc., one must immediately be struck by the readily acknowledged paucity of facts. Where there are facts, marketing managers are able to evaluate situations and draw conclusions. Where facts do not exist, marketing managers are presented only with images of bold new life styles, alternative futures, and sheer speculation regarding future events upon which to base their decisions.

Clearly such alternative futures represent ideologies, values, implications and conclusions which do not necessarily deal with perceived reality. The farther into the future predictions are made, the less those who predict are constrained by what is known and the more such predictions are influenced by what the forecaster would like to see or not like to see. Such a situation is certainly uncomfortable for marketing management. Nevertheless, it may be unavoidable in the immediate future.

Should senior Canadian marketing management spend time and effort to engage in the evaluation of speculations about the future? This paper argues that the response should be YES - and with a vengence. Some of the reasons for spending such time, effort and resources have to do with being positive in the face of unknowns and being defensive in the face of perennial "doom-predictors" or "doomsayers;" other reasons have to do with facing up to clear facts with respect to some issues - for example, energy - coupled with clear speculation with respect to others - such as the various states of social organization and society.

That the Federal government funded the Gamma group's efforts, that the Science Council saw fit to issue <u>Canada As A Conserver Society</u>, that the Ministry of State for Science and Technology sponsored a series of meetings across the country to open a public dialogue on conserver themes is enough to underscore "official" recognition of the reality of the situation. Marketing managers have additional reasons for recognizing this reality. There are major changes in the way in which energy utilizing products are being designed, the way in which gasoline is being distributed, the way in which consumers are reacting towards price increases and so on. In total, organizations have faced extraordinary cost increases in many areas, extraordinary levels of regulation and suasion, and varied patterns of product/service market, capital, and labour market responses and pressures. The realities come through for marketing management in daily operations and forward planning problems.

The question of urgency and how to proceed falls into a clearer perspective if attention is turned from the realities of the present and near future situation (where, in some sense, marketing managers know what they are facing) to longer term matters. Right now, for example, product/service costs (energy, materials, skills, capital, etc.) are being dealt with by management in primary, secondary and tertiary industry through the normal price mechanisms. These factor prices are being distorted from what might be called normal market reality by government views (primarily through regulations and taxes) of social requirements. This is not to say that distortions are wrong, only that they exist and are currently having effects. Thus, we are in transition - some would say we always have been - with respect to our realities.

The urgency of the situation has already been well recognized on some fronts. (Marketing managers have been dealing with shortages, waste and other social problems insofar as they are reflected in factor prices, market and competitive conditions and regulations. Product ingredients and promotional themes are being changed; no-name brands and box-stores are appearing. Canadian marketing managers are working on those real issues which are most urgent - those reflected in price, market and regulatory mechanisms. However, where there is not adequate information and a high degree of uncertainty, management does not readily act.

Marketers should now be moving forward (as undoubtedly many are) to lengthen planning horizons and to generate information in those areas that are amenable to a high degree of validation as opposed to a high degree of speculation. They bear a special burden here, for in most firms, it is marketing management that has the expertise and ability to generate and organize information from the environment for the use of the entire organization.

What has traditionally been called "market research" will have to expand and become a more important task for Canadian marketing managers if organizations are to effectively meet the challenge of rapidly changing environments. Future oriented research aimed at probing how changes in various environmental factors affect life styles will be crucial both from a public policy and individual firm and industry perspective. Several life style options will have to be tracked on a consistant basis so that industries and companies will be able to determine which sectors, which markets will grow, decline or change in

various ways. The development of consumer typologies will be
important. The sociology of consumption will have to become well
developed in order for life-style trajectories to be developed
and used in forward planning.

INTERNATIONAL AND NATIONAL EXIGENCIES

This section moves from the planning imperative and its
implications to the amplification of a series of factors whose
locii are both international and national. These factors are as
important in indicating the kind of business and industrial activity currently in transition, as in providing direction for
planning and action. The discussions and papers which deal with
future worlds, various scenarios of social and market segments
and industrial and market structure, do not, in our opinion, explore these exigencies and draw implications in any fashion com-
mensurate with their importance.

Foreign Dependence

The most obvious and crucial factor to examine is the extent of Canadian dependence on foreign countries as important
markets for primary and some secondary goods, as competitors in
such markets, as sources of investment capital, as sources of
necessary imports and as the homes of many important subsidiaries. The implication should be stated very clearly: moves
which Canada makes in a unilateral fashion where the effect is
to threaten the competitive position of any dependent sector
must be viewed as heavily cost laden for an intermediate period.
The key problem areas include foreign responses to the limits to
growth theorem, the bases for such responses, their effects on
both domestic and foreign market interests and the manner in
which they constrain and provide Canadians with avenues and opportunities for dealing with, and moving towards, conserver concepts and practices. It should also be underscored that, in the
cases of foreign owned subsidiaries in Canada (particularly U.S.
owned), there will be great pressure from the parent to have the
subsidiary accept U.S. solutions to U.S. defined problems.

The operative term in this discussion is unilateral. Changes in regulations and the shifting of costs from external to
internal categories, which are reflected in different product
specifications, different quality and performance levels and
higher net export prices, can only be successful if competing
suppliers are adjusting to conserverism problems in a fashion
which produces similar price and product effects. Close attention must be paid to the manner in which the United States,
Western Europe and Japan handle similar situations in both export and import oriented sectors important to Canada. Both the

nature and timing of responses have a great effect on Canadian marketing's ability to adjust in the least painful fashion. Canadian subsidiaries will have to strive to be truly compara- tive in order to stand up against parents when product specifi- cations and operating standards are at issue.

Eschewing unilaterial moves and concentrating on concerted action does not mean that Canadians should model needed adjust- ments on others. Some of the countries on which Canadians are dependent are more self-sufficient than are we; others are less. Industrial and business organization systems differ; elements of social structure and social values differ; strengths of eco- nomies and sectors differ. Being comparative will require care- ful sifting and analysis of the actions of others. It should allow Canada to develop truly domestic options where required and lead to low cost adaptation where appropriate.

Other aspects of dependency concern GATT and the nature of development in the Third World. In the Tokyo round of trade negotiations, the members of GATT have moved towards a lowering of tariff barriers over the next ten years and have agreed to dismantle many "non-tariff" barriers. This movement will put pressure on all secondary manufacturing, particularly those sectors which are domestically oriented and vulnerable to im- port competition. As long as Canada's major competitors face similar costs and reflect them in product specifications and prices, competitive parity, at least, is maintained. If not, domestic desires to cope with some conserver concepts (for ex- ample, full costing) will be severely constrained.

As countries in the Third World proceed with their own de- velopment plans they will increasingly pre-empt those manufac- turing sectors which operate with low technology and high lab- our content. Further, the development of many new resource sup- pliers can be expected, which could cause interesting problems in our resources markets abroad. It is fair to say that the reality and urgency which Canada may associate with the limits to growth thesis does not exist in the developing countries. They have their own problems of an extreme and immediate nature which are viewed as the obverse of our own. With respect to many conserver society concepts, however, Canada can learn from their experiences as either traditional societies or in terms of attempting to develop appropriate and intermediate technologies.

National Strains

Two closely related domestic issues should be emphasized; regional disparity, and the centralization of business and gov- ernment. Canada is in transition with respect to centralization of government. The dialogue between the provinces and the

277

Federal government will very likely result in the granting of wider powers to the provinces to deal with their perceived needs and priorities. The implication is that Canada will have more regionalism than now exists. The positive aspect of this is that a regional approach can very well be more productive than a centralized one. Senior marketing management will have to reconsider such questions as location, acquisition, merger, and distribution and product policies in the light of the growth in power (particularly fiscal) of provincial governments. It is through the leadership of the provinces that decentralization of business and industry will take place. It will be beyond what is now seen in the case of Alberta.

The immediate reaction of management to the exercising or shifting of political power appears to be one of business as usual, unless and until constrained or provided with incentives. In the short-run this may be the only sensible response, but the evidence of shift should be read more closely. It should be viewed, not just in terms of pressure to be responded to, but in terms of the restructuring implications for centralized operations where they may be amenable to restructuring. Then the positive dimension of such actions becomes apparent. Lack of responsiveness may, for example, invite a host of provincial crown corporations and assorted institutions into the picture.

Changing Behaviour and Values

Most of the future worlds that are being urged upon Canadians are said not only to require a change in the use of material and consumption patterns, but also to require changes in values and attitudes. The exhortations to change values on the assumption that this will change behaviour in general, and material consumption in particular, is very heady stuff for social engineers - be they academic or bureaucratic. One clear effect of such exhortations is to frighten people, including many managers. Marketing managers are all too well aware of the fact that normal marketing techniques are not effective in altering basic societal attitudes and values. The idea that they would be asked to perform such a task would be viewed as ethically undesirable by many Canadian marketing managers.

The better option is that, where necessary, behaviour be changed by providing either incentives (or what is currently termed disincentives), and that the behaviour change advocated is reinforced in traditional terms - not new terms. The price system is well understood by all Canadians; they know how to adapt to increases and decreases in price. They are currently becoming conservers through this kind of adaptation. They will continue to do so. As a result of this form of adaptation, their attitudes towards some material goods and services will

change and such goods and services will no longer be associated
or identified with whatever social and cultural values exist.
Exhortations to change attitudes and values without clear behavioural incentives or disincentives are likely to have only
modest effect.

COPING WITH INTERNATIONAL AND NATIONAL EXIGENCIES

The long-range planning imperative has to be undertaken
with all seriousness and dispatch. Those sectors and organizations where limited scope for unilateral action exist must be
ascertained and concentrated on first to assure their viability.
Canada is so dependent in some cases that we can do nothing
other than accept a situation. In other cases we can work mul-
tilaterally for industrial adjustment. The time frame for action will be determined outside of Canada in most types of dependence situations.

The real question is the shifting between private, and
public or social costs. The conserver concept of developing
total or full costs for product systems, production systems, or
distribution systems must be pursued. All relevant constituen-
cies must be involved in tax and social accounting. But decisions with respect to the internalizing of external or social
costs and reflecting them through product/service prices is
clearly not just an economic decision, it is a political one as
well. It makes sense to load full costs only in some situations.
The root answers to the loading of full direct and social costs
onto a sector must arise from broader business and industrial
strategy issues. Governments and the sectors must work in con-
cert on these matters.

Incentives for Action

Business and industry will generally attempt to operate in
the future as they did in the past, by incremental adjustments
to changes in prices and expected returns. Insofar as the difference between internal costs and full costs can be ascertained,
this discrepancy potentially provides the lever for adjustment
in a sector. We propose the consideration of the Value Added
Tax (V.A.T.) approach as the mechanism for dealing with the internal cost - full cost difference.

With a value added tax approach, organizations in a sector
pay a specified rate on the value added by their operations.
(Value added = value of goods sold - cost of materials, supplies,
fuel.) The value added component is the contribution of labour,
management and capital for a sector (or for an individual firm).
The applicable rate is the interesting question: a rate can

279

reflect none, some, all, or more than all, of the social costs
(based on a systematic approach) associated with the sector.
And here we add a caveat: the present sector definitions are
not necessarily the most appropriate and could well stand with
review - thirty or forty may make more sense.

It is through the tax rate set for a sector that the firms
involved can respond to conditions. For those sectors which are
heavily export oriented, the rate must reflect the realities of
competitive parity. In some cases an industry may face an almost non-existant rate regardless of the social costs. These
will be absorbed elsewhere in the economy because of the national and regional priorities set by the political and economic
climate. In other cases, medium or high rates will apply. Regardless, the rate set provides the incentive to the sector. It
may make sense in some sectors to reduce rates with increases in
value added, in others to increase them. Thus if energy costs
can be reduced, this can be reflected in a levered V.A.T. If
renewable inputs are substituted for non-renewables on a percentage basis, again a levered V.A.T. could apply.

There are other advantages inherent in a V.A.T. approach.
It is generally simpler and less costly to administer than the
existing plethora of sales taxes. When used in an inverse
fashion (the greater the value added the lower the rate), it is
an appropriate incentive in some sectors to integration. It is
of selective aid in job creation, import substitution and international marketing. V.A.T.'s are acceptable under GATT insofar
as they are perceived as sales taxes and are appropriate for
drawback with respect to export sales. A low corporate income
tax may be necessary to ensure V.A.T. drawback under GATT rules.

Moving Towards Decentralization

Important aspects of the conserver society are quality of
life, quality of workplace, humanism, independence, self-sufficiency and choices of lifestyle. These elements are all part of
the regional disparity and centralization/bureaucratization exigencies. A better job must be done with respect to what can be
termed as pre- and post-industrial dualism. Outside of the
twelve major metropolitan areas in Canada there exists a great
deal of what has been called relative "under-development."
While provincial governments and DREE have worked at developing
such areas, the record is not good. One reason for the lack of
success has been the attempt at miniature replication of major
metropolitan area development. Intermediate or appropriate
technology approaches have not been attempted often enough. The
most glaring examples of this kind of miniature replication and
its attendant consequences exist in the native peoples' communities. Other examples exist close enough to our large cities to

make the point. Two types of development are necessary in such areas: pre-industrial, which brings the quality of life and life-styles of inhabitants to a locally approved level and post-industrial, which provides alternative life-styles and qualities of life-alternatives to those that exist in the major metropolitan areas.

This paper will not "paint the scenarios" for these two forms, but rather will indicate the types of structural changes which can enable them to develop. Regional and local control of requisite resources and their utilization is a necessary condition. This kind of control is most appropriate for those sectors which are primarily internally oriented; tertiary sectors such as retailing, other services, banking and insurance. Some secondary sectors may also be appropriate. This can best be discerned when a picture of a sector's direct and social cost becomes available.

Very few economices of scale exist in tertiary industry on a full cost basis and thus centralization is inimicable to both pre- and post-industrial types of development. Wherever vertical integration and horizontal marketing systems exist in tertiary industries, they are potential bottlenecks to local and regional development. It may make a great deal of sense to have national chains and franchises reduced to regional size. Some insurance agents should be local brokers offering a locally relevant portfolio from competing suppliers, some of which are regional. Some banks should be locally owned and controlled single or small chain units. All that has to be done to achieve this is to rationalize the present local banking system in Canada, the credit union.

Some secondary industry, if reviewed in full cost terms would also be found to offer little if any advantages of scale. The development of regional suppliers for various products sold regionally would become feasible. This is simply a form of regional import substitution which can make use of either locally developed or appropriately adapted technology. More employment alternatives as well as variety of life-style would result from successful decentralization based on regional import substitution. To illustrate, the Atlantic Provinces Economic Council estimates that, in general, residents of the Atlantic Provinces spend twice as much as they earn, the shortfall being made up by various transfer and equalization payments. These tax dollars, generated from Ontario, for example, arrive in the region and then move right back out to pay for goods and services produced in central Canada. The estimate is that if one per cent of the goods and services the region imports could be sourced in the region, the gain would be $85-million. Such an amount would not make much difference in central Canada; but it is one-third of

281

P.E.I.'s budget. If national retailers operating in Atlantic
Canada can work to develop local sources rather than having a
centralized buying office deal with a few large suppliers, the
local and regional effects would multiply. Local communities
could become more attractive as population concentration points
with life-style options not available in major metropolitan
areas.

A number of structural changes must be seriously considered
for this kind of decentralization – rather than the miniature
replication variety – to have a chance to develop. If provinces
or regions were able to set V.A.T. rates, in conjunction with
the Federal government, that reflected regional sourcing and
value added in regionally defined useful terms, business and industrial decentralization incentives will become sensible. Some
will say that the country will be balkanized in development
terms and marketing managers will worry about fractured markets
and cost duplications. However, for many years, and for many
dollars, this has been the case. Rather than dealing with regional disparity on a transfer payment basis and with national
problems which fit no region or province except the eleventh
(the average one), it would seem appropriate that regions be enabled to attempt to solidify regionally appropriate levels and
styles of living. The concept of regional disparity may be the
largest structural problem Canada has. The substitution of acceptable regional alternative styles, with real provincial control over incentives to enable appropriate development and div-
ersification, appears more likely to satisfy people than continually discussed and demonstrated relative deprivation.

One more proposal for structural change must be enter-
tained. If it is sensible to decentralize organizations and re-
gionalize markets and production centres, it is equally sensible
to decentralize organized labour. Where sectors have a heavy
foreign inter-dependence, there is a case for the international
co-ordination of unions relevant to such a sector. Where international inter-dependence does not exist, and where Canada is
dependent on foreign markets, competitive parity is appropriate,
not simple wage parity. Competitive parity refers to the full
cost concept; wage parity to the direct cost approach. It would
seem inappropriate in such cases for Canadian locals of U.S.
based unions to exist – just as it may be inappropriate for some
chains to exist or some mergers to take place. Wage standards
and reference points for negotiations of wages must also be decentralized for decentralization to take place. National unions
should exist where national employers exist; regional unions
with regional employers. In any event, the value of work and of
the life-styles such work sustains, are regionally determined
and the development of labour market structures which are based
on an Edmonton or Vancouver or Toronto wage rate is as ineffic-

ient in total cost terms as is the centralized sourcing in southern Ontario of a major retail chain with significant sales in Atlantic Canada.

The spheres of responsibility of Federal and Provincial governments and sector/trade associations should be underscored in concluding this section. We propose a Federal government which uses incentives for consumers and business and industry (including crown corporations), rather than exhortations or direct involvement in operations. We envision a Federal government which provides clear regulations based upon research and planning, and which co-ordinated with the provinces. While the Federal government should maintain national responsibility for base line social programs, and for sectors with heavy international dependencies, the major responsibility for local development in economic and social terms should be at the provincial or regional level. It is here where relevant standards can best be set.

The Federal government will have to become much more of a co-ordinative apparatus than it is at present. There will be growing contention among the provinces and regions that will have to be refereed.

The provinces and regions will have to become more sophisticated with respect to planning and priorities. The ever present danger exists at the local level of becoming overly responsible to vocal pressure groups. Similarly, sector and trade associations will have to become stronger in order to carry out effective long-range forecasting and planning activities as well as to develop systematic approaches to total costing.

MANAGING ORGANIZATIONS UNDER CONSERVER CONCEPTS

It is sometimes claimed that organizations are too large; that many have become unmanageable. This may be true for a small number of highly centralized not-for-profit organizations and monopolies of both the public and private variety. However, even these kinds of organizations are probably not unmanageable. Rather, they lack clear mandates, explicit performance criteria and monitoring systems that report on performance according to some plan or set of expectations. The decentralization of large scale organizations can be expected because, if for no other reason, information and communication technology is exploding so rapidly that people will not have to be in the same building or city to communicate effectively. Physical proximity as a reason for centralization and control is rapidly becoming less important.

Shifting powers to the provinces will aid in the problem of contending with large scale organizations. Various types of activities will be decentralized because incentives will exist and technology will ease the burden of co-ordination control. More and more organizations will be decentralized simply because new venture groups seem to have a better record of being able to capitalize on new ideas and technologies when established as separate entities and moved out of the shadow of the parent. More personnel appear to be interested in the intermediate and smaller scale organizations as working environments which provide scope, responsibility and variety in work tasks.

Organizational Commitment

As individuals are able to pick and choose among a greater variety of life-styles, many of which stress either autonomy or opting for a larger number of experiences phased over time, the question of organizational commitment becomes a greater problem. Turnover rates will increase, putting pressure on organizational planning and operating systems to capture important information and keep it in the organization. More innovation will be required for training and motivational purposes. On the other hand, firms have the capacity to respond to these issues. They are doing so now and there is no reason why they cannot continue to do so in the future. Another factor to be kept in mind is that there will not be massive changes. Rather, changes will likely be predictable with appropriate environmental monitoring - selective, and incremental. Jobs are being designed and redesigned in various ways to broach the commitment problems as they materialize.

Product Planning and Development

If any phase of business activity comes under great pressure as a result of the development of conserver society concepts, it is the product planning and development area. Being more and more systematic, both in terms of product use and system effects and associated direct and indirect costs, will be more time consuming, more expensive, more difficult and will likely result in fewer "new" products. On the other hand, the new product success ratio may very well go up as a result of this process.

Many innovations in a conserver mode will be imported from the U.S. and Western Europe. Care will have to be taken to assure that there is appropriate local development to meet Canadian needs. There will be much entrepreneurial activity of an import nature which can very well become wasteful. With the advent of local or provincial banking and moves towards decentralisation, small and medium sized businesses should become more important in innovation.

Promotional Activities

Fuller disclosure of product information will be necessary
as the systematic nature of product use and effects become
known. Marketers should move quickly to more comprehensive and
stricter self-regulation in order to defend against a plethora
of regulations and disclosure requirements. Such regulations
will add to costs without necessarily adding to greater efficiency in the market-place. It is likely that all kinds of product efficiency rating schemes will be devised by governments
for the benefit of consumers. It is equally likely that most
consumers will misunderstand them, pay no attention to them, or
at best, take a long time learning to understand them.

Some critics of the marketing process have underscored the
materialistic approach of promotion. It is to be expected that
where this was the case, it will be ameliorated. This will come
about as a result of the changes in product planning and development which will produce more explicit and accurate product use
information relating to safety, proper handling and product
functions and attributes. More factual information will move
through the promotional system and replace common unsubstanti-
ated puffery and some elements of life-style promotion.

A final word with respect to promotion concerns the role of
national brands and brands in general. Price escalation and
consumer price sensitivity has weakened the position of many
national brands. With decentralization and the development of
clearer standards for performance, national brands should become
even weaker as the "information" inherent in a national brand-
name per se becomes less relevant. This should operate to weak-
en the brand owners' position in the entire marketing system and
should mean that many U.S. owned brands and subsidiaries will
lose their current dominant positions to the gain of regional
Canadian brands and firms.

Capital Accumulation and Stakeholders

Decentralization in banking and insurance should cause
greater search for investment opportunities at the local and regional level. The effective setting of Federal and Provincial
V.A.T. rates should attract capital. More profit-sharing and
employee stock plans would help, not in raising capital but in
increasing productivity and reducing costs.

A recent development in Britain is worthy of study. A task
force studying possible revisions to the British tax system has
suggested replacing the progressive tax on income with a

285

progressive tax on expenditure. An individual would record his income, plus receipts from the sales of assets, and deduct from that total payments such as the purchase of securities or mortgage interest. The balance, "consumption", would be subject to a progressive expenditure tax subject to an exemption indexed to the rate of inflation. Such an expenditure tax is said to promote savings and investment generally, remove disincentives to high-income earners, and encourage the small businessman and self-employed workers. There would be problems in refining and applying such a concept, but it deserves study as it could have some of the characteristics of a personal V.A.T. to encourage capital formation and modity life styles and consumption patterns.

Management's Responsibilities

As a concluding comment, we would like to point out that we are not ignoring such matters as the environment, quality of work-life and urban life, and the lack of humanism in daily affairs - all of the things that we come up against on a daily basis. Rather what we are saying is that these and other matters of everyday concern will be well looked after if we make some adjustments in our system so that people can be given the scope to act responsibly. In this we include management at all levels as well as all others who work in Canadian business and industry.

The coming years will be difficult because we will most likely have to deal with relatively slow growth coupled with the need for relatively rapid rates of adjustment. For the last twenty-five years Canadian marketing managers have lived with easy change and growth which submerged adjustments. Canada will no longer have the excess of resources to cover up both errors and slow rates of adaptation. The easy growth has made us less responsible than might otherwise have been the case.

REFERENCES

Anderson, Robert C. (1977), "Public Policies Toward the Use of Scrap Materials," American Economic Review, 67, 1 (February), pp. 355-358.

Anonymous (1977), Agenda for Co-operation: A Discussion Paper on Decontrol and Post-Control Issues, Ottawa: Government of Canada, (May).

Anonymous (1976), The Way Ahead: A Framework for Discussion, Ottawa: Government of Canada,(October).

Cardinal, Robert J., Ronald J. Sanderson and George J. Wingerter (1977), "The Changing Private Market System," Journal of Advertising, 6,3,pp. 34-40.

Carpentier, Michel (1977), "The Background To Consumer Affairs: The European Perspective," speech presented in London, England before European Association of Advertising Agencies, December 5.

Coleman, John T. (1977), "Alpha Society Briefing Paper: Gamma Report on the Selective Conserver Society," March 1.

Elgin, Duane and Arnold Mitchell (1976), Voluntary Simplicity, Stanford Research Institute Business Intelligence Program Long Range Planning Service Guidelines, June, no. 1004.

Firth, Raymond (1976), Tikopia Ritual and Belief, Boston: Beacon Press.

Fisher, Anthony C. and John V. Knitilla (1975), "Resources Conservation, Environmental Preservation, And The Rate of Discount," The Quarterly Journal of Economics, LXXXIX, 3, (August), pp. 358-370.

Fisk, George (1973), "Criteria for a Theory of Responsible Consumption," Journal of Marketing, 37, 2, (April), pp. 24-31.

Gordon, Myron J. (1978), "A World Scale National Corporation I Industiral Strategy," Canadian Public Policy, IV, 1, (Winter), pp. 44-56.

Haines, George H. (ed.) (1976), Problems in Consumer Affairs: A Research Symposium, Toledo, Ohio: Business Research Center, College of Business Administration, The University of Toledo.

Harman, Willis H. (1976), An Incomplete Guide to the Future, San Francisco: San Francisco Book Company, Inc.

Louis Harris and Associates Inc. for Sentry Insurance, Consumerism at the Crossroads.

Henderson, Hazel (1973), "Ecologists vs. Economists," Harvard Business Review, (July-August).

_____(1974), "The Decline of Jonesism," The Futurist, (October).

_____ (1974), "The Entropy State," Planning Review, 2,3 (April-May).

_____ (1975), "Limitations of Traditional Economics in Making Resource Decisions," Transactions of the 40th North American Wildlife and Natural Resources Conference.

_____ (1976), "The Coming Economic Transition," Technological Forecasting and Social Change, (March).

_____ (1976), "A Farewell on the Corporate State," Business and Society Review, 17.

_____ (1977), "Constraints Affecting the Futures of the Packaging Industry," Human Resource Management, 16,1, (Spring).

_____ (1978), Creating Alternative Futures: The End of Economics, New York, N.Y.: Berkeley Publishing Co.

Hotelling, Harold (1931), "The Economics of Exhaustible Resources," Journal of Political Economy, 39, (April).

Kahn, Herman, William Brown and Leon Martel (1976), The Next 200 Years: A Scenario for America and the World, New York: William Morrow and Co. Inc.

Kotler, Philip and Sidney Levy (1971), "Demarketing, Yes, Demarketing," Harvard Business Review, 49,2, (November-December) pp. 74-80.

Marien, Michael (1976), Societal Institutions and Alternatives: A Critical Guide to the Literature, Information for Policy Design, LaFayette, N.Y.

Mathias, Philip (1971), Forced Growth, Toronto: James Lewis and and Samuel, Publishers.

Meadows, Donella H., Dennis L. Meadows, Jorgen Randers, William W. Behrens III (1972), The Limits to Growth, New York: Signet Books (New American Library).

Mermelstein, David (ed.) (1975), The Economic Crisis Reader, New York: Vintage Books.

Mesarovic, Mihajlo and Edward Pestel (1976), Mankind at the Turning Point, The New American Library of Canada Limited.

Mishan, E.S., The Costs Of Economic Growth, Harmondsworth, Middlesex, England: Penguin Books Limited,.

Moyer, Mel, Consumerism in the Future: Complex Questions and Collaboration Answers, unpublished working paper, Faculty of Administrative Studies, York University.

Nelson, Ruben F.W. (1976), The Illusions of Urban Man, Ottawa: Ministry of State for Urban Affairs.

Quirin, Davis, "Economic Problems in A Conserver Society," unpublished working paper, Faculty of Management Studies, University of Toronto.

Reich, Charles A. (1970), The Greening of America, New York: Random House.

Rotstein, Abraham (1976), Beyond Industrial Growth, Toronto: University of Toronto Press.

Science Council of Canada (1975-1976), Conserver Society Notes Vol. 1, No. 1 through Vo. 2, No. 1, Ottawa: Science Council of Canada.

Science Council Committee on the Implications of a Conserver Society (1977), Canada as a Conserver Society: Resource Uncertainties and the Need for New Technologies, Ottawa: Science Council of Canada.

Simon, Leonard S., Examination of Techniques Used For Demand Reduction Or Re-Allocation in the Financial Industry, Working Paper Series 7524, Graduate School of Management, University of Rochester.

Smith, J. Graham (1977), "Consumer and Conserver Societies: A Choice, and a Challenge for Canada," Notes for luncheon address before Canadian Advertising Advisory Board, Royal York Hotel, Toronto, (November 15).

_____ (1977), "Not Gloom and Doom But Profit and Boom In a Conserver Society," draft of remarks presented at conference on Business Opportunities in a Conserver Society, sponsored by Economic Development Advisory Council of Manitoba, Winnipeg, (April 26).

Stavrianos, L.S. (1976), The Promise of the Coming Dark Age, San Francisco: W.H. Freeman and Company.

Thorelli, Hans B., Helmut Becker and Jack Engledow (1975), The Information Seekers: An International Study of Consumer Information and Advertising Image, Cambridge, Mass.: Ballinger Publishing Co.

Tomczak, Michael (1978), "The Impact of a Business Cycle on the Candian Urban System: Changes in Manufacturing Employment 1972-76," Discussion Paper Series, University of Toronto, Department of Geography, (February).

Valaskakis, Kimon, Peter S. Sindel, and J. Graham Smith (1975), Tentative Blueprints For A Conserver Society in Canada, Preliminary Draft Report, Gamma Conserver Society Project, Universite De Montreal and McGill University, (July).

_____ (1977), The Selective Conserver Society, Montreal: GAMMA (Universites de Montreal/McGill University), (February).

290

CONSUMER ENERGY CONSUMPTION
AND CONSERVATION RESEARCH

John D. Claxton, University of British Columbia
C. Dennis Anderson, University of Manitoba
Gordon H. G. McDougall, Wilfred Laurier University
J.R. Brent Ritchie, University of Calgary

ABSTRACT

Energy use and conservation are becoming critical areas of public policy. In particular, there is a need to develop effective policy initiatives to curb energy demand in the residential sector. There is a definite role for consumer research in the formulation, selection and evaluation of energy conservation policies. The focus of this paper is on research in the area of consumer energy consumption and conservation (CECC). A framework which provides a structure for cataloguing conservation policy initiatives and CECC research studies, is presented. Policy initiatives are classified on two dimensions: (1) stage of intervention (whether they affect the availability, purchase decision or use behavior of energy forms or energy consuming products) and (2) policy type (whether they are financial or non-financial in nature and whether they are mandatory or persuasive). Research must determine: (1) the extent of energy savings (technical/potential) from alternative policy initiatives and (2) consumer reaction (attitudinal and behavioral) to the policy. CECC research focused on the latter area will help determine the extent to which actual energy savings will match the technical/potential energy savings of conservation policy initiatives.

The purposes and conceptual and methodological issues facing CECC researchers are discussed and illustrated. This is followed by an overview of CECC research activity, much of which has been initiated by the Canadian Department of Consumer and Corporate Affairs and the U.S. Department of Energy. This research activity is classified according to the conservation policy framework. The paper closes with an indication of future CECC research directions.

L'utilisation et la conservation de l'énergie sont devenues des propros critiques dans le domaine des affaires publiques. Il y a surtout un besoin urgent de développer des principes d'initiatives efficaces pour réduire la demande d' énergie dans les secteurs résidentiels. La recherche auprès des consommateurs a un rôle bien défini dans la formulation, la sélection et l'évaluation des principes sur la conservation de l'énergie. Cet article se concentre surtout sur la recherche dans le domaine de l'utilisation du consommateur et la conservation de l'energie (UCCE). Un système y est présenté fournissant une structure capable de cataloguer les principes d'initiatives et les études des recherches faites à ce sujet. Les principes d'initiatives sont classé en deux dimensions: (1) le stage d'intervention (à savoir s'ils affectent la disponibilité, les dédisions d'achats et le comportement dans l'usage) et (2) les genres de principes adoptés (à savoir s'ils sont d'ordre financier ou non non et s'ils sont obligatoires ou persuasifs). La recherche doit determiner: (1) la mesure d'économie de l'énergie (technique/potentielle) réalisée par d'autres principes d' initiatives) et (2) la réaction du consommateur (attitude et comportement) vis-à-vis ces principes. Les recherches de UCCE concentrées sur la deuxième dimension aideront à déterminer si l'étendue de l'économie d'énergie actuellement réalisée peut se comparer à l'économie d'énergie technique/ potentielle des principes d'initiatives sur la conservation.

Les buts et les questions conceptuelles et méthodolo- giques à lesquelles les rechercheurs de la UCCE doivent faire face, sont discutés et illustrés. Le tout est suivi d'une vue d'ensemble sur l'activité de recherches de la UCCE, laquelle a été en grande partie promue par le Ministère Canadien du Consommateur et des Corporations et le départe- ment de l'Energie des Etats-Unis. L'article se termine sur une indication des directions que devraient prendre les recherches du UCCE dans le futur.

INTRODUCTION

Energy use and conservation are among Canada's most critical areas of public policy. Though much attention is given to policies designed to maintain or increase energy supplies, it is also important to curb energy demand by developing policies to encourage energy conservation. In particular, there is a need for conservation in Canada's residential energy sector.

The urgency of residential sector conservation is clearly illustrated in an Energy Strategy Report (Department of Energy Mines and Resources 1976) which presents a 1990 energy conservation scenario for Canada. The conservation scenario envisages that in-house or residential demand for energy will drop from 19% of total energy demand in 1972 to 13% in 1990. In comparison, the industrial sector demand is viewed as increasing from 25.5% to 29% during the same period. Clearly, if the 1990 scenario is to become a reality, in-home energy conservation must be achieved.

The focus of this paper is on research in the area of consumer energy consumption and conservation (CECC). The view taken is that CECC within the home are not a series of unrelated events. Rather, they are components of an inte- grated lifestyle. though CECC can be interpreted narrowly to signify actual energy consuming and conserving behaviors of householders, it is more appropriate to use the term more broadly to refer to consumers' household energy patterns in terms of their knowledge, attitudes, values and actual behaviors. To be successful, policy initiatives will have to be based on a thorough understanding of all these dimensions of CECC.

The purpose of this paper is to privide an overview of CECC and to discuss the role of consumer research in this area. The first section of this paper presents an overview of CECC in which the following issues are discussed:

(1) the concerns that have brought this area into prominance,

(2) the complexities facing CECC initiatives, and

(3) a framework for CECC actions.

The second section considers CECC research in terms of:

(1) the purposes of CECC research,

(2) CECC research concerns, and

(3) an overview of existing CECC studies.

The paper closes with an indication of future CECC research directions.

CECC OVERVIEW

Background Concerns

There are three concerns that provide the impetus for and
guide the development of CECC research. The first concern is
evidence of impending energy shortages. The second is the
research indicating that consumers do not feel a need to make
significant individual efforts to reduce energy consumption.
The third factor is a need to provide information which will
guide energy conservation policy. Each of these three background concerns will be discussed in turn.

"Energy problem" concerns. Given the apparent abundance
of energy resources currently available to Canadians, it is
useful to be reminded of the serious energy shortages that are
likely to occur in the non-too-distant future. A pointed re-
minder is provided by Energy Futures for Canadians (1978), a
report published by the Federal Department of Energy, Mines
and Resources. In summary, this report indicates that, if
Canada is to be energy-self-reliant by the year 2000, all of
the following must occur:

. reduction of the energy demand growth rate of
  one-half the historic 5.3 percent rate.
. increase of Canadian oil production by 50 percent.
. increase of natural gas production by one-third.
. increase of coal production by four or five-fold.
. increase of electrical energy from one-third to
  one-half of total primary energy.
. supply of at least 5 percent of primary energy
  from renewables other than hydro.

One of the major action recommendations put forward by the
Energy Futures report was for an "Energy Information and Participation Program." Three of the objectives suggested for this
program parallel the general purposes of CECC research. These
are:
. to ensure that the public is aware of the national
  threat posed by the evolving energy situation in
  Canada and abroad and that the public is continually
  able to evaluate the implications of changing developments.
. to assist members of the public to appreciate how
  their active, responsible participation in energy-
  related activities contributes to a satisfactory
  energy transformation.

294

. to ensure that up-to-date information is always available to participants in all parts of the country in order to permit meaningful discussion, debate, evaluation and participation in energy-related programs.

Evidence of impending energy shortages is clear. The need to acquaint the general public with the seriousness and urgency of the energy situation and the need to alter their consumption patterns, provides the major impetus for CECC research.

"I'm alright, Jack" concerns. A number of factors may contribute to consumers' opinions about the seriousness of the energy supply situation. The 1973 oil embargo and subsequent shortages prompted many Canadians to realize that energy supplies should not be taken for granted. However, more recent oil discoveries, disagreements between government and industry as to reserve levels, and the apparent lack of any major conservation initiatives undoubtedly explain consumer complacency regarding household conservation efforts.

Evidence of dwindling consumer interest in conservation is provided in a longitudinal study commissioned by the Office of Energy Conservation, Department of Energy, Mines and Resources. Consumer perceptions as to the seriousness of the energy shortage gradually increased from 1975 through 1977. However, in 1978 this trend reversed. Consumers considered energy shortages to be less serious than they had the year before (McDougall and Keller 1979).

Other evidence is provided by a recent survey (McDougall, Ritchie and Claxton 1979). This study indicates that consumers were largely unaware of how their household energy consumption compared with other households. Even householders with extremely high consumption levels felt they used "about the same" amount of energy as other householders. Further, consumers generally felt they were doing as much for energy conservation as most other people. Hence, the phrase "I'm alright, Jack" aptly describes this apparently common attitude toward conservation. Consideration of the "I'm alright, Jack" syndrome suggests the need to look for means of using CECC findings to increase consumer awareness.

Energy policy concerns. From the perspective of policy formulation and selection, it is possible to assess in a technical sense the energy savings that could result from any particular policy. However, consumer reaction to a policy will influence the degree to which potential savings become actual savings (Evans Ritchie and McDougall 1978). The implication for CECC research is that an integrated picture of household energy consumption is needed not only to provide factual information as to types and amounts of energy consumed, but also information regarding consumer feelings about the importance of various energy consuming activities. How much energy is consumed in various household areas? In which areas would consumers be most willing to reduce? What types of energy restrictions would consumers find least objectionable? Which consumers will be most affected? Questions of this type should be addressed during the formulation and selection of energy conservation policy, and answers to these questions require a thorough understanding of household energy consumption and conservation patterns.

Three background concerns, then, shape CECC research. "Energy problem" concerns provide the initial impetus. The "I'm alright, Jack" outlook of consumers focuses attention first on the problem of increasing consumer sensitivity to household energy consumption, and seond, on how best to accomplish this task through the provision of CECC information. Finally, conservation policy concerns required CECC research to focus, not only on the quantitative dimensions of household energy consumption behavior, but also on linkages between this behavior and householder energy related attitudes and values.

Complexities Facing CECC Initiatives

In attempting to select policy initiatives which will encourage energy conservation, policy makers face a series of complexities such as:

. multiple jurisdictions.
. energy action interdependencies.
. incomplete technical data on consumption.
. fragmented expertise.
. philosophical - political issues.

After each of these complexities is discussed below, a framework which has been developed to minimize the problems presented by these complexities will be outlined.

Multiple jurisdictions. Consumer energy conservation is not the responsibility of a single agency. Insulation standards for new houses, highway speed limits, prices of residential electricity, and energy consumption labels all have potential for stimulating consumer energy conservation. Yet, each of these areas is the responsibility of a different federal or provincial agency or department. From the perspective of developing a meaningful conservation strategy there is a clear need to view the issue from a broader vantage point than that of any single jurisdiction.

Incomplete technical data on consumption. To make informed judgments regarding the impact of particular actions on
energy consumption requires consumption data obtained through
standardized technical procedures. Although this type of
technical data base is improving, it is far from complete.
For example, the only household appliance for which Canadian
data is available to enable comparisons of energy consumption
across models is refrigerators. On the other hand, recent
research efforts have been directed to the important task of
cataloguing the potential energy savings that might result
from various conservation actions (Cullen 1979).

Fragmented expertise. Although there is clearly a great
deal of expertise on which to draw for energy related concerns,
this expertise is dispersed among many agencies and organizations. For example, the expertise for each of the following
would be found in a considerable variety of places: the
effect of increasing home insulation by two inches; the impact
on consumers of increasing the prices of inefficient cars; the
feasibility of implementing standard test procedures to provide life cycle cost data for appliances; the development of
an effective media and message campaign to get consumers to
lower thermostat settings. Because these types of expertise
may be dispersed, the task of evaluating alternative conservation initiatives is made more difficult.

Philosophical-political issues. In addition to comparing
alternative energy conservation actions in terms of maximum net
benefit-cost, attention must be given to the nature of the
action. Is the consumer response voluntary or mandatory? Is
the impact uniform across all Canadian consumers or does the
action present hardships for particular consumer groups? At a
time when policy makers are striving for de-regulation, it is
clearly desirable to have conservation initiatives based on
voluntary response rather than regulation. Further, the potential impact of conservation policies on voter preferences is a
continuing political concern.

In order to cope with this complex range of issues, a
framework providing an overview of consumer energy conservation
areas would seem particularly appropriate. A framework developed for this purpose is presented in the following discussion.

A Framework for CECC Initiatives

As reported elsewhere (Anderson and Claxton 1978; Evans
Ritchie and McDougall 1978), a framework for formulation and
analysis of energy policy has been developed over the past year.
This work was initiated by the Consumer Research and Evaluation

Branch of the Federal Department of Consumer and Corporate Affairs. The general purposes of the framework are: (1) to provide a means of enumerating energy conservation policies, (2) to provide a structure for cataloging conservation research information, and (3) to provide a systematic mechanism for assessing the probable impact of alternative energy conservation policies.

Figure 1 captures the essential elements of the conservation policy framework. As indicated at the left of Figure 1, there are three major intervention stages or foci for consumer conservation policies: policies may be designed to affect (1) the availability of energy forms or energy consuming products to consumers, (2) the purchase decision sued by consumers to select a particular energy form or energy consuming product, and (3) the nature and extent of consumption behavior exhibited by consumers subsequent to the purchase decision. It should be noted that interventions aimed at energy forms can be considered direct while those targeted at products can be considered indirect.

For each intervention foci there may be several types of policies that are appropriate. The two major alternative policy types identified in Figure 1 are financial and non-financial. Within each of these major categories, policies can be subclassified on the basis of whether they are mandatory or persuasive. The examples contained in Figure 1 are illustrative of policy actions that are currently in place or that might be contemplated by various levels of government.

A third dimension of the framework (not indicated in Figure 1) is the nature of the energy consuming activity. Four major consumer energy activities are home heating, water heating, appliances, and travel. When these four activities are combined with the six intervention foci and the four policy types, a total of 96 possible policy categories can be enumerated. This is not to say that it is possible to identify a policy in each of these categories. However, the framework can stimulate creative search for policy alternatives.

A major outcome of this policy framework is the concept of pay-off matrix (McDougall Ritchie and Claxton 1979). As indicated in Figure 2, this matrix is defined by "Intervention Focus" and "Nature of Energy Consuming Activity." The purpose of this pay-off matrix is to identify the extent of energy savings possible from each policy category generated by the pay-off framework. What potential energy savings could result from a particular increase in home insulation? What potential energy savings could result from consumers' shift from frost-free to manual defrost refrigerators? Answers to these types

FIGURE 1

CONSERVATION POLICY FRAMEWORK AND SOME EXAMPLE POLICIES

POLICY TYPES

INTERVENTION FOCUS	FINANCIAL		NON-FINANCIAL	
	MANDATORY	PERSUASIVE	MANDATORY	PERSUASIVE
(1) Availability				
(i) energy supply	X	Grants for R and D of solar energy systems.	Rationing.	Programs to encourage substitution of oil by natural gas for home heating.
(ii) energy consuming products	X	Removal of taxes on energy efficient products.	Product restrictions.	Provide energy "seals of approval" to persuade appliance retailers (manufacturers) to stock (design) energy efficient appliances.
(2) Purchase Decisions				
(i) energy supply	Tax non-renewable energy types.	Subsidies available for renewable energy types.	X	Advertise merits of adopting renewable energy heating systems.
(ii) energy consuming products	Tax inefficient products.	Subsidies available for energy efficient products.	X	Energy labeling programs (eg., energuide) for major energy consuming durables.
(3) Consumption Behavior				
(i) energy supply	Increase price of electricity.	Rebates for staying within an energy quota.	Ban use of energy for certain purposes (eg., heating pools).	Advertise merits of discrete use of gasoline, electricity, etc.
(ii) energy consuming products	Increase price of inefficient products.	Subsidize furnace maintenance.	Reduce highway speed limits.	Advertise merits of furnance maintenance.

FIGURE 2

CONSERVATION POLICY

PAY-OFF MATRIX

NATURE OF ENERGY CONSUMING ACTIVITY

INTERVENTION FOCUS	Home Heating	Water Heating	Appliances	Travel
(1) Availability				
(i) Energy source				
(ii) Energy consuming products				
(2) Purchase Decisions				
(i) Energy source				
(ii) Energy consuming products				
(3) Consumption Behavior				
(i) Energy source				
(ii) Energy consuming products				

of questions are currently being compiled (Cullen 1979).

The significance of the pay-off matrix concept for CECC research is that matrix pay-offs are defined on a <u>technical</u> basis. It remains for CECC research to assess consumer views and preferences regarding various types of energy, various energy applications, and various government actions. Understanding these consumer energy values is seen as critical to the task of judging consumer reaction to any policy alternative, and hence the extent to which <u>actual</u> energy savings will match <u>potential</u> energy savings specified by the pay-off matrix.

CONSUMER RESEARCH AND CECC

The first part of this section, which deals with consumer research and CECC, discusses the general purposes of CECC research and is followed by an outline of conceptual issues facing **researchers involved in this work.** The section concludes with an overview of existing CECC research.

CECC Research Purposes

The intention here is to suggest two general purposes that provide the rationale for the study of CECC. Briefly, these general purposes are:

. to provide a description of household energy
  consumption and conservation patterns so that
  consumers may become more aware of the importance
  of energy conservation.
. to provide an understanding of household energy
  consumption and conservation patterns that will
  assist in the evaluation of energy conservation
  policies.

The first purpose, the development of information to increase consumer energy awareness, is based on two premises: (1) consumers do not see dwindling energy supplies as a major concern at present, and (2) consumer understanding of energy consumption is hampered by a lack of factual information on consumers' own consumption relative to that of their neighbours and consumers in other parts of Canada. These premises were considered earlier under the heading, "I'm alright, Jack" concerns. The implication of this for CECC research is that an integrated approach to household energy consumption must be developed that will provide consumers with a straightforward means of putting their own consumption into perspective. In other words, CECC findings should provide a simple summary of major types of household energy consumption. As will be discussed later, this might be accomplished by using a household energy consumption profile that would indicate consumption in three major areas: home heating, electricity, and automobile gasoline.

The second general purpose, the provision of information to aid in the evaluation of energy policies, evolves from the conservation policy concerns discussed earlier. In summary, it is clear that consumers represent a major potential target for energy policy efforts. Examples of policy alternatives include restricting energy consuming products, persuading consumers to reduce consumption, increasing energy prices and subsidizing energy conserving products. The potential impact of alternative policy initiatives must be judged by (1) evaluating in a technical sense the potential energy savings that could accrue from any particular policy, and (2) assessing, in a behavioral sense, probable consumer reaction to the policy. It is the latter area that provides a major focus for CECC research.

CECC Research Concerns

With the aforementioned purposes in mind, attention will now be directed to three conceptual areas. The first area is the formulation of a model which will incorporate the factors that might be expected to influence household energy consumption and conservation decisions. This will be followed by a discussion of issues involved in the development of a household energy consumption profile. The third area involves the evaluation of potential measurement problems associated with obtaining information on household energy consumptions.

Household energy decision model. Figure 3 presents the conceptual model that has been developed to suggest areas of CECC data collection and analysis. The lower half of the model identifies three major sets of dependent (or resultant) variables. One set is behavioral, dealing with ongoing household consumption and conservation actions. The two other sets are action preferences, one dealing with female conservation preferences and one dealing with male conservation preferences.

The upper half of the model identifies three major sets of explanatory (or predictor) variables. One set is existing situational factors, such as type of dwelling, electrical products and automobiles owned by householders. The other two sets are variables which focus on the energy views and values of each household head.

The model also identifies several anticipated linkages between and among variable sets. The views and values of the female household head are expected to be related to her

FIGURE 3

HOUSEHOLD ENERGY DECISION MODEL

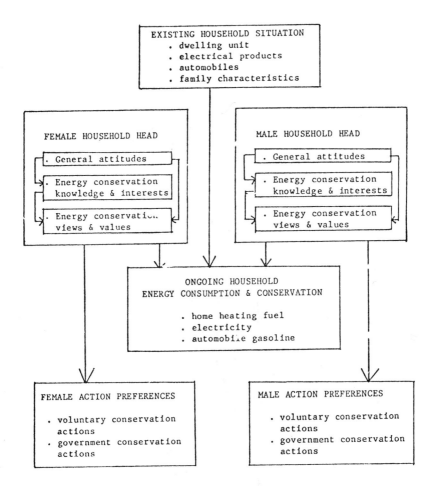

303

FIGURE 4

EXAMPLE OF HOUSEHOLD ENERGY
CONSUMPTION PROFILES

ENERGY CONSUMED

Home   Household   Automobile

Heating   Electricity   Gasoline

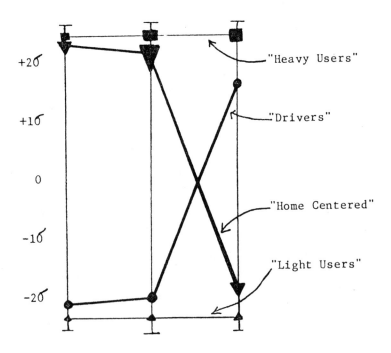

conservation action preferences. A similar linkage is expected for the male household head. A more complex and, to some extent, more interesting linkage is that three sets of variables are potentially **related to ongoing household energy** actions. The energy views and values of both household heads, together with existing situational variables, all have potential for affecting ongoing consumption and conservation. Clearly, prior research on family decision making, as reviewed so well by Davis (1976), has much to offer in terms of guidance for future CECC studies.

Household energy consumption profiles. The second area of conceptual importance is the issue of how to summarize energy consumption. In a major American study (Newman and Day 1975), energy consumption was summarized and discussed by considering various end uses, one at a time. However, to understand household energy consumption more fully it may be useful to be able to recognize differing patterns of household energy usage. Some households might be expected to use a modest amount of energy for each of home heating, appliances and travel, while others might use relatively little energy for heating and applicances and a large amount for travel. Being able to recognize differences in consumption patterns is considered an important step to understanding household energy consumption. One such approach might use a household energy consumption profile based on three major energy uses: home heating, household electricity and automobile gasoline.

Figure 4 indicates examples of household types that might be identified by analyzing consumption profiles. Clearly the profiles suggested in this figure are somewhat simplistic. However, they indicate that concentrating on energy profiles, rather than single energy uses or aggregate consumption, provides a more complete picture of household energy usage. An understanding of household consumption can then be sought by relating energy profiles to (1) enabling and constraining factors in the household situation, and (2) energy views and values of household members.

CECC measurement issues. A major primary concern of CECC research is to determine an approach that will obtain accurate measures of household energy consumption. There are many unresolved questions in this area. Do householders save heating fuel and electricity bills? Would they be willing to look them up? Could they provide an accurate estimate of total miles driven per year and miles per gallon for their vehicles?

Guidance in this area is provided by a recent study done in London, Ontario (McDougall 1979) and by a major study of American household energy consumption (Newman and Day 1975).

The former indicates that, although many households do keep records of heating and electricity expenditures, an equal number of households do not. The same concern led Newman and Day to obtain heating and electricity expenditures directly from public utilities. Each respondent in their sample was asked to sign an authorization that would allow the applicable utilities to release energy consumption information.

The utility authorization procedure is obviously a cumbersome approach. Although it has been adopted in two major studies (Newman and Day 1975; McDougall Ritchie and Claxton 1979), it is impractical to suggest that it be used as a standard practice for CECC research. Thus, the concern for obtaining accurate measures of consumer energy consumption will continue to require serious research attention.

Overview of Existing CECC Research

Bibliographic works. Over the last year three major bibliographic works centering on energy research have been compiled. The first is an annotated bibliography (Anderson and Cullen 1978) which reviews in excess of 200 pieces of energy related consumer research. In addition to annotating each piece of research, the bibliography classifies studies based on: (1) major attitude and behavior categories, (2) country where the research was done, (3) year in which the research was reported, (4) type of energy being researched, and (5) energy usage situation. The second work is an annotated bibliography of research studies centered on the impact of economic incentives on energy consumption (Nemetz 1979). This work also provides extensive categorization on such dimensions as incentive, energy consumption activity and target consumer group.

Finally, a review by Cullen (1979) provides an excellent summary of existing data on potential energy savings that could be expected from a broad range of domestic conservation activities. For example, existing evidence indicates that: (1) improved home insulation can result in savings ranging from 20 to 50 percent of projected national sector demand, (2) use of radial tires may lead to savings of approximately 25 percent of projected sector demand, and (3) use of manual versus frost-free refrigerators could lead to savings of approximately 50 percent in energy used. This type of conservation estimate can thus be used to estimate the potential impact of various conservation initiatives - a major step in estimating the probable pay-off of alternative conservation policies.

Energy life-styles and attitudes research. The Anderson and Cullen bibliography indicates an extensive list of attitudinal research studies which relate to CECC. The discussion here is limited to two Canadian studies. The first is an important longitudinal study completed for the Department of Energy, Mines and Resources, Ottawa (Contemporary Research Centre 1975, 1976, 1977, 1978). Each year for the past four years telephone interviews were conducted in seven cities across Canada. Respondents were asked their views on a range of energy issues such as perceived seriousness of the energy shortage, the role of individual efforts in energy conservation, preferences for voluntary versus regulatory conservation initiatives, the role of technology in alleviating energy shortage, and current household conservation actions.

The results of this research **have** been reported in annual research papers. In addition, the data has been analyzed on a longitudinal basis (McDougall and Keller 1979). This latter analysis indicates, for example, that after a substantial increase in the perceived seriousness of an energy shortage between 1975 and 1977, this consumer concern has stabilized and possibly started to decline.

A second Canadian study that focused on household energy issues was one sponsored by the Department of Consumer and Corporate Affairs, Ottawa. This research went beyond consumer attitudes to a composite analysis of household life-styles with respect to energy consumption/conservation. The purpose of the study was to classify households based on consumption profiles and energy values. The consumption profiles were composed of the extent of home heating, electricity usage, and automobile gasoline consumption. The energy values reflected dimensions of social responsibility and concern. To help provide an understanding of why household consumption profiles differ, the profiles were related to situational and demographic factors.

The data collection for this study was carried out during the fall of 1978, and involved three questionnaires from each household in a national panel of approximately 2000. One questionnaire gathered factual information on household energy consumption and situation/demographic descriptors. The second questionnaire assessed the energy views and values of the female household head. The third questionnaire did the same for the male household head. Energy consumption information was also obtained from the particular energy suppliers serving each household.

The analysis of this data is currently in progress. However, an overview paper (McDougall Ritchie and Claxton 1979) indicates the following general findings:

(1) Energy Consumption: average household energy

expenditure is $1,400 per year (or $760 if no gasoline expenditures).

(2) Seriousness of energy shortage: the energy shortage is seen as the least serious of five national concerns; however, approximately 20% see it as a "very serious" problem.

(3) Views on energy: indications are that householders tend to push the energy problem into the future, want to avoid major sacrifices in the present, and tend to view others (such as business) as being more responsible for the problem than themselves.

(4) Energy knowledge: householders tend to underestimate the energy saving that would result from alternative conservation actions.

(5) Current energy conservation actions: indicates a number of minor actions, such as turning down thermostat and changing furnace filters; 10% use public transportation, 12% have modified furnace, and 30% have added insulation.

(6) Future voluntary conservation actions: willingness to reduce home thermostat by three degrees, turn down hot water heater, and drive 1600 miles less per year.

(7) Government action preferences: preferences of householders indicate a desire to minimize the direct impact of government policy on themselves; doubling of energy prices is consistently seen as the worst type of conservation action.

Although aggregate statistics of this type provide an important overview of householder energy consumption and conservation, a major research effort centres on identifying and understanding energy patterns as they differ from household to household. This analysis of household patterns is currently underway.

"Availability" research. As previously discussed, energy conservation can be focused on three alternative stages of intervention: (1) on the availability/design of energy supplies or energy consuming products, (2) on consumers' purchase decisions, and (3) on the manner in which consumers use energy sources or energy consuming products. There appears to be considerable potential for conservation through changes in design or restrictions in market offerings. The research documented by Cullen (1979) indicates, for example, that if all homes were modified to 6 inches of insulation the equivalent of approximately 60,000 barrels of oil per day would be saved. Further, if all automobiles averaged 21 miles per gallon, approximately 50,000 barrels of oil per day would be saved.

"Purchase decision" research. The annotated bibliographies mentioned earlier indicate considerable research focused
on conservation through consumer selection of energy efficient
products. A number of information programs have been advocated
as means of encouraging energy efficient choices. For example,
Lune (1977) and other researchers at the Centre for Policy
Alternatives at MIT have promoted the potential of a product
life cycle cost (LCC) information scheme. The major components
of LCC are purchase price, energy operating costs and repair
and maintenance costs. The hope is that the provision of LCC
information to consumers will lead to purchase decisions based
on total lifetime costs rather than simply on lowest initial
price. To the extent that more energy efficient models have
the lowest life cycle costs, consumer use of the LCC purchase
criterion will result in energy savings. The only reported
test of the impact of objective LCC information on attitudinal
and behavioral dimensions of consumer decision making is a
study conducted by Hutton (1977). His results provided a preliminary assessment of how consumers actually do respond to
the LCC concept. Hutton's study involved consumers in simulated purchasing of major appliances. His major findings
included: (1) strongest results being seen in measures reflecting levels of consumer response in a more cognitive, as
opposed to behavioral, sense, (2) consumers using the LCC information when it is provided with positive results, (3) more
positive attitudes being seen in relation to energy saving
features and less favorable toward energy using features, and
(4) in a simulated purchase condition, subjects in the LCC
condition did purchase appliances that were significantly
more energy efficient.

Another second study centering on energy efficient purchase choices was sponsored by the U.S. Department of Energy
(National Demographics Ltd., 1978). The study, called ECO
(Energy Cost of Ownership), was carried out in Denver, Colorado.
It involved an integrated marketing communications program
designed to motivate consumers to use the concept of ECO when
purchasing energy consuming products. The communications included paid multi-media advertising, a home energy retrofit
contest and a shopping centre display of a home energy use
simulator. Before and after measures of consumer acceptance
of energy conservation and conservation related products were
taken both in Denver and in a control city, Salt Lake City,
Utah. The results of the ECO demonstration are very encouraging. Significant changes in consumer attitudes and knowledge
about a variety of conservation dimensions were achieved as
well as some small shifts in behavior (e.g., greater belief in
personal contribution to solving the energy problem, greater
knowledge about costs and savings of specific conserving
measures, greater willingness to purchase energy consuming

products even though initial price is higher, increased purchases of energy conserving devices such as automatic set back thermostats). At present, a major demonstration profject is being conducted in five market areas in the U.S.

Finally, a recent Canadian study also focused on conservation via informed purchase decisions. As of October, 1978 refrigerators manufactured for sale in Canada are required to be labeled as to the kilowatt hours of electricity consumed per month. This ENERGUIDE labeling program was the focus of an 18 store field experiement (Anderson and Claxton 1979). The experimental manipulation consisted of two forms of the ENERGUIDE label (kwh vs. $) and two levels of salesperson emphasis on the energy aspects of refrigerators (emphasis vs. no emphasis). The major conclusions of this study are presented below:

- There is a clear potential for achieving worthwhile energy savings via shifts in consumer refrigerator choices.
- To date, only a relatively small proportion of consumers has considered energy consumption to be important when selecting a refrigerator.
- A majority of consumers has depended on retail salespeople at least for information and often to recommend which refrigerator to buy.
- Retail salespeople, although not in the habit of discussing energy information with customers, have indicated an interest in using a sales aid that would help compare operating costs of the models on display.
- EIPS had no observable impact on the mix of refrigerator models sold during the experiment. Given the range of factors influencing model mix, this was not viewed as surprising.
- Of consumers purchasing refrigerators at a store providing EIPS, the following was observed:
  ..only 33 percent recalled seeing the energy labels.
  ..25 percent said they understood the labes.
  ..5 percent reported noticing major differences in energy consumption from model to model.
  ..1 percent indicated the label information was the most important consideration in the choice. (Another 9 percent said it was one of a few important considerations).
  ..The analysis that assessed differences between "kwh per month" and "$ per year" labels indicated minimal differences.

These results will be utilized for ongoing management of the ENERGUIDE program which calls for energy consumption labels for all other major household appliances.

"Energy use" research. The final place at which conservation initiatives can be centered is consumer usage patterns associated with energy consuming products. Perhaps the most significant studies in the "energy use" area involve feedback of energy consumption information to consumers. The basic premise is that timely feedback about the cost implications of present household energy consumption levels will act as a powerful means of shpaing future energy consumption behavior. Research evaluating feedback initiatives are annotated by both Anderson and Cullen (1978) and Nemetz (1978). Hayes and Cone (1979), for example, assessed the impact of monetary payments, energy information, and daily feedback on electricity consumption rates. The Connecticut Power and Light Co. (1976) evaluated the effects of seven types of communication appeals on the decision to add insulation to the home. An excellent review of the energy feedback literature is contained in Mauser, Kendall and Filiatrault (1979). Many of the studies produced positive results.

A most promising "energy feedback" project is currently underway as a joint effort between Canadian and American CECC researchers (Mauser, Kendall and Filiatrault 1979; Collins 1979). The study involves use of an energy feedback monitor or energy cost indicator (ECI) which is a mechanical device, approximately the size of a kitchen clock, capable of measuring total household gas and electricity consumption and displaying this energy usage in dollars and cents both cumulatively and instantaneously. An ECI demonstration project will begin in four American and two Canadian cities (probably Boston, Minneapolis, Dallas, San Francisco, Montreal and Vancouver) in the fall of 1979 and will run for a full year. In each city, the gas and electricity consumption of approximately one hundred homeowners with ECI's will be compared with the consumption of a matched sample of homeowners without ECI's. This demonstration is co-sponsored by the U.S. Department of Energy and Consumer and Corporate Affairs Canada.

The studies cited above are only a small part of the work that has been completed in the CECC area. The purpose of this brief review has been to indicate the extensive nature of this research field and to provide the reader with a sample of the research undertaken.

THE FUTURE FOR CECC RESEARCH

Policy Impact Research

In attempting to forecast the future for CECC research,
it is useful to return first to a consideration of conservation
policy selection. Policy selection was described earlier as
requiring (1) a determination of potential policy pay-offs, and
(2) an assessment of the extent to which these pay-offs will
likely be achieved. In a somewhat futuristic situation this
might be accomplished by developing a policy impact model
using computer simulation. If this model included both technical energy savings and behavioral reactions, policy makers
could use it to determine what the probable net energy savings
from a particular policy would be and which consumers would be
affected.

The reason for suggesting this somewhat futuristic picture
is to indicate the directions currently being pursued. This is
not to say that the ultimate purpose should be to develop a
deterministic computer model that will simplify policy decisions. Rather, the need is to piece together behavioral information about energy consumption so that policy makers can bet-
er understand the proportion of potential pay-offs that would
likely accrue to alternative conservation initiatives. In
other words, further progress is needed on a matrix of potential policy pay-offs. Cullen's efforts are a major step in
this direction but more are needed. In addition, CECC
research must build the corresponding behavioral understanding
needed to assess policy impact in terms of probable consumer
reaction.

Trends in CECC Research Methods

It appears at this point that there is relatively less
need for one-shot attitudinal surveys. The vast majority of
studies referenced in the annotated bibliographies are of this
type. Instead, general consumer views on conservation might
better be monitored by means of well designed, compact surveys
that efficiently tap consumer views on a longitudinal basis.
This approach could be used to provide an ongoing macro view
of energy conservation. On the other hand, evaluation of
individual conservation initiatives requires the utilization of
two other types of research. First, the development of conservation programs could benefit from greater use of field experi-
mentation and field testing. To date, these methods have been
used in only a limited number of situations, yet, from a program management perspective they have much to offer. Second,

ongoing conservation programs have rarely been subjected to formal impact evaluation research. Formal impact assessment not only offers program managers the opportunity to identify program weaknesses but it also provides guidance for the extension of existing programs and the development of new ones.

REFERENCES

Anderson, C. **Dennis,** and John D. Claxton (1978), "Energy Information at Point of Sale: An Overview," Unpublished working paper, University of Manitoba.

Anderson, C. Dennis, and John D. Claxton (1979), Impact on Consumer Refrigerator Purchases of Energy Consumption Information At Point of Sale, Report for Consumer Research and Evaluation Branch, Consumer and Corporate Affairs, Ottawa, Canada.

Collins, Lynn D. (1979), "A Demonstration Program for Energy Cost Indicators," Memorandum, Department of Energy, Washington, D.C.

Connecticut Power and Light Co., Hartford, CN experimental study, reported by the Associate Press in the New York Times, Saturday, August 21, 1976.

Contemporary Research Centre (1975, 1976, 1977, 1978), A Study of the Canadian Public's Attitudes Towards the Energy Situation in Canada, Reports on Wave I through Wave IV of a study for Department of Energy, Mines and Resources, Ottawa, Canada.

Cook, Stuart W., et al (1977), "A Comparison of Three Methods of Encouraging Homeowners to Install Insulation," Unpublished papers, University of Colorado.

Cullen, Carman W. (1979), The Potential for Energy Conservation in the Residential Sector, Unpublished report, Consumer research and Evaluation Branch, Consumer and Corporate Affairs, Ottawa, Canada.

Davis, Harry L. (1976) "Decision Making Within the Household," Journal of Consumer Research, Vol. 2, No. 4. (March), 241-260.

Department of Energy, Mines and Resources (1976), An Energy Strategy for Canada: Policies for Self-Reliance, Ottawa, Canada.

Department of Energy, Mines and Resources (1978), Energy Future for Canadians, Ottawa, Canada.

Evans, John L., J. B. Brent Ritchie and Gordon H. G. McDougall (forthcoming), "Energy Use and Consumer Behavior: A Framework for Analysis and Policy Formulation," Journal of Business Administration.

Hayes, S.C. and J.D. Cone (in press), "Reducing Residential Electric Use: Payments, Information and Feedback," Journal of Applied Behavior Analysis.

Hutton, R. Bruce (1977), "Life Cycle Costs: The Impact on the Processing of New Information for Durable Goods," Unpublished doctoral dissertation, University of Florida.

Lund, Robert T. (1977), "Life Cycle Costing as a Societal Instrument," Centre for Policy Alternatives, M.I.T., Report No. CPA-77-15, Cambridge, Massachussetts.

Mauser, Gary A. Kenneth W. Kendall and Pierre Filiatrault (1979) Feedback and Household Energy Use: A Literature Review and Research Proposal, Report for Consumer Research and Evaluation Branch, Consumer and Corporate Affairs, Ottawa, Canada.

McDougall, Gordon G.H. J.R. Brent Ritchie and John D. Claxton (1979), Energy Consumption and Conservation Patterns in Canadian Households: Overview and Aggregate Statistics, Report for Consumer Research and Evaluation Branch, Consumer and Corporate Affairs, Ottawa, Canada.

McDougall, Gordon H.G. and G. Keller (1979), "The Energy Issue: A Four Year Canadian Investigation of Attitudes and Behaviors," Proceedings, Reno, American Institute for Decision Sciences, 478-481.

McDougall, Gordon H.G. (1979), "Profiling the Socially Responsible Consumer," Working Paper, School of Business and Economics, Wilfrid Laurier University.

National Demographics Ltd. (1978), Evaluation of a Marketing Program Designed to Increase Consumer Consideration of Energy-Efficient Products in Denver, Colorado, Report for Department of Energy, Washington, D.C.

Nemetz, Peter N. (1979), Economic Incentives for Energy Conservation at the Consumer Level: An Overview and Preliminary Synthesis, Report for Consumer Research and Evaluation Branch, Consumer and Corporate Affairs, Ottawa, Canada.

314

Newman, Dorothy K. and Dawn Kay (1975), <u>The American Energy Consumer</u>, Cambridge, Mass.: Ballinger Publishing Co.

PARTICIPANTS

Third Triennial Canadian Marketing Workshop
York University, June 1979

Larry M. Agranove
Wilfred Laurier University

Dennis Anderson
University of Manitoba

Stephen B. Ash
University of Western Ontario

Bryan Barbieri
Concordia University

Donald W. Barclay
Memorial University of
  Newfoundland

James G. Barnes
Memorial University of
  Newfoundland

J.A. Barnhill
Carleton University

Roger Bennett
McGill University

Ken Blowatt
Brock University

Dave Boag
University of Toronto

Gordon R. Bond
University of Prince
  Edward Island

Lorne Bozinoff
University of Toronto

S.A. Brown
University of Alberta

Gerald L. Byers
Humber College

Robert Caco
Humber College

Roger Calantone
McGill University

David R. Cameron
Federal/Provincial
  Relations Office

Terry Cameron
Lambton College of Applied
  Arts and Technology

Dr. R. Chaganti
University of Alberta

John Claxton
University of British
  Columbia

Chris Commins
York University

Alice E. Courtney
York University

Carman W. Cullen
Consumer and Corporate
  Affairs

316

George S. Day
University of Toronto

Jack F. Defayette
Algonquin College

Brian Dixon
York University

Carole Duhaime
University of Western Ontario

Pierre Filiatrault
Universite de Quebec a
Montreal

J.D. Forbes
University of British
Columbia

James Graham
University of Calgary

Jerry Grevstad
Lambton College of Applied
Arts and Technology

George H. Haines
University of Toronto

Louise Heslop
University of Guelph

Vernon J. Jones
University of Calgary

John R. Kennedy
University of Western Ontario

Peter J. Lawton
Queen's University

John Liphardt
Humber College

Werner Loiskandl
Humber College

R.M.A. Loyns
University of Manitoba

Hiro Matsusaki
University of Calgary

G. McDougall
Wilfred Laurier University

Peter McGrady
Mount Allison University

Barbara Michalos
York University

Ted Mitchell
University of Toronto

Mel S. Moyer
York University

Michael R. Pearce
University of Western
Ontario

John A. Quelch
University of Western
Ontario

Stanley Reid
York University

J.R. Brent Ritchie
University of Calgary

Robbie Robinson
Humber College

Christopher A. Ross
University of Western
Ontario

Ronald Rotenberg
Brock University

Rolf Seringhaus
York University

Hart E. Sernick
York University

Stanley J. Shapiro
McGill University

Patricia Simmie
York University

Henry A. Skinner
York University

M. Sommers
University of Toronto

Peter Thirkell
University of Western Ontario

Donald N. Thompson
York University

Douglas J. Tigert
University of Toronto

Ronald E. Turner
Queen's University

Linda Van Esch
York University

Rob Wilson
York University

Robert G. Wyckham
Simon Fraser University